Sunset

Vegetable Gardening
ILLUSTRATED

By the Editors of Sunset Books and Sunset Magazine

Harvest colorful summer squash by the basketful

Lane Publishing Co. ■ **Menlo Park, California**

Book Editors:
Cynthia Overbeck Bix
John K. McClements

Contributing Editors:
Susan Warton
Philip Edinger

Special Consultant:
John R. Dunmire
Associate Editor, Sunset Magazine

Coordinating Editor:
Suzanne Normand Mathison

Design:
Roger Flanagan
Kathy Avanzino Barone

Photo Editor:
JoAnn Masaoka

Illustrations & Maps:
Sandra Popovich
Rik Olson
Joe Seney

Juicy blackberries, ripe for picking

Fresh from your garden...

When you plant a vegetable and berry garden, not only will you experience the special satisfaction of growing your own produce from the ground up, but also you'll benefit from having the freshest possible food to put on your table. Moreover, you'll spend lots of hours outdoors in the sunshine and save on food costs at the same time.

Whether you're a novice or an experienced gardener, you can use this book to help plan your garden, to find out about varieties of vegetables and berries, and even to learn some basic gardening skills.

To inspire you, we lead off with a colorful photo gallery of special gardens. In Chapter 2, you'll find practical information on garden planning and layout. Chapter 3 provides basic information about a wide variety of vegetables and berries. And in Chapter 4, we give you an in-depth look at the steps in preparing, planting, and maintaining a produce garden.

Preparing this book took a team effort by many people. We'd like to extend special thanks to John Bracken, Nurseryman, Dallas, Texas; Gene Joyner, Urban Horticulturist, West Palm Beach, Florida; Jane Guest Pepper, Executive Director, Pennsylvania Horticulture Society, Philadelphia, Pennsylvania; and Gil Whitton, County Extension Director, Largo, Florida.

We're grateful also to Bob Thompson for his ideas on editorial organization, and to the many people who let us into their gardens for firsthand research and photography.

Cover: Juicy, sun-ripened tomatoes and plump, golden corn are just a sampling of the good things that come to your table when you plant and lovingly tend your own vegetable garden. Photograph by Lloyd Hryciw. Photo styling by JoAnn Masaoka. Design by Naganuma Design & Direction.

Editor, Sunset Books:
Elizabeth L. Hogan

Fourth printing April 1990

Photographers:

Bill Adams: 46 bottom. **William Aplin:** back cover. **Glenn Christiansen:** 90. **Rosalind Creasy:** 3, 4, 7 top, 10, 11 top. **Derek Fell:** 6, 15 top, 52 top. **Lee Foster:** 36 left, 73 top. **Gerald Fredrick:** 12 bottom right. **Horticultural Photography:** 5 top, 11 bottom. **Michael Landis:** 5 bottom, 12 bottom left, 16 top and bottom. **Jack McDowell:** 34 bottom, 38, 41 top, 43 top, 44, 45, 47 top, 50 bottom, 56 top, 60 bottom, 61 bottom, 62 top, 66, 67 top and bottom, 68, 72, 74 top and bottom left, 80 bottom, 82 top, 88, 91 bottom, 96 bottom. **Steve W. Marley:** 55, 61 top, 75 bottom right, 81 bottom, 83, 85, 87, 92 bottom. **Ells Marugg:** 34 top, 35, 41 bottom, 42, 43 bottom, 46 top, 47 bottom, 51, 52 bottom, 53 top, 54 top, 58, 62 bottom, 63, 64 top and bottom left, 73 bottom, 81 top, 82 bottom, 91 top, 94 bottom, 96 top. **Don Normark:** 48. **Norman A. Plate:** 8 right, 12 top, 60 top, 94 top. **Bill Ross/West Light:** 7 bottom, 77. **Teri Sandison:** 76, 78. **David Stubbs:** 14 top. **Michael Thompson:** 8 left, 9 bottom, 13 bottom, 36 right, 39, 40, 50 top, 53 bottom, 54 bottom, 56 bottom, 64 bottom right, 70 (all), 74 bottom right, 75 bottom left, 79, 80 top, 84, 92 top. **Darrow M. Watt:** 1, 13 top, 33, 86, 93. **Tom Wyatt:** 2, 14 bottom.

Contents

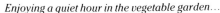

Enjoying a quiet hour in the vegetable garden...

A Gallery of Special Vegetable Gardens

When you grow your own vegetables and berries, you reap a two-fold reward. Of course, you'll harvest a wealth of delicious, fresh-from-the-garden produce for your table. But you may also be pleasantly surprised by the visual delight a colorful, well-planned produce garden can lend to your yard.

To inspire you, we've put together a photo "album" featuring an array of vegetable gardens that are as pretty as they are productive. Our album is divided into six sections that show you a full range of garden types, sizes, and planting methods.

On pages 6–9, you'll find a potpourri of gardens, from colorful front-yard displays that mix ornamental plants with vegetables, to no-nonsense home "farms" that yield a bountiful and diverse harvest. On pages 10–11, you'll see examples of vegetable plantings in tidy raised beds that hold a carefully prepared soil mix *and* give structure and definition to your garden. Page 12 features produce in containers you can tuck into any space, no matter how tiny. Spacious gardens, planted for superhigh yields using the French intensive method, appear on page 13. On pages 14–15, a selection of smaller gardens demonstrates techniques you can use to put every corner of your garden to work. And on page 16, you'll find examples of special structures that help protect your young seedlings from the elements.

Whatever your available space or your needs, there's a vegetable and berry garden that's just right for you. In these next pages, you may find the very ideas you need to create your own "dream" garden.

'Pancha' melon vine spills exuberantly over the edge of its raised bed. In neighboring beds, tomatoes ripen by the bushel; pink Madagascar periwinkles add a sprightly touch of color.

Neighbors over the fence, roses and petunias in full bloom keep company with waving green corn.

Well-contained garden features feathery carrots in neat wood boxes (front). Other vegetables and flowers—even a pummelo tree—flourish in containers, too.

Glorious gardens

Does your vegetable garden *have* to be a backyard rectangle planted with straight rows of carrots, lettuce, and tomatoes? It can be…or it may also be anything you can dream up, from a graceful curved plot winding its way across your front lawn to a neat series of edged beds set side-by-side near your kitchen door. You can create a colorful display by mixing vegetables with bright ornamental annuals and perennials, or plant a vegetables-only garden. Your garden may include elaborate raised beds and trellises—or it can be a simple, down-to-earth plot. On these pages, you'll find a sampling of all the ways your garden can grow.

Vegetables are right at home with flowers in this cheerful front-yard garden. Zinnias rub elbows with corn; scarlet runner beans climb an arched trellis alongside a bright display of petunias and coreopsis.

Dad and young helper harvest vine-ripened bush beans from their easy-to-tend backyard garden. Salad greens, strawberries, tomatoes, eggplant, herbs, and more flourish—but stay under control in neat wood-edged beds.

Evoking the quiet charm of an old-fashioned summer, this traditional kitchen garden occupies neat rectangular plots set in a lush lawn. Spinach, carrots, cabbage, beets, and chard, among other crops, form orderly rows across the plots.

…glorious gardens

This spectacular forest "farm" has it all, from asparagus to broccoli to loganberries. Terraced to hold the soil on its hillside site, the garden is surrounded by a wire fence that keeps woodland deer out but allows them a few nibbles around the perimeter. An ample coldframe lets owners start seeds throughout the season.

Vigorous grapevines and beans clamber up from raised beds onto a sturdy trellis; sunny gloriosa daisies bloom below. This ambitious garden features no fewer than 15 raised beds, packed with over 25 kinds of edibles and multitudes of flowers.

This graceful curved bed proves a garden can be good-looking and highly productive. Salad crops grow in neat rows; the greenhouse does double duty for starting seeds and extending the growing season for heat-loving vegetables.

Shipshape beds

Planting your vegetables or berries in raised beds has plenty of practical advantages. Raised beds built of wood or stone can hold a light, rich soil mix that drains well and warms up quickly in the sun. They're a special boon where your garden soil is poor. In addition, raised beds are easy to weed, tend, and water, and they give your garden a neat, well-organized look, as these pictures amply illustrate. For information on the "nuts and bolts" of creating a basic raised bed, see page 101.

Raised beds constructed of stone lend a sense of permanence to this distinguished garden. Beans and onions grow in the beds; behind, a trellis bright with scarlet runner beans completes the elegant tableau.

Well-mannered enough to be "on show," these low raised beds sport a pleasing mix of flowers and edibles. Petunias mix with onions, basil, and tomatoes (front); nasturtiums and daylilies add color to a bed planted with squash, cabbage, and other vegetables (back).

Roomy wood beds accommodate a bountiful crop of corn, squash, and chard, plus a rainbow of zinnias and marguerites in full bloom.

Bountiful containers

Even when your outdoor space is limited to a balcony or patio, you can harvest a surprising variety of vegetables and berries—just plant them in containers. Anything will do, from a basket to a wooden tub. The right size pot and the right location—plus vigilant watering and feeding—will insure good results. For more information on planting in containers, see page 122.

Seven kinds of basil fill this basket herb garden; to create it, simply add a plastic lining and soil mix, then plant young herbs from 2- and 4-inch pots.

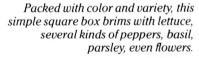

Packed with color and variety, this simple square box brims with lettuce, several kinds of peppers, basil, parsley, even flowers.

Plump for the picking, clay pot cucumbers dangle temptingly from a vine that's been carefully trained on a wire frame for neat, disciplined growth.

Super-achievers

If you want a garden that's all business, dig in with a full-scale French intensive garden. The French intensive method, which features thorough soil preparation, mounded beds, and close planting, gives a high yield of produce per square foot. It's a lot of work, but the results can be abundant, as these pictures show. Your garden may be large or small—whatever the size, you'll harvest loads of tender, flavorful vegetables all season long when you use this high-yield method. To learn how to plant a French intensive garden, turn to pages 20 and 125.

A blue-ribbon harvest is the reward for hours of loving care in this thickly planted French intensive garden. Mounds lush with vegetables are separated by redwood bark paths that keep down weeds, allow easy access.

Geared for high production, this no-nonsense French intensive garden features 4-by-16-foot planting mounds composed of carefully worked soil. Closely planted crops will cover the mounds by season's end.

Space-saver gardens

Tucked into a 9-by-15-foot front courtyard, this carefully planned garden yields astonishing variety. A discreet drip irrigation system facilitates watering.

The only magic you need to conjure up an abundant, varied harvest from a relatively small space is good planning. These gardens demonstrate ways you can make every square foot count. Techniques include vertical planting, where trellises, stakes, and fences allow climbing plants to grow upward, and carefully defined beds where a variety of vegetables can be neatly contained. For some suggested small-space plans, see page 21.

In this handsome front-yard enclosure, vegetables flourish in four neat raised beds. Tomatoes, squash, onions, parsley, and herbs have plenty of room to grow to maturity, yet can't overrun the allotted space. Around the perimeter, flowers add a bright note of welcome.

Simple wood frames tied with string netting make the most of available space by training aggressive bean and tomato plant growth upward. A bonus is "easy pickings" at harvest time.

Protective environments

Getting your garden off to a good start usually requires a little coddling of your seedlings and young plants during periods when temperatures may dip. Structures like coldframes and greenhouses provide a protected area for starting seedlings and hardening off young plants. Composed of a frame (usually wood) and transparent material such as glass, acrylic plastic, or plastic sheeting, coldframes collect the sun's daytime heat and hold some of it to warm tender plants during chilly nights. For more information on coldframes and greenhouses, see page 123.

Here's a coldframe handsome enough to put on display; slatted wood covers and glass panels beneath slide off easily to expose tender plants tucked cozily inside.

Ingenious mini-greenhouse protects cucumbers from seedling stage to maturity. Plastic bubble wrap forms a removable blanket around the entire frame.

Planning for Blue-Ribbon Harvests

*T*houghtful planning is the important first step toward creating a healthy, productive vegetable and berry garden. In this chapter, you'll find helpful ideas for selecting plants and laying out your garden (pages 18–21), as well as climate maps (pages 22–25) and a brief step-by-step review of the preparation-to-harvest sequence you can expect to follow (pages 26–29).

Deciding on a site

If you pay attention to these few "do's" and "don'ts," you'll greatly enhance your chances for success.

• Select a plot of ground that receives at least 6 hours of full sun daily.
• Avoid planting the garden close to shrubs and trees, which may cast shade and can compete with crops for water and nutrients.
• Choose a spot that's protected from cold winds in spring and hot, drying winds in summer.
• Steer clear of "frost pockets." Cold air seeks the lowest level, so late frosts will strike harder in garden low spots.
• Place the garden near a convenient water source (usually a hose bib).
• Try to select a level piece of land: in a level garden, watering and care are easier. If you have only sloping land available, look for ground that slopes toward the south or southeast to take full advantage of the sun.

Soil considerations. Well-drained soil is important. Generally the best, well-drained garden soils are a combination of sand, clay, and silt particles plus ample organic matter. If your soil is predominantly clay ("heavy") or sand ("light"), or is low in organic matter, be prepared to incorporate large amounts of organic amendments into it before planting. And for the first-time garden, at least, it's a good idea to test the soil (see pages 27 and 99).

Determining garden size & variety

Determining which vegetables and berries and how much of each you want to grow will greatly influence how large you'll make your garden. Another crucial factor is the amount of time you'll want to spend tending the garden.

Start small. If you're new to vegetable gardening, you'll have more success if you start with a fairly small plot—say 100 to 130 square feet—and a limited variety and number of plants. As you gain experience, you'll be able to expand the garden with confidence.

What to plant. First, decide which vegetables and berries you and your family really enjoy. Then determine how much of each you'll have to grow to satisfy your needs.

Your climate and length of growing season will also affect your choices. Other factors to consider are how much room individual vegetables and berries will occupy; how productive they are for the amount of space they take up; and how long they will bear a crop.

Laying out your garden

The best garden starts with a plan you draw on paper, then lay out in the actual garden plot using a tape measure and string. Whether your garden is large or small, a thoughtful plan can insure that you'll have no wasted space and, at the same time, that the vegetables and berries you select will have enough room to grow successfully to maturity.

To help you visualize how your garden might be laid out, we've provided several sample plans on the next few pages. Our plans show a variety of efficient, highly productive gardens that take the greatest advantage of available spaces and growing periods.

Draw your own intended garden to scale on graph paper (our examples show 1 square to 1 foot). Start with a grid, then indicate rows or blocks of plants. As you plan, be sure to allow for the suggested spacing between plants (consult our catalog of crops, pages 32–96).

On level ground, plan to run rows north to south; that way the plants get the maximum amount of sunlight as the sun travels in its east-to-west path. If you'll be planting on a slope, run the rows along the contour of the hill. Be sure to place tall crops, such as corn and pole beans, on the north side of the garden so that as they mature they won't shade the lower-growing plants.

Put perennial plants, such as asparagus and berries, in their own section of the garden. This way you won't disturb their roots each year (or season) when you prepare the soil for other crops.

As you draw up your plans, consider how you intend to supply water—by overhead sprinkler, by flood irrigation, or by drip irrigation (see pages 106–107). You won't want, for example, tall or large-leaved plants blocking sprinklers, or irrigation rows that run downhill.

And finally, consider how you'll gain access to the plants. Be sure to allow yourself enough room to get in easily when you want to harvest the crops.

A continuous-harvest garden

With a little extra planning, you can lay out a garden that will produce a continuous supply of crops from spring all the way through autumn/winter. The plan below shows one way to push a single garden's productive season to the maximum and increase the number and variety of crops you can grow.

This basic 22-by-16-foot garden plot is divided into halves, separated by 4 feet of space to allow access for cultivation. In early spring, plant the left half of the plot with cool-season vegetables—carrots, lettuce, cabbage, peas—that will mature before the heat of summer (see the plan on the left). One end of the plot is reserved for cane berries, such as raspberries.

In later spring, after all danger of frost is past, plant the right half of the plot with warm-season vegetables such as corn, squash, and tomatoes (see the center plan).

In mid- to late summer, when most of the left plot is harvested or "played out," you can rework the soil and replant that plot as shown at right, rotating placement of crops like cabbage to avoid fostering soil-borne diseases. At this time, you can add new cool-season vegetables, such as broccoli and cauliflower, for harvest in late summer and autumn.

With this continuous-harvest plan, you can use three special techniques—succession planting, double-

This 22-by-16-foot garden is divided into two halves (shown at left and center). The left side is planted in early spring with cool-season vegetables; the right side is planted with warm-season vegetables in late spring. In mid- to late summer, the left side is replanted, as shown in the diagram at right, with a second crop of cool-season vegetables.

1 square = 1 foot

Left side (plant in early spring)

cropping, and intercropping—to further increase the amount and variety of your garden's output.

Succession planting. For vegetables that come to maturity all at once, or within a short period of time, you can stretch the harvest period by staggering plantings of seeds or young plants at roughly 2-week intervals. These successive plantings will produce a continuous supply of a given vegetable. In our plan, for example, the carrots are planted in two side-by-side plots, one planted 2 weeks after the other. (The plantings of bush beans in the right half of the plot could also be divided into halves for successive sowing.)

In addition, replanting the entire left half of the plot in mid- to late summer enables you to harvest two cool-season crops from the left half while the crops in the right half, planted later, mature through the longer warm season.

Double-cropping. Some vegetables—radishes, lettuce, and green onions are classic examples—grow so quickly that you can raise a second crop in the same spot within the same season after the first crop has been completely harvested. The space for carrots on the left side of our plot, for example, could be replanted for a second harvest within the spring growing season if your climate permits.

Intercropping. Two vegetables can occupy the same allotted space if one matures quickly before the slower-growing one crowds it out. In the left side of our plot, the green onions (scallions) will mature and be pulled before the cabbage plants fill out the entire space. Similarly, fast-growing spinach occupies the fringe of the berry area before the berries completely take over.

Spinach, lettuce, green onions, and radishes are good intercrop choices for cool-season gardens. You also can grow them in summer gardens (between tomato plants, for example) and harvest them before the weather heats up.

Right side (plant in late spring)

Left side (replant in mid-to late summer)

A French intensive garden

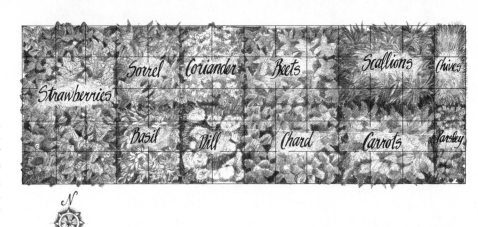

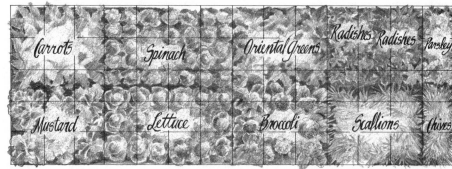

French intensive gardening relies on close planting in wide, mounded beds to conserve soil moisture and thereby promote steady, abundant growth. To avoid crowding, plants are thinned frequently as they grow (the thinnings go to your kitchen). French intensive gardening starts with very thorough soil preparation followed by specific seeding and planting methods (see page 125). Not all vegetables and berries lend themselves to this treatment; choose plants that will produce all season and lend themselves to regular thinning.

Our plan shows two ways to plant the same 14-by-5-foot plot. Above is a cool-season planting; below is a warm-season planting (or an all-season planting in mild climates). Each includes crops that give generous yields in small spaces. Note that the beds are just narrow enough for easy reach; the length can vary according to your available space.

1 square = 1 foot

A vegetable and flower "landscape"

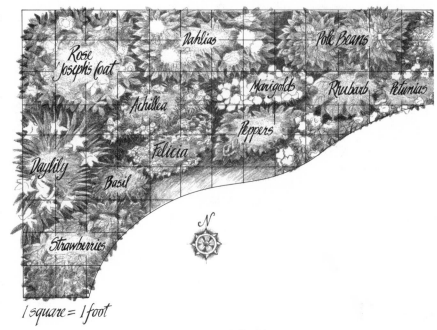

If you hesitate to set aside space for a purely utilitarian food garden, or if your front yard is the only sunny spot for the lettuce or strawberries you want to grow, try mixing crop plants with your ornamental plantings. Many vegetables, berries, and herbs display a diverse array of showy "fruits" as well as foliage textures and colors. Our example shows edibles mixed with flowering plants in a gracefully shaped bed that would look good anywhere.

When you interplant your garden, plan carefully and make sure you have access to the crops for harvest. In addition, read cautions on the labels of any fertilizers or pesticides you're considering; the products used on some ornamentals could contaminate nearby edibles. For further suggestions about crop plants in the landscape, see pages 31 and 124.

1 square = 1 foot

Two small-space gardens

Although some gardeners might consider small space a handicap, the small produce garden offers an exciting challenge: how to reap a diverse and bountiful harvest from a limited plot. The examples here show you ways to organize two small plots—one rectangular, the other square—for maximum productivity and variety. The keys to a good harvest are thorough preparation and careful plant selection and placement.

Soil and water. In a small-space garden, you'll need to spend extra time on soil preparation. With a small plot you can add a liberal amount of soil amendments (see page 98). You might even consider double digging the ground (pages 100 and 125), or try planting the whole garden as a raised bed (page 101).

In addition, you may want to install a drip irrigation system (see page 107). As in any size space, a drip system entails a minimal outlay of time and cost and insures that the entire plot is watered evenly and without waste.

What to plant. The small-space garden rules out space-grabbing crops with low yields per square foot, such as corn, melons, and some squash. For maximum yields, seek out varieties that are especially productive. Plant ideas can be found in "Catalog of Flavorful Crops" (pages 32–96) and in seed catalogs.

You can also maximize your small-space productivity by planting both early-maturing and late-maturing varieties of the same vegetable.

Garden layout. To get maximum production, use techniques that make the most of available space. Whenever possible, use vertical supports such as stakes, frames, and trellises (see pages 109 and 110) to conserve space. In addition, pay special attention to the various modes of continuous-harvest planting (pages 18–19). Take advantage of any chance you have to interplant fast-growing crops among those of slower growth. Spinach, lettuce, scallions, and radishes are proven intercroppers. And whenever season and climate allow, practice double-cropping as soon as the first crop is harvested. In the plans below, lettuce, scallions, carrots, and bush beans might be double-cropped.

Note that the examples show blocks rather than rows of lettuce, carrots, and scallions. These (and other vegetables not shown) could also be planted thickly in French intensive bed fashion, with the thinnings from these plots being the first to reach your kitchen.

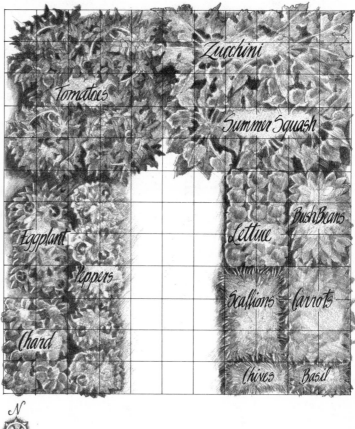

1 square = 1 foot

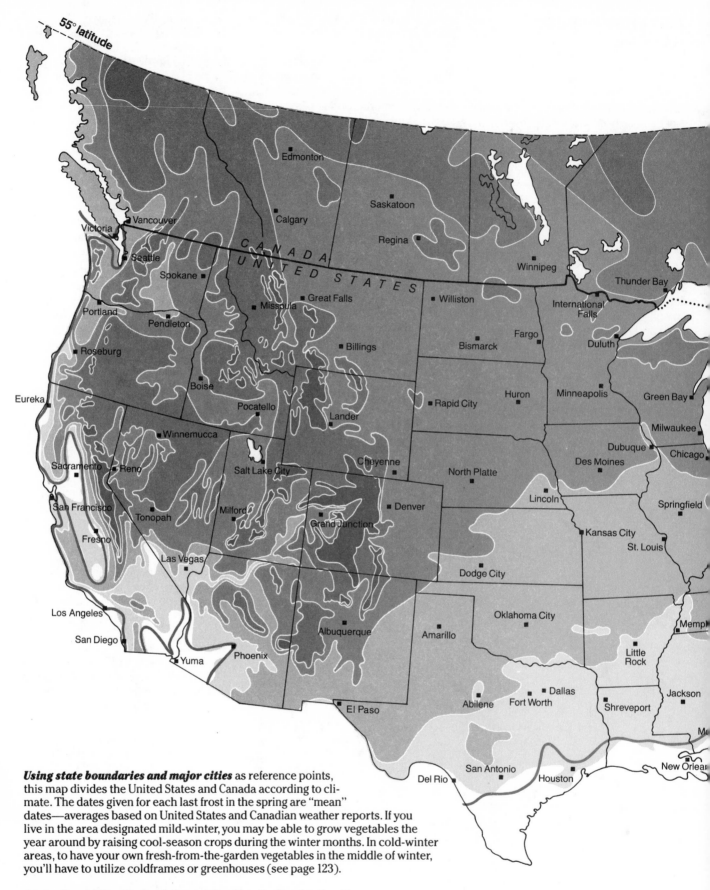

Using state boundaries and major cities as reference points, this map divides the United States and Canada according to climate. The dates given for each last frost in the spring are "mean" dates—averages based on United States and Canadian weather reports. If you live in the area designated mild-winter, you may be able to grow vegetables the year around by raising cool-season crops during the winter months. In cold-winter areas, to have your own fresh-from-the-garden vegetables in the middle of winter, you'll have to utilize coldframes or greenhouses (see page 123).

Australia and New Zealand. Consult local horticultural authorities about the proper time to plant in spring.

A climate map for vegetables

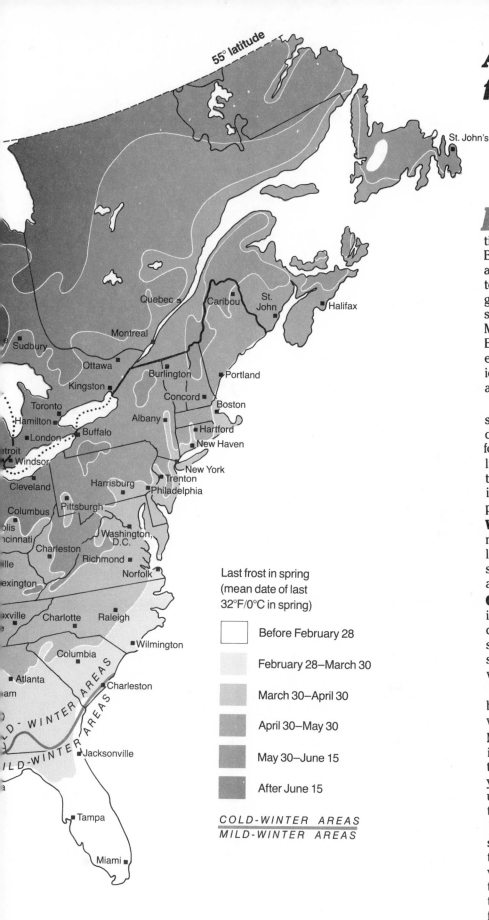

55° latitude

St. John's

Quebec
Caribou
St. John
Halifax
Montreal
Sudbury
Ottawa
Burlington
Portland
Kingston
Concord
Toronto
Boston
Albany
Hamilton
Buffalo
Hartford
London
New Haven
etroit
Windsor
New York
Cleveland
Harrisburg
Trenton
Philadelphia
Columbus
Pittsburgh
olis
cinnati
Washington, D.C.
Charleston
Richmond
lle
Norfolk
exington
xville
Charlotte
Raleigh
Wilmington
Columbia
Atlanta
Charleston
am
MILD-WINTER AREAS
MILD-WINTER AREAS
Jacksonville
Tampa
Miami

Last frost in spring
(mean date of last
32°F/0°C in spring)

Before February 28

February 28–March 30

March 30–April 30

April 30–May 30

May 30–June 15

After June 15

COLD-WINTER AREAS
MILD-WINTER AREAS

By checking the climate map, you can determine the right planting time in your area for each vegetable. But don't consider the lines on the map as rigid. Frost dates aren't so consistent that we can draw a line on the ground with a stick and say "on this side of the line the last frost will be March 29; on the other side, April 1." Be sure to consider local conditions, especially elevation and nearby bodies of water, and seasonal fluctuations as you do your yearly planting.

Vegetables are divided into warm-season and cool-season categories, depending on the weather that's best for their growth. On pages 30–31 are lists of warm and cool-season vegetables; see the individual descriptions in the catalog (pages 32–96) for more precise information.

Warm-season vegetables, the summer crops, need both soil warmth and long days of high temperatures (or short days and early heat) to form fruit and ripen.

Cool-season vegetables grow steadily at average temperatures 10 to 15 degrees below those needed by warm-season crops. Many of the cool-season crops—cabbage, for instance—will even endure some frost.

Generally you plant these vegetables in very early spring so the crop will mature before the summer heat.

Mild-winter areas. Beneath the solid line on the map are the mild-winter areas. Here, there is no frost one year out of every two; snowfall measures less than one inch per year; and the ground does not freeze.

Under these conditions, many cool-season vegetables can be grown throughout the winter. Mild-winter vegetable gardeners can plant vegetables in late summer and early autumn while days are still warm enough for good plant growth but nights are lengthening.

Climate maps for berries

Unlike most vegetables—which are annuals, growing from seed to harvest within a year's time—berries are perennials or woody plants that live on in your garden year after year. Success in growing them depends on your selecting plants whose year-round growth requirements are compatible with your climate.

Many climatic factors affect each berry's performance: severity of winter, summer humidity and temperature, for example. The climate maps here show areas of best adaptation in the United States and Canada for each popular home berry crop. Information for Australia and New Zealand appears at the end of each description.

Strawberries

Strawberries—unlike the other berries—can be grown nearly anywhere in the United States and Canada. Numerous varieties have been developed to perform in different climates, so it's important to choose those that are adapted to your particular region (see page 88 for more information).

Australia. They'll succeed in Victoria, New South Wales, and Tasmania, and in the semiarid and Mediterranean-like areas of Western Australia and South Australia. Choice of variety is important.

New Zealand. Commercial growing is centered around Auckland, but home crops can be grown throughout the country.

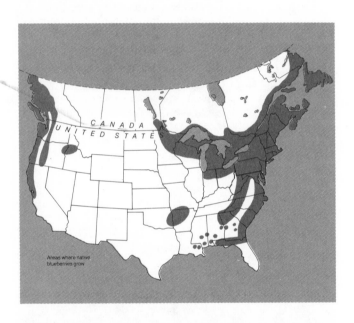

Areas where native blueberries grow

Blueberries

Best regions (where plants grow with the least amount of effort) in the United States and Canada are shaded on the map. Native types occur there. Edible blueberries consist of several different species and many named hybrids, and cultural requirements vary. Be sure to choose varieties that are appropriate for your area.

Australia. Best areas are cool highland and tableland districts. Most varieties need winter chill. Recent hybrids from southern United States succeed in warmer-winter districts.

New Zealand. Central North Island probably offers the best environment, but with proper care and the right variety, blueberries may succeed in all parts.

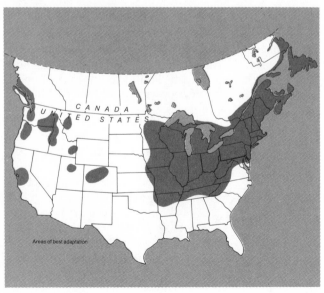

Areas of best adaptation

Raspberries

Generally speaking, all raspberries perform best where summers are cool, winters are cold, and water is always available. Heat—both humid and dry—is raspberry's enemy. You can moderate the effect of heat by choosing a cool planting location. But the less favorable your overall climate is, the more erratic your results are likely to be.

Australia. Winter chill plus coolness and shelter during summer are necessary for success. This limits raspberry growing to Tasmania and to regions of Victoria and New South Wales.

New Zealand. Raspberries grow easiest in northern and central South Island, but with proper care they can bear some fruit in all areas.

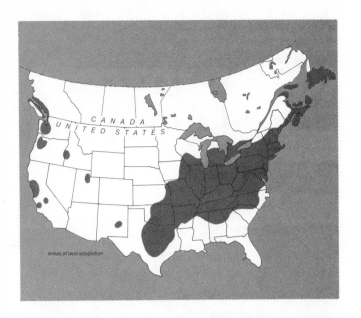

Blackberries

In contrast to their close relatives, the raspberries, blackberries will tolerate warmer climates. Like strawberries, many blackberry varieties have been selected for their ability to produce in different climatic regions. The map shows the areas of the United States and Canada where the most popular varieties grow best.

Australia. Best districts are where both summer heat and winter cold are moderate. Everywhere, blackberries need shelter from drying winds. Check with local agricultural specialists for recommended varieties.

New Zealand. Blackberries are easy to grow throughout the country.

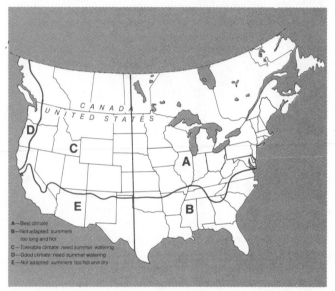

Currants/Gooseberries

Currants and gooseberries share similar climate requirements. Currants, though, generally need colder weather and cooler summers than gooseberries (gooseberries have been grown successfully in parts of area B on map).

Australia. Currants are restricted to the colder-winter areas of Victoria, New South Wales, and Tasmania. Gooseberries grow in the same districts, but they will also succeed in other areas as long as there is some winter chill and if summer heat is moderate.

New Zealand. Southern South Island is best for currants, central South Island is best for gooseberries. With care, though, both kinds can be grown throughout the country.

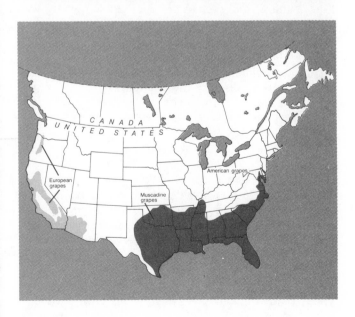

Grapes

A map that shows areas where grapes will grow tells only part of the story. There are several types of grapes, and each has requirements that limit it to only a portion of the total grape-growing territory; see pages 55–57 for a detailed explanation of types and their adaptability.

Australia. European types are best in districts with dry, warm-to-hot summers. American grapes will successfully bear fruit in northern New South Wales and Tasmania, where warmth and summer and autumn rains create problems for European kinds.

New Zealand. Eastern North Island and northern South Island have the best climate for European types. With special care they will bear fruit in most of North Island and central South Island.

Step 1. Find a site for your garden

Step 2. Make a plan to fit the site

Picking the right place to grow vegetables and berries is a major step to success with gardening. When you choose a site, consider these factors:

• Sunlight. Almost all vegetables and berries like to grow in full sunlight. Choose a spot that gets at least 6 hours of sunlight a day. Avoid gardening where trees, shrubs, fences, or other structures will cast a great deal of shade.

• Soil. The best soil for growing vegetables and berries is rich enough to nourish the crops, has good drainage, but holds ample moisture to keep plants from wilting between waterings. Choose a spot where the soil is far away from trees and shrubs with invasive, competing roots. If your soil is very poor, consider gardening in raised beds or containers, or at a nearby community garden.

• Water. Most vegetables and berries need a steady supply of moisture. In some areas, gardeners can depend on rainfall to supply their water needs, but in many areas, especially in the West, gardeners have to water all summer. Is water available at the site? It's helpful to have a spigot within one or two hose-lengths of the garden.

• Climate protection. Try to choose a spot that's sheltered from cold winds in spring and hot, drying winds in summer. (However, avoid a place with completely stagnant air which can encourage some plant diseases.)

• Geography. What sorts of places can you use for a garden? You can enlarge an existing garden, dig up a patch of lawn, or plant in a sunny side yard. Also you can grow some vegetables and berries in containers on a patio, deck, or porch, or even at a nearby community garden.

Make a plan before you purchase seeds or plants. A plan will help you decide what to get and will help you keep track of what to do, in what sequence, at planting time. To make a plan for your garden, use the information in this book and from other sources such as mail-order catalogs, seed packets, and cooperative extension service bulletins. Things to consider when making a plan include the following:

• What kinds of vegetables and berries does your family like? When in doubt, plant the ones you know they will like to eat.

• What are your reasons for gardening—to reduce food costs, for tastier vegetables and berries, or for recreation?

• How much time do you have to garden? Initially, it takes a lot of work to prepare the soil and do your planting; on the average, though, the majority of home gardeners spend less than 4 hours a week in their garden.

• How much space is available? A 10 by 10-foot garden is a good size for a beginning gardener. In a season you can expect to harvest about 1 to 1½ pounds of vegetables for every square foot of garden space.

• How much to plant? It depends partly on what you want to do with your harvest—use it fresh or preserve it. Information in the catalog (pages 32–96) can help you learn how productive each kind of vegetable can be.

Once you've decided what you want to grow, make a scale drawing of the garden (see page 18) showing the rows (or wide beds) for each vegetable and berry. When you're ready to plant, take the drawing to the garden.

Step 3. Buy or order seeds and plants

Step 4. Prepare the soil

To start your garden you'll need seeds and plants. Most vegetables can be started from seeds (though for convenience, some are purchased as started plants); almost all berries are purchased as plants.

You can purchase seeds and plants, including cane berries, from local nurseries and garden centers or order them from mail-order catalogs (see pages 126–127).

If you buy from mail-order catalogs, read the descriptions of vegetables and berries carefully. Compare the conditions that the plants need with the climate of your area, and order plants that will do well in your locale.

To help discover what varieties of vegetables and berries will do well in your area, several sources of information are available: local nurseryworkers, cooperative extension service agents, and gardening friends.

The earlier in the year that you order seeds and plants by mail, the better. Mail-order companies do most of their business in the first months of the year, so the sooner you send your order in to the company, the less delay there will be in getting your order back to you.

It's wise to shop carefully at your nursery or garden center. Purchase young, healthy plants that will grow quickly after you plant them. Never choose plants that are crowded or straggly; they've been around too long. You want compact plants with good leaf color and a vigorous appearance.

When browsing through seed packets, check the suggested planting times and look for a date stamp. Be sure the seeds are intended for the current or coming season of the current or coming year.

Preparing the soil properly is possibly the single most important thing you can do to gain success in a garden. Properly prepared soil will be fertile, will drain well yet retain enough water to meet the needs of plants, and will allow enough air to enter to keep roots healthy. More information on soil is on pages 98–101.

It helps to test the soil before you begin to till or spade it. Relatively inexpensive soil test kits are available at many nurseries and from mail-order houses. Most tests kits will tell you how much nitrogen, phosphorus, and potassium are in the soil and the soil pH (a measure of acidity and alkalinity). From the results of the test, you can tell what soil amendments and fertilizers to add.

To prepare the soil, add a layer of compost or similar soil amendment, or sprinkle commercial fertilizer over the top of the soil according to directions on the package. Then spade or till the layer into the soil. When the soil is well broken up, rake it, and form it into furrows, hills, mounds, or raised beds.

Don't till or spade the soil when it's wet. Pick up the soil in your hand and squeeze it into a lump. Poke the lump with a finger of your other hand. If the ball of soil crumbles, it's ready to be worked. If the lump holds together, the soil is too wet. (If the soil won't form a lump at all, then it's probably too dry.)

Once the soil has been tilled or spaded, raked, and formed into rows or beds, it is ready to be planted. Some gardeners prefer to let the soil sit for a few days before they plant; others go right ahead and plant.

Step 5. Sow the seeds...

Step 6. ...or set out seedlings or plants

Seeds are planted two ways: 1) indoors in flats, trays, or packs; and 2) in the garden. By starting seeds indoors, you can carefully control the light, heat, and moisture. You can also get a head-start on the growing season. On the other hand, some vegetables are difficult to transplant and are customarily sown directly in the garden.

Sow seeds outdoors, or transplant young seedlings, when the weather is right for the kind of vegetable you're growing. Use the information on the seed packet, the climate map on pages 22–23, and the description in the catalog (pages 32–96) to determine the right time.

For vegetables that were started indoors, it's best to give them an opportunity to harden, or become gradually adjusted to the out-of-doors, before you transplant them into the garden. Do this by moving the plants outdoors each day for increasing lengths of time until they can stay out overnight, or place them in a coldframe.

Most seed packages give clear instructions on how to plant seeds: how deep and how far apart, as well as when. For information on techniques, see pages 102–103.

Remember that seeds are very delicate when they are sprouting. Be sure they have enough moisture, but not too much. In hot weather you may have to water seedlings growing outdoors twice a day or more. If the weather is extremely hot, you may want to shade seedlings for the first few days until their roots are well established.

When the vegetables are well established, usually 3 or 4 weeks after planting, thin crowded seedlings to the distances recommended on the seed packets.

Another way to start your garden is with plants purchased from a nursery or garden center. If you are planting only a few of each kind of vegetable or fruit, it may be more convenient to purchase them as started plants. For more information on planting, see pages 103–105.

Usually these purchased plants are ready to go directly into the garden. When the soil is ready and the weather is right, you can set out your plants. Follow the instructions in the catalog (pages 32–96) about the timing for setting out various kinds of plants. For an early start in climates where summers are short, cover the transplants with cloches or plant caps each night until the weather becomes steadily warm.

When you set out transplants, dig a hole twice as wide and deep as the root ball, mound up soft soil at the bottom of the planting hole, and set the transplant in place. Fill in soil around the root ball and water the plant thoroughly before going on to the next plant. Some people give a dose of vitamin B-1 with the first watering to lessen transplant shock; not everyone agrees with this practice.

Most berries are planted slightly deeper in soil than the plants grown in the nursery. They also need pruning right after planting.

If the weather is very hot, shade the plants with boards or netting for the first few days after transplanting. Water all transplants thoroughly so their roots will grow deep.

Protect transplants from scavengers such as birds by covering them with netting or chickenwire. Also, you may have to set out bait or traps for earwigs, snails, and slugs.

Step 7. Set up a plant care program

Step 8. Harvest and store

*O*nce your vegetables are planted, you need to care for them—water, weed, fertilize, and protect. Plant care information is on pages 106–111 and 114–117. Another important chore, pruning, is discussed on pages 118–121.

You'll need to water often enough to keep plants growing steadily throughout the season. When plants are young, you must water often enough to keep the soil around the shallow roots moist. That may mean watering two or three times a day. Later, as the roots grow deeper, you can water less often. When seedlings are well established, you can put down a mulch to help conserve moisture in the soil.

The best way to tell how often to water is to look at the plants and to examine the soil. One good way to test soil moisture is to dig down an inch or so and feel the soil with your finger. If the soil is damp, you probably don't need to water immediately; but if it's dry, water right away.

Weeding is another important task in food gardens. It is necessary to weed when seedlings are sprouting and growing, because weeds can rob the young plants of vital moisture and nutrients. Once plants are well established, putting down a mulch will help keep weeds from growing.

Depending on how well you prepared the soil, you may want to give plants an extra boost of growth by fertilizing them. If you do fertilize, wait until plants are well established.

Inspect your garden regularly for signs of damage by insects and other devouring creatures. Early in the growing season, take the proper preventive measures. Take action when plants are being seriously attacked. Light damage is usually acceptable unless you're extremely fastidious.

*H*arvesting and enjoying your own unbeatably fresh crops is the reward you receive for working diligently in your garden.

Different vegetables and berries are harvested at different times, in different ways. You will need to look at each plant for its special signs of readiness for harvest. You'll find precise information for each kind of plant in the catalog descriptions on pages 32–96.

Generally, it's a good idea to pick leafy vegetables and herbs in the early morning while they are still moist with dew. For best flavor, harvest just before you plan to eat or preserve the produce.

Most vegetables and berries should be watched and picked at the peak of ripeness. Blueberries and corn are two familiar examples. However, some vegetables, such as carrots and celery, can be left in the ground or on the vine until it's convenient for you to harvest them. Piling up straw and soil as insulation can delay the harvest of some vegetables beyond the first frosts. Parsnips, late cabbage, and kale require little frost protection.

When harvesting root crops for immediate use, keep a bucket of water close by so you can wash the dirt off before you take them in; then return the muddy water to the garden instead of pouring it down the drain.

Once picked, crops can be eaten immediately, stored at room temperature or below, kept in the refrigerator, frozen, dried, canned, or pickled. More information on which crops are suitable for storage, and the best methods of storage, are given on pages 112–113.

Quick ideas for planting

*E*veryone has favorites among the vegetables and berries, and the natural desire is to grow them in quantity. But before you plant them at all, be sure that the crops' requirements match up with the conditions your region and your garden have to offer. Some vegetables are fairly foolproof in nearly all regions—tomatoes, for example—but the raspberry aficionado, to choose an example of the other extreme, had better live in a raspberry climate; otherwise it's go to the market and pay the going price.

The lists on these two pages categorize the vegetables and berries into groups that will be useful to the broadest range of growers.

Cool-season edibles

Artichoke
Asparagus
Beets
Broccoli
Brussels sprouts
Cabbage
Carrot
Cauliflower
Celery and Celeriac
Collards
Cress
Endive
Garlic
Kale
Kohlrabi
Leeks
Lettuce
Mustard greens
Onion
Oriental greens
Parsnip
Peas
Potato
Radish
Rhubarb
Roquette
Rutabaga
Salsify
Shallots
Spinach
Swiss chard
Turnip

Warm-season edibles

Amaranth
Beans
Chayote
Chicory
Collards
Corn
Cucumber
Eggplant
Herbs (most)
Jerusalem artichoke
Jicama
Melon
Okra
Oriental melons
Peanut
Peppers
Pumpkin
Southern peas
Spinach, New Zealand
    and Malabar
Squash
Sunflower
Sweet potato
Tomatillo
Tomato
Watermelon

More than one edible part

Beets
Chayote
Chicory
Kohlrabi
Onion
Pumpkin
Roquette
Rutabaga
Turnip

Roots that store in ground

Horseradish
Jerusalem artichoke
Parsnip
Rutabaga
Salsify
Turnip

Container candidates

Amaranth
Beans
Beets
Broccoli
Cabbage (some)
Carrots
Collards
Cress
Cucumber
Eggplant
Herbs
Kale (some)
Lettuce
Mustard greens
Onion (scallion)
Oriental greens
Peas
Peppers
Radish
Roquette
Shallots
Sorrel
Spinach, New Zealand
Swiss chard
Tomato

Of basic importance is whether a crop needs warm to hot weather to mature, or whether cool conditions are the requirement. To some extent these needs can be managed if you set out plants so that the edible part will mature at the time of year when the weather is suitable. But there are always the "impossibles"—watermelons in Seattle and artichokes in Houston, just to single out two illustrations.

Beyond the basic climate needs, there are other ways to categorize crop plants that will help the gardener plan or organize the garden. Here we present some of the most useful of these classifications—those that are colorful on the plate, decorative in the garden, the most productive for amount of space used, vining crops, good choices for containers, early maturers, or winter producers in mild-winter regions. Two other classifications are root crops that store in the ground and vegetables that have more than one edible part.

Prolific producers

Beans
Brussels sprouts
Cucumber
Herbs
Jerusalem artichoke
Mustard greens
Oriental greens
Peas
Radish
Spinach, New Zealand
Sprouts
Squash (some)
Sunflower
Tomato

Decorative garden plants

Artichoke
Asparagus
Cabbage (some)
Carrot
Cardoon
Chicory
Eggplant
Herbs (most)
Jerusalem artichoke
Kale (some)
Lettuce (some)
Mustard greens (some)
Oriental greens
Peppers
Rhubarb
Sunflower
Swiss chard

For colorful cooking

Beans
Beets
Cabbage
Carrot
Cauliflower (some)
Corn
Eggplant
Kohlrabi
Lettuce
Melon
Onion (some)
Peppers
Potato (some)
Pumpkin
Radish
Rhubarb
Squash
Sweet potato
Swiss chard
Tomato
Watermelon

For winter harvests in frost-free regions

Beets
Broccoli
Brussels sprouts
Cabbage
Carrot
Cauliflower
Celery
Cress
Lettuce and celtuce
Oriental greens
Peas, green and edible pod
Spinach
Swiss chard
Radish
Turnip

Fast-maturing crops

Amaranth
Cress
Herbs (most)
Lettuce
Mustard greens
Onion (scallion)
Oriental greens
Radish
Roquette
Spinach
Sprouts
Turnip

Vines and sprawlers

Beans (some)
Blackberry
Chayote
Cucumber
Gourds
Grapes
Jicama
Melon
Oriental melons
Peas (some)
Pumpkin
Raspberry
Southern peas (some)
Spinach, Malabar
Squash (most)
Strawberry
Sweet potato
Tomatillo
Tomato
Watermelon

A Catalog of Flavorful Crops

*H*ow do you decide what vegetables and berries to plant? First, you need to determine where you're going to locate your garden and how much space you have. Then, use the information on the following pages to help you decide what and how much to plant.

Favorites and lesser-knowns

On pages 33–96, we acquaint you with the most familiar and favorite vegetables and berries, some lesser-known ones that deserve wider appreciation, and the most useful culinary herbs. For each plant we describe the appearance, edible parts, culture, and other helpful facts.

Using the check lists

Following each description is a check list that tells you at a glance whether the crop is annual or perennial, cool or warm season, and its edible parts, soil preference, and expected yield. The check list also suggests when and how to plant and harvest, how to care for the plants, and how to deal with pests and diseases.

Use these check lists as guides to the planting and care of vegetables and berries. For example, the check list suggests the general planting season for each crop in most areas of the country. But where you live, the planting season for some crops may be different. Consult your county farm advisor for precise information about when to plant and harvest vegetables and berries in your area.

What about varieties?

A number of the descriptions of vegetables and berries mention some varieties, but many more exist than those listed. Some varieties do well in most parts of the country; others do well only in small areas. If you like to experiment, try different varieties to find the ones that do best in your garden. For more certain results, consult local gardeners, nurserymen, and your county farm advisor.

Making choices

Still bewildered by the range of choices? Then consider these suggestions: first, grow the kinds of vegetables and berries that your family likes to eat. Second, select crops you have the space to grow and the time and energy to take care of, and plant in amounts you can use. Finally, even though raspberries may be as precious to you as rubies, don't try to grow them—or any other crop—in a climate unsuited to their cultivation.

A bright and bountiful harvest at your table is your just reward for a garden carefully planned and lovingly tended.

Amaranth

A spinachy green, scarcely known in the U.S.

Tell people that you're serving them a lovely amaranth soufflé, and they may look a bit perplexed. Not many Americans are yet acquainted with this nutritious hot-weather spinach substitute. But elsewhere in the world, it has been cultivated for many centuries.

A time-honored vegetable of China, amaranth, or *hin choy*, is popular as a leafy addition to soups and stir-fry dishes. In the Western Hemisphere, the Aztecs relied on native kinds of amaranth as a staple crop, grinding their high-protein seeds into meal. In parts of Mexico, amaranth continues to be a market crop, prized both for its seeds and spinachlike leaves.

Young leaves, spinachy-flavored

You'll find the kinds of amaranth that are grown for their edible leaves listed in catalogs under names such as "Tampala," "Chinese Spinach," "Hin Choy," and "Edible Amaranth."

Plant the edible-leaf amaranths in spring, when the weather has warmed up. Unlike spinach, they like warm weather and won't go to seed when the temperatures get hot.

Serve the leaves steamed or add them raw to salad. Cook the stems as you would asparagus.

Amaranth ...at a glance

Type of vegetable. Leafy; warm season.

Edible parts. Leaves; stems.

Best soil. Fertile, well drained.

When to plant. *Cold-winter and mild-winter climates: For summer crop,* sow seeds in spring (3 to 4 weeks after last frost date).

How to plant. Sow seeds ¼ inch deep, ½ inch apart, in rows spaced 2 feet apart; thin seedlings to 2 to 24 inches apart, depending on variety.

When to harvest. 40 to 56 days after sowing seeds when plants are 6 to 8 inches tall.

Care. Keep soil moist. Weed regularly.

Pests and diseases. Mites. (For treatment, see page 115.)

How to harvest. For greens, use whole plants when they are small. Cut off 4 to 5-inch tips of leaves on large plants.

Artichokes

This prickly thistle hides a tender, tasty heart

Artichoke buds, prime for picking

Appearances can be deceptive. In the plant kingdom, just as in the human realm, a prickly exterior may hide a tender heart. The prickly-looking artichoke is a case in point: its heart, the base of the bud, is the most tender and delicious part. And despite its rugged appearance, the artichoke plant is fussy about climate. It needs mild winters and cool summers (it won't grow in Florida).

The rewards for growing this unusual edible perennial go beyond the harvest of buds. A massive, beautiful plant, the artichoke develops into a silvery green fountain that can spread to 6 feet wide. Buds that escape harvest reveal the artichoke's family ties: they blossom into purple thistles that can be dried for arrangements.

Here are two little-known facts about this remarkable edible thistle. First, the name comes from an Arabic word, *al-kharshuf,* and doesn't have anything to do with the English word "choke." Second, the bud contains a chemical that makes food eaten after it taste sweet. Eventually it may become a noncaloric sweetener.

Artichokes ...at a glance

Type of vegetable. Perennial, hardy to 30°F/−1°C; cool season.

Edible parts. Flower buds: bracts (leaves) and heart (base of bud).

Best soil. Rich, well drained, pH 6.0.

When to plant. *Mild-winter climates:* Set out root divisions or plants in winter or in spring.

How to plant. Set out root divisions or plants in garden 4 to 6 feet apart in rows spaced 6 to 8 feet apart.

Yield. A dozen or more buds per plant.

When to harvest. In spring while buds are tight, first year after planting. Autumn to spring in following years.

Care. Water weekly during growing season. Apply fertilizer in spring or autumn.

Pests and diseases. Slugs, snails. (For treatment, see page 115.)

How to harvest. Cut buds from stems 1 to 1½ inches below bud base.

Asparagus

Delicate, delicious spears, plentiful for years & years

After a winter of slush, wet boots, and sniffles, the first tender harvest of asparagus—lightly steamed and drizzled with butter—can renew your springtime determination to plant a veritable Eden of vegetables.

Asparagus is a perennial. And since its bright green spear-fingers reach up to the spring sun year after year—possibly for decades—you'll want to plan a permanent location for your patch.

Because growing asparagus takes 3 years from seed to harvest, most people buy 1-year-old crowns—rhizomes (food storage stems) with scraggly dry roots growing downward and nubbly growth buds sticking up.

Give the roots a soft, rich bed and they'll reward you with years of plentiful spears. Dig a foot-deep, foot-wide trench. If you're planting more than one row, space trenches 3 to 5 feet apart. Pile soil to one side. Into the trench put a 2 to 3-inch layer of well-rotted manure. Sprinkle in a complete fertilizer—2 pounds of 5-10-10 per 25-foot row works well. Mix manure and fertilizer with the loose soil in the trench and bank it up about 6 inches.

Atop the length of the banked planting mix, space crowns 12 to 18 inches apart and spread each crown's roots down over the sides of the ridge. Partially fill the trench with loose soil to cover the crowns 2 inches deep. As shoots grow, fill in soil around them but *do not cover the tips of the shoots.* Keep the bed well watered.

The first year let all the spears shoot up and leaf out; the feathery foliage nourishes the growing roots, which in turn supply the rhizome with nutrients to tide the plant through the winter and give the next season's spears strength for growth. The second spring you can harvest the first few spears. When spears begin to look spindly (less than ¼ inch in diameter), let them grow up and leaf out. By the third spring, the asparagus will produce spears in full force over a long season.

Asparagus ...at a glance

Type of vegetable. Perennial, hardy to −40°F/−40°C; cool season.

Edible parts. Young shoots (spears).

Best soil. Fertile, well drained, sandy loam to clay loam, pH 6.0 to 6.7.

When to plant. *Cold-winter and mild-winter climates:* Set out plants in spring (when danger of frost has passed). Set out crowns (clumps of roots and dormant buds) in winter or in early spring. Sow seeds in flats 12 to 14 weeks before you intend to set out plants in garden.

How to plant. Set out plants 18 inches apart in 1-foot-deep trenches spaced 3 to 5 feet apart. Cover plants with 1 inch of soil and fill in trenches as they grow. Set out crowns 6 to 8 inches deep, 12 to 18 inches apart, in the same size trenches. Cover crowns with 2 inches of soil. As plants grow, fill in trenches with soil. (Where drainage is very bad, make mounds of soil, rather than growing in trenches.)

Yield. 3 to 4 pounds per 10-foot row.

When to harvest. In spring when shoots appear, second year after planting. Third year harvest will be fuller.

Care. Apply high-nitrogen fertilizer (such as 10-10-10) twice each year (except year of planting), once in spring before spears emerge and again at end of harvest. If soil pH is lower than 6.0, apply lime with first application of fertilizer. Weed regularly; cut down ferny foliage when it turns brown.

Pests and diseases. Aphids, asparagus beetle. (For treatment, see page 114.)

How to harvest. Snap or cut off all spears 7 to 10 inches long, leaving tough, white stubs on plants. Stop harvesting when emerging spears are less than ¼ inch wide; let these spears turn into foliage.

Tender, first-of-season asparagus spears

Beans

Abundant variety, bushy or pole-climbing

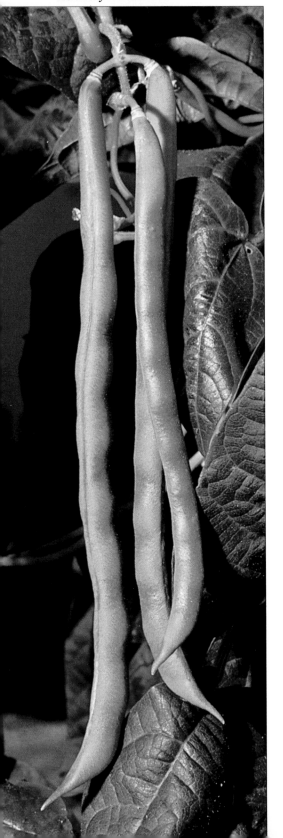

What takes the most effort in growing beans? Some people think it's deciding which kind to grow. For instance, there are snap beans (also called green or string beans), beans for shelling when the seeds are mature but still green, beans to dry for long storage, lima beans, soybeans, and fava beans. Once you've decided which kinds to grow, then you have to choose among the many varieties of each. Poring over seed catalogs can become an all-winter occupation once you start investigating beans.

Snap beans—garden favorites

The whopping number of varieties of snap beans attests to this vegetable's continuing popularity with home gardeners. You can buy seeds for either bush or pole varieties, each with a choice of color—green, yellow (wax), or, for novelty, purple.

Bush beans are compact plants, 1 to 2 feet tall, depending on variety and growing conditions. Pole or climbing beans grow 8 feet or more and need firm support. Bush beans bear 10 days to 2 weeks earlier than pole beans, but the crop is not as prolific.

Snap beans can be easily grown from seeds, but wait until the soil warms up to at least 60°F/16°C or the seeds will just sit and sulk or rot. Either check the soil with a soil thermometer or wait until late-leafing trees—oaks, hickories, pecans—uncurl new spring foliage.

Plant seeds of bush varieties 1 to 1½ inches deep and 2 inches apart in rows spaced 2 to 3 feet apart, or sow them in wide bands with seeds spaced about 6 inches from each other. Since some bush beans require only 7 weeks to mature in warm weather, they can be grown successfully in areas with fairly short summers.

Pole bean plants are much larger and need 3 feet between rows and 6 to 12 inches between plants. Seeds should be planted 1 to 1½ inches deep. Provide poles 6 to 8 feet tall and 6 to 12 inches apart, or let beans climb a trellis.

Romano beans, also known as Italian green beans, are another type of snap bean you might enjoy growing. This delicious bean has a flat, wide pod that's tender and meaty. Pole and bush

Colorful *Golden Wax beans*

Romano beans are available. For eating, you prepare the pods as you would snap beans. Planting and growing requirements of Romano beans are the same as for other bush or pole snap beans.

Though there are probably 50 varieties of snap beans, we can mention only a few. Your local cooperative extension service agent can recommend specific varieties for your area. For green bush beans, reliable varieties include 'Tender crop', 'Tendergreen', and the 'Bush Blue Lake' types. For yellow (wax) bush beans, consider 'Kinghorn', 'Eastern Butterwax', or 'Gold Crop'. For novelty, there's 'Royalty', a purple-podded snap bean that turns green when cooked.

Pole bean varieties include the famous 'Kentucky Wonder', 'Dade', and 'Blue Lake' varieties. 'Kentucky Wonder Wax' is a yellow pole-type snap bean.

Harvesting snap beans takes a certain amount of diligence to keep up with the ready crop, but not much skill. At the ideal point, beans should not have started to bulge the sides of the pods. Pick bean pods when they are at least 3 inches long but before they begin to get tough and stringy. The more faithful you are about frequent picking, the longer the plants will yield.

Beans for shelling or drying

Everyone knows about snap beans and dry beans—but beans for green-shelling? Sometimes called shellies or shuckies in the South, and often called horticultural beans in the seed catalogs, beans for green-shelling are varieties that are grown until their seeds are full-size but not dry.

Some beans are particularly delicious harvested at the green-shelling stage. These include the flageolet bean, a popular variety in the south of France, and the 'French Horticultural Bean', also known as the 'October Bean'. 'Vermont Cranberry Bean' is yet another tasty, succulent shelling bean, and the 'Great Northern White' bean, though mainly known as a dry bean, is delicious harvested early as a shellie. All of these green-shelling favorites grow on bush-type plants and require the same plant spacing and care as bush snap beans. You'll have to wait an average of 65 days to harvest mature green pods.

Cook fresh shellies 5 to 20 minutes until tender (time varies with size of bean and maturity), then serve with butter, salt, and pepper. Or add them to hearty soups or casseroles, or marinate for salads. Left to dry, the shellies, especially the creamy-textured, mellow-tasting flageolet, are delicious cooked by themselves or in casseroles.

Beans cultivated especially for their flavor when they are cooked after drying include the familiar navy bean, pinto bean, and red and white kidney bean, as well as rare varieties known only to the home gardener who loves to scan seed catalogs—'Jacob's Cattle Bean', 'Dalmatian Bean', 'Soldier Bean', 'White Marrowfat', and 'Red Peanut Bean'.

The culture for these beans is the same as for the bush type of snap bean. The main difference is that you let the beans remain on the bush until the pods turn dry or begin to shatter. Shell the ripe beans from their hulls and dry them well before storing.

Limas—king of the garden

Lima beans come in frozen blocks, right? You disliked them as a child, and you haven't tried them since. Well, give fresh-from-the-vine limas a chance before you reject this tasty vegetable. Lima bean is a different plant species from other common beans, but its cultural requirements are nearly the same as for snap beans.

Limas come in either bush or pole form. Bush lima beans develop more slowly than snap beans, requiring 65 to 75 days to mature; pole limas take 78 to 95 days. Limas do not produce as reliably as snap beans in extremely dry, hot weather.

Among the bush limas are 'Improved Bush', 'Henderson Bush', 'Fordhook 242', 'Jackson Wonder', and 'Dixie White Butterpea'; the last two are especially useful in hot-summer areas. 'Prizetaker' and 'King of the Garden' are good large-seeded pole limas. 'Small White Lima' or 'Sieva' is usually grown for drying, but it yields an abundance of green-shelled beans, too.

Soybean—for a protein bounty

Soybeans are newcomers to home gardens. Their seeds, shelled from the short, plump, fuzzy pods, are delicious when cooked as you would cook green-shelling or lima beans. The protein content of soybeans is outstanding. Soybeans grow best in the warm, humid climates of the South and Midwest and do poorly in most dry climates.

The soybean bush is about the same size as that of bush lima beans. Plant seeds 1 inch deep, 4 to 6 inches apart in rows spaced 30 inches apart. Harvest soybeans when the seeds have reached full size but the pods are still green. Pour boiling water over the pods to soften them before shelling.

Fava, a cool-weather bean

The fava bean, like flageolet bean and 'Great Northern', is delicious used when the seeds are still green or when the seeds are dry. The fava, also called broad bean or horse bean, is the only bean to come from the Mediterranean area; all the other well-known beans are New World plants. Unlike other beans, this is a cool-season vegetable (actually a giant vetch). It grows 2 to 4½ feet tall and produces prodigious amounts of oversize pods, up to 18 inches long.

In cold-winter areas you can plant fava beans in early spring as soon as the soil can be worked. In mild-winter climates, plant in autumn for late winter or early spring crops. Plant seeds in rows spaced 18 to 30 inches apart; sow seeds 1 inch deep, 4 to 5 inches apart along the row. Beans mature in 120 to 150 days, depending on the temperature. You can harvest pods for shellie beans before that, though.

A cautionary note: Most people can eat fava beans with safety; a very few (principally of Mediterranean ancestry) have a genetic enzyme deficiency that can cause severe–even fatal–reactions to the beans and the pollen.

Beans ...at a glance

Type of vegetable. Seed-bearing; warm season (except for fava bean).

Edible parts. Harvested seed pods or seeds.

Best soil. Fertile, well drained, pH 6.0 to 6.8.

When to plant. *Cold-winter and mild-winter climates:* Sow seeds in spring (when danger of frost has passed). To increase productivity, inoculate seeds with a legume inoculant. Best soil temperature for germination is 60° to 85°F/16° to 29°C. Lima beans should be planted 2 weeks later than other varieties. Fava beans should be planted in early spring or autumn. Make successive plantings of beans.

How to plant. Sow seeds 1 to 1½ inches deep. (For exact spacing of beans within rows and distance between rows, see entries for specific beans.) You can broadcast bush snap beans in wide rows. Thin seedlings to 6 inches apart. Set up supports for pole beans at planting time.

Yield. 3 to 10 pounds per 10-foot row, depending on variety.

When to harvest. 50 to 100 days after sowing seeds, depending on variety (see entries for specific beans).

Care. Beans will tolerate drier soil than many vegetables, but you should keep soil moist when beans begin to flower and while they are forming pods. Beans have shallow roots, so don't hoe or cultivate soil deeply.

Pests and diseases. Aphids, leafhoppers, Mexican bean beetle, mites; damping off, downy mildew. (For treatment, see pages 114–116.) To prevent spread of leaf diseases, avoid working among beans when leaves are wet.

How to harvest. Carefully pull ripe pods from plants.

Beets

Deliciously enjoyable, leafy top to ruby root

There's a satisfying "thonk" when the earth releases a big fat beet. Beet harvesting has its toothsome rewards, too, and the root isn't the only crop that beets have to offer. The tops are delicious, as well. You can add the small, tender leaves of beet thinnings to salads and prepare the larger leaves as you would spinach.

You may be surprised to find that beets come in colors and shapes other than red and round. Seeds are available for white and yellow beets and for long, cylindrical red beets. White and yellow varieties are sweeter than red beets, and their tops have a milder flavor. Cylindrical beets, though red-fleshed, seem milder and tenderer than most ordinary red kinds. Their elongated roots usually grow 8 inches long and uniformly 1¼ to 2 inches in diameter. Look for seeds of these varieties in mail-order catalogs.

Because the beet root is a storage unit that expands to accommodate food sent down from the green top, the faster the food is produced, the greater the root growth. The best conditions for food production are warm, bright days and cool nights.

Beets like fertile soil without lumps or rocks. Both lumpy soil and heavy clay soil produce misshapen roots. Because beet seeds are slow to germinate, you might want to mark the seed rows by sowing a few fast-sprouting radish seeds. Besides reminding you where the beets are planted, they'll keep your interest while you water the beet bed and wait for the beets to sprout.

After the beets sprout, consistent watering keeps the roots tender as they grow. If you inflict a drought on them, they'll respond by becoming hard and woody.

Beets—roots and tops—at young, tender stage

Blackberries

For heavenly pies, jam— or nibbles as you pick

Blackberries have much the same growth cycle and cultural needs as their close cousins, raspberries. They send up canes one year and produce berries on them the second year. They prefer areas with cool, moist summers, though some kinds are native to the warm, moist regions of southeastern United States.

Included in the blackberry category are cane berries known as dewberry, loganberry, boysenberry, and olallieberry. Berries range in color from jet black to red, from sweet to tart, and have a variety of flavors.

Blackberries develop in two distinctly different forms. Varieties typical of the West Coast, so-called "trailing blackberries" or dewberries, produce long vinelike canes that need to be trellised. Blackberries of the Midwest and East grow upright, shorter canes. In general, blackberries have wicked thorns, though thornless varieties have been developed. Different varieties do best in different parts of the United States and Canada. Though most kinds are self-pollinating, some varieties in the South need a second variety as a pollinator.

Blackberries thrive in a rich, well-prepared soil and sunny location. Most kinds are fairly hardy, but some can't take hard freezing unless you completely cover their canes with mulch. To avoid verticillium wilt, don't plant blackberries in soil where you have raised potatoes, eggplants, peppers, or tomatoes in the last 2 years.

As is true of raspberries, blackberries are more likely to produce well if you start with certified stock from a reliable nursery. At planting time, set plants an inch deeper into the ground than they grew in the nursery. Give trailing varieties of blackberries plenty of room to grow, and set up a trellis to support them. (See drawings on pages 105 and 109.)

Unless they get ample rainfall, water blackberries liberally during their growing season until the harvest is complete. Reduce watering after fruit is picked.

Blackberries have perennial roots, but biennial canes. As "primocanes," canes grow to their full length or height in the first year. After flowering and fruiting in the second year, the canes, now called "floricanes," die and should be cut down.

If you are raising trailing blackberries, allow the first-year canes, the primocanes, to grow undisturbed along the ground. At the end of the first season, where winters are cold, cover the canes with mulch for winter protection from freezing. At the start of the second year's growth, tie these year-old canes, now called floricanes, to a trellis to bear fruit. The canes can be shortened to 5 to 6 feet to fit the trellis.

Plants that produce upright canes do not need to be trellised. When first-year canes have grown 24 to 30 inches tall, pinch off their tops to force the growth of side branches. In the second year, as new growth starts in spring, shorten all of the side branches to 12 to 15 inches long. Fruit will be borne on these short side branches.

Blackberry cluster *with ripe and half-ripe fruits*

Blackberries ...at a glance

Growth habit. Berries borne in clusters on 2-year-old canes.

Climate preference. Plants do best where summers are cool and moist and winters are cold, but not colder than −15°F/−26°C. Some kinds do well where summers are warm and moist. Some varieties of thornless blackberries, boysenberries, youngberries are hardy only to 0°F/−18°C.

Best soil. Rich, well-drained, sandy loam, pH 5.5 to 6.8.

When to plant. *Cold-winter climates:* In early spring before new growth starts. *Mild-winter climates:* In early spring or autumn.

How to plant. Erect blackberries: Set out bare-root plants in trenches 24 to 30 inches apart in rows spaced 6 to 10 feet apart. Cover crowns with 1 inch of soil. Trailing blackberries: Set out bare-root plants in holes 5 to 8 feet apart in rows 9 to 10 feet apart. Cover crowns with 1 inch of soil. Set up supports for trailing varieties.

Yield. A quart of berries per plant; 10 to 15 quarts of berries per 10-foot row.

When to harvest. Spring or summer, when berries are full-size, fully colored.

Care. Keep soil moist. Weed regularly. Tie trailing kinds to trellis. Prune according to instructions in text and on page 119.

Pests and diseases. Aphids, borers, mites, strawberry root weevil; verticillium wilt. (For treatment, see pages 114–116.)

Blueberries

Bobbing in cream, a blue-ribbon dessert

Today's backyard blueberries descend from solid Yankee stock. Members of the heath family (and therefore cousins of azaleas, rhododendrons, and cranberries), their forebears were wild, upright-growing bushes from New England. Hybrids that would produce well in gardens were first achieved in 1909; before that, if you wanted blueberry pancakes for breakfast, first you had to roam the countryside and harvest blueberries wherever they grew.

Today, you can raise blueberries in many areas of the United States and Canada, provided you can give plants certain conditions. Highbush blueberries need climates with cold winters. Rabbiteye blueberries are better adapted to the mild-winter regions of the south. Plants can last for 25 to 30 years.

Blueberries need a very acidic soil (pH between 3.5 and 4.5) that is rich in organic matter. To increase soil acidity, you can mix 1 pound of soil sulfur per 100 square feet of sandy soil or 3 to 4 pounds per 100 square feet of loam. Maintain acidity by using fertilizers formulated for acid-soil plants. Most soils will benefit from the addition of generous amounts of peat moss or other organic material.

Plant blueberries in the autumn if your winter is mild (compared to New England), otherwise in early spring. Buy 2 or 3-year-old certified plants that are 12 to 36 inches high. To allow for essential cross-pollination, choose two or three different varieties to raise together. Prune transplants down to 3 or 4 of their strongest shoots, and prune off the plump fruit buds.

Prepare planting holes by digging holes 18 inches deep and as wide. Blend soil with organic matter before backfilling and planting. Set plants 4 to 6 feet apart, in rows 8 to 12 feet apart. Put down a thick mulch around each plant to help shallow roots to retain moisture and to keep down weeds.

During the first critical 3 years, blueberries need at least an inch of water per week in the growing season. But don't overfertilize: each bush needs only an ounce of fertilizer per year of age up to a maximum of 8 ounces per plant (use a fertilizer blended for azaleas and rhododendrons). Apply fertilizer by dividing it into several applications during the first 2 years. After that, apply fertilizer just once a year in early spring.

During the first few years, prune bushes lightly in early spring, removing low, overlapping, or weak canes. After 3 years, also cut back the tips of vigorous canes, leaving 6 to 8 buds, to promote side branching. The goal is to keep canes well spaced to give berries ample exposure to sunlight, to force side branching, and, in later years, to keep bushes from growing too tall.

Blueberries ...at a glance

Growth habit. Berries borne along 1-year-old branches of bushes.

Climate preference. Highbush blueberries: Plants do best where winters are cold and summers are not too hot and dry. Rabbiteye blueberries: Plants do best where winters are mild and summers are warm. Best in southeastern states.

Best soil. Abundant organic matter, well-drained, sandy loam, pH 3.5 to 5.0.

When to plant. Highbush varieties: In early spring before growth starts. Rabbiteye varieties: In late autumn or winter.

How to plant. Highbush varieties: Set out bare-root plants in holes 12 to 18 inches deep, 4 to 5 feet apart, in rows spaced 8 to 10 feet apart. Rabbiteye varieties: Set out bare-root plants in holes 12 to 18 inches deep, 5 to 6 feet apart, in rows spaced 10 to 12 feet apart. (See page 105.)

Yield. 2 to 7 pounds per plant.

When to harvest. 60 or 80 days after bloom, when berries are entirely blue and taste sweet.

Care. Keep soil moist. Mulch soil with organic matter. Weed regularly. Prune in late winter or early spring before growth starts; plants need only light pruning first 3 years. (See page 118.) Cover with netting to protect berries from birds.

Pests and diseases. Leafhoppers, mites, nematodes; powdery mildew. (For treatment, see pages 115–116.)

Plump blueberries, *ready for pies and muffins when they turn blue and taste sweet*

Broccoli

Bunches of tasty flower buds from a cole cousin

Full, *firm head of broccoli*

Broccoli is one of the easier-to-grow members of the cole family (cabbage, cauliflower, Brussels sprouts, and so forth). Given its basic requirements, broccoli grows without giving the gardener a great deal of grief, and it bears over a long season.

Broccoli shares the cole family preference for a cool growing season. If the temperature goes too high, it will bolt—not out of your garden, but into premature flower stalks that will bloom and go to seed before you can pick them.

In cool weather, broccoli first sends up a central stalk that bears a cluster of green or purple flower buds. This unopened central bouquet, along with 6 to 8 inches of stem, is what you harvest. The central cluster may reach 6 inches in diameter—but don't wait too long or the buds will open into yellow flowers, and you'll have broccoli of inferior quality. After the main broccoli stem is cut, side branches will lengthen and produce smaller but good-tasting clusters for you to harvest throughout the growing season.

Broccoli ...at a glance

Type of vegetable. Bud-forming; cool season.

Edible parts. Flower buds; stems.

Best soil. Fertile, pH 6.0 to 6.8.

When to plant. *Cold-winter climates:* For *summer crop*, set out plants in spring. *For autumn crop*, set out plants or sow seeds in mid and late summer. *Mild-winter climates:* For *summer crop*, set out plants in spring. *For winter and spring crops*, sow seeds or set out plants in autumn.

How to plant. Set transplants 15 to 24 inches apart in rows spaced 2 to 3 feet apart. Sow seeds ½ to 1 inch deep, 1 inch apart, in rows spaced as above. Thin seedlings to 15 to 24 inches apart.

Yield. 4 to 6 pounds per 10-foot row.

When to harvest. 50 to 100 days after setting out plants, before buds open.

Care. Keep soil moist. Weed regularly.

Pests, diseases. See Cabbage, page 42.

Brussels sprouts

Baby cabbages with good, grown-up flavor

Bountiful crop *of Brussels sprouts*

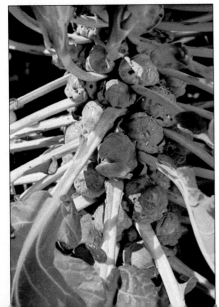

Brussels sprouts are peculiar-looking plants that would be worth growing just for the novelty even if they weren't such good food. They look like miniature palm trees with lumps growing on their trunks. The lumps—sprouts—have the flavor of sweet tiny cabbages. Unlike most true palm trees, Brussels sprouts prefer to grow during cool weather—their flavor is improved by light frosts, and they are often planted as an autumn crop.

Like the rest of the cole family, Brussels sprouts are happiest growing in fertile, well-drained soil. Harvest begins when the big bottom leaves start to turn yellow. Each plant should produce 50 to 100 sprouts clustered closely around the main stalk. You harvest the sprouts from the bottom of the stem to the top, snapping off firm green sprouts that are slightly smaller than a golf ball. Remove any side leaves growing below the harvested sprouts. Continue harvesting upward along the stem as the sprouts mature.

Brussels sprouts ...at a glance

Type of vegetable. Bud-forming; cool season.

Edible parts. Sprouts (swollen buds).

Best soil. Fertile, pH 5.5 to 6.8.

When to plant. *Cold-winter climates:* Set out plants or sow seeds in midsummer. *Mild-winter climates:* Set out plants or sow seeds in autumn. Sow seeds 4 to 6 weeks before you intend to set out plants.

How to plant. Set out plants 15 to 24 inches apart in rows spaced 2 to 3 feet apart. Sow seeds ½ inch deep, 1 inch apart, in rows spaced as above. Thin seedlings to 15 to 24 inches apart.

Yield. 3 to 5 pounds per 10-foot row.

When to harvest. 80 to 100 days after setting out plants, when green and firm.

Care. Keep soil moist. Weed regularly.

Pests, diseases. See Cabbage, page 42.

Cabbage

"Old King Cole" in a royal banquet of varieties

Cabbage is the Old King Cole of the vegetable patch. "Cole," the Old English word for cabbage, is also the general name for a group of vegetables that share a common ancestry, a family preference for cool weather, and a family susceptibility to certain pests and diseases. Cabbage's garden relatives include kohlrabi, broccoli, cauliflower, and Brussels sprouts.

True, seeing them placed side by side in a family portrait, you would be hard pressed to see what cabbages have in common with kohlrabi or broccoli. But the diverse appearance of cole family members comes from a single remarkable family trait—the ability to thicken various plant parts. Thus the kohlrabi has thickened stems; broccoli has thickened immature flowering branches; and cabbage—well, with cabbage, the ability to thicken went entirely to its head. Cabbage heads are formed by a rosette of thickened leaves on a short stem.

You'll probably be surprised not only at the variety of shapes of cabbage heads—round, pointy, and flat—but also at the variety of rich colors and leaf textures. In addition to green cabbages, you can choose from among several red varieties and the Savoy varieties with their crinkly leaves.

Besides these, you'll also find miniature cabbages, such as 'Dwarf Morden' and 'Earliana'; varieties that develop early to midseason, such as 'Early Jersey Wakefield', 'Emerald Cross', 'Harvester Queen', 'King Cole', 'Salad Green' (for cole slaw), and 'Stonehead' (a firm head that develops well in hot weather) late-maturing varieties, such as 'Premium Flat Dutch' and 'Penn State Ballhead'; varieties that are good for storage, such as 'Danish Roundhead' and 'Winterkeeper'; and varieties that are good for kraut, such as 'Surehead', 'Ultra Green', and 'Superslaw'.

For red cabbage, you can select such varieties as 'Red Head' (good winter variety) and 'Ruby Head' (heat resistant).

For a late-maturing Savoy type, try 'Savoy Chieftain'. Other Savoy types include 'Savoy Ace' (develops early) and 'Savoy King'. Your county farm advisor can tell you which varieties do best in your area.

Spectacular Savoy cabbage is not for the small-space garden (unless you want just one or two for show); the mature plant can be 2 feet in diame-

Crinkly leaves *distinguish Savoy cabbage*

ter. Full-grown, 8-inch Savoy heads can weigh 4 to 4½ pounds. Savoy leaves are sweet, juicy, and somewhat milder than other cabbages, and the heads are looser. Though this variety is something of a newcomer to many home gardens, it is actually an old variety, developed in ancient times in southern Europe; today's more common solid-headed varieties were developed during the Middle Ages in northern Europe.

Flowering cabbage is another decorative—but edible—cabbage. The leafy 10-inch heads of these cabbages look like giant peonies of deep blue green, which are marbled and edged in white, cream, rose, or purple. Flowering cabbage requires the same soil, care, and timing as conventional cabbage. The "flower" color is most dazzling after the first frost touches the plants. They can either be planted 15 to 18 inches apart in garden beds, or potted singly or together. You can eat the loose-leafed heads cooked or raw, just like ordinary cabbage.

Cabbages of all varieties mature best during cool weather. You can grow spring and fall crops where summers are hot. Plant early-maturing varieties or hybrids in spring; these mature from transplants in 7 to 8 weeks. Later-maturing varieties, such as the king-size kraut cabbage, need up to 12 weeks to mature from seeds and should be planted after midsummer for autumn harvest.

A planting precaution: Cabbages and members of the cabbage family are susceptible to a wide variety of soil-borne diseases. One way to avoid them is to rotate cabbage crops (and other members of the cole family); don't plant any cole crop in the same spot again for at least 4 years.

Round, *green cabbage, a typical kind*

Cardoon

Not for the impatient, it takes its own sweet time

Cardoon plants, tied for blanching

Though by the time it reaches the kitchen, tender and blanched, it will remind you more of celery, cardoon is actually a close cousin of the artichoke, which it resembles. Both are native perennials of southern Europe.

We eat the flower buds of artichoke plants; cardoon, though, is grown for its thick, fleshy leaf stalk. Cut in chunks and then steamed like asparagus, these stalks make an unusual and tasty delicacy.

Frost-tender and slow to mature, cardoon needs a long, mild growing season. Start seeds indoors in spring where winters are cold and the summer growing season is short; set out plants when the danger of frost is past. Where the frost-free growing season is 180 days or more, sow seeds directly in the garden in spring.

Give cardoon plants plenty of elbow room: they may reach 4 feet tall and 6 feet wide.

To assure mild flavor, 4 or 5 weeks before the expected harvest date you should wrap the leaf stalks to blanch them. Tie up the leaf stalks with string. Then encase the stalks either with heavy paper or a sheath of straw bound with string. Avoid covering the leaf tips.

Cardoon ...at a glance

Type of vegetable. Leaf stalk; tender perennial.

Edible parts. Leaf stalks.

Best soil. Rich, well drained, pH 6.0.

When to plant. *Cold-winter climates:* Set out plants in spring. *Mild-winter climates:* Sow seeds in garden in spring.

How to plant. Indoors, sow seeds in peat pots. Set out 3-inch-tall seedlings 20 inches apart in rows spaced 3 feet apart. Outdoors, sow 3 to 5 seeds in clusters ¼ inch deep, 20 inches apart, in rows spaced as above. When seedlings are 3 inches tall, thin to one plant per cluster.

Yield. 1 to 2 pounds per plant.

When to harvest. 180 days after sowing seeds, after blanching stems 4 to 5 weeks.

Care. Keep soil moist. Weed regularly.

Pests and diseases. Aphids. (For treatment, see page 114.)

Carrots

For straight-arrow growth, give them fine, loose earth

Well-grown carrots, *firm and straight*

"Eat your carrots!" is a parental command guaranteed to make children's mouths turn down in stubborn pouts if those orange mounds are overcooked canned or frozen carrots. But when the carrots are fresh, sweet, finger-size roots that were planted, watered, and plucked by the children themselves—that's another story at suppertime. You're more likely to hear, "Let's have some more!"

Though not a quick-and-easy task, growing carrots can be child's play once the ground is prepared. Plan on spending time refining the soil unless your garden is blessed with fine, sandy loam—without lumps, rocks, rusty nails, skate keys, or other archeological treasures. You see, carrots are very sensitive; they grow straight until they hit the least obstruction, then they make a sharp turn, or fork, or otherwise grow misshapen. They also grow misshapen if you put fresh manure in the soil. Time invested in breaking up clods and removing debris will help increase your yield of perfectly formed carrots.

There are several ways to grow carrots in spite of problem soil. One way is to select a short variety of carrot; they tend to be sweeter, anyway. You can find baby-size carrots in heart, finger, and even golf ball shapes.

Another way around fractious soil is to soften the soil by soaking it. Then, when the soil has dried enough to work, dig for each row a V-shaped planting trench 6 to 8 inches deep that is 2 to 3 inches wide at the top for each row. Fill the trench with fine planting soil; a combination of your best garden soil sifted with well-rotted (fine textured) compost is ideal. The trench lets the roots expand without twisting or forking.

Yet another way to by-pass difficult soil is to grow carrots in containers, where you have complete control over soil quality. A good mix for container-grown carrots is two parts sand, two parts well-rotted (fine-textured) compost, and one part garden soil—lump-free, naturally. Or you could use commercial potting soil.

Once you've sown the tiny seeds as thinly as possible and covered them with ¼ to ½ inch of fine soil, keep them moist for the 2 to 3-week germination period. During hot weather, covering your bed of carrots with moist burlap will help keep seeds moist until they sprout. Remove this burlap cover once seedlings emerge. If you live in a very cool climate, try growing carrots in a heat-absorbing metal or wooden container.

Carrots ...at a glance

Type of vegetable. Root; cool season.

Edible parts. Roots.

Best soil. Fertile, sandy loam (should never contain fresh manure); pH 5.5 to 6.8.

When to plant. *Cold-winter climates: For summer crop,* sow seeds in early spring. *For autumn crop,* sow seeds in late summer. *Mild-winter climates: For summer crop,* sow seeds in spring. *For autumn, winter, and spring crops,* sow seeds 30 to 80 days before you intend to harvest.

How to plant. Sow seeds ¼ to ½ inch deep, ½ inch apart, in rows spaced 12 to 30 inches apart; or broadcast seeds in wide beds. Sow seeds directly in garden or in deep containers. Seeds take 7 to 21 days to germinate. Thin seedlings to 2 inches apart in rows, about 4 inches apart in wide beds when they are 1 inch tall.

Yield. 7 to 10 pounds per 10-foot row.

When to harvest. 30 to 40 days after sowing seeds (for baby carrots); 50 to 80 days after sowing seeds (for mature carrots). Harvest first carrots when they are finger-long. Continue harvesting until carrots are full-grown; if left in ground, they become hard and woody. In *cold-winter climates,* harvest all carrots before hard frosts occur. Where winters are not severely cold, you can store carrots in the ground all winter; after the first hard frost, cover carrots, tops and all, with 6 to 8 inches of shredded leaves. Wherever summers are hot, harvest spring-planted carrots before hottest weather arrives.

Care. Keep soil moist. Remove weeds while they're still small so they won't hinder growth.

Pests and diseases. Aphids, leafhoppers, nematodes; damping off. (For treatment, see pages 114–116.)

How to harvest. Pull up carefully. Before harvesting entire crop, pull up one or two roots to see how large they are.

Consistent watering is important throughout the growing season. If carrots dry out while growing, their flesh hardens; then when water is restored, their roots tend to split.

There is one watering trick you can use to encourage long, slender carrots. Sow seeds in fine, rich soil and keep the seeds evenly moist while they germinate. When the little plants reach about 1 inch tall, withhold water until they start to wilt. This forces the roots to grow deeper. Then resume normal watering—you perform this trick only once.

Harvesting actually starts with thinning. Nothing is as tasty as miniature carrots thinned from the garden. Try chopping them up, tops and all, to add to tossed salads for a fresh surprise. Keep thinning until carrots are about 2 inches apart, then wait and harvest when they reach your favorite eating size.

There are well over 80 varieties of carrots. Many of them are hybrid variations on such carrot standards as 'Chantenay', 'Danvers', 'Nantes', 'Imperator', or 'Spartan'.

For long-rooted carrots (up to 8 inches), try 'Gold Pak' or 'Imperator.' For medium-rooted ones (6 to 7 inches) there are 'Nantes Coreless', 'Danvers Half-long', or 'Spartan Bonus'.

Short-rooted carrots (5 inches or less) include 'Red Core Chantenay', 'Short 'n' Sweet', 'Tiny Sweet', 'Little Finger', and golf ball shaped 'Gold Nugget'.

Cauliflower

A fancy, blanched cabbage cousin with an education

Perfect head of cauliflower: *solid and white*

According to Mark Twain, a cauliflower is just a cabbage that has gone to college. That places you, the gardener, in the role of professor. Your task? To groom this member of the cole family for the dining table.

A pure white, solid head of cauliflower, such as you see in the produce section of the market, has been "educated" in ideal cole-family conditions: cool, humid growing season and fertile, well-drained soil that's watered often to keep it moist. If you live where summers are hot and dry, set out transplants early enough that you'll be able to harvest well before or well after the midsummer heat.

Snowy white, solid, high-quality cauliflower has also gone through a process called blanching. To blanch a cauliflower head, tie the large outer leaves over the head when it's about 2 inches wide. Elastic bands are good for this purpose. Blanching keeps the sun and rain from damaging the tender head as it matures.

If blanching sounds like too much trouble, you might try growing varieties that are self-blanching. On these varieties, the outer leaves naturally grow up and over the heads and cover them.

Self-blanching varieties include 'White Top', 'Self Blanche', 'White Summer', and 'Purple Head'. 'Purple Head', as the name indicates, has a head of deep purple, which fades to green when you cook it; this variety tastes somewhat like broccoli, cauliflower's less-educated first cousin. 'Chartreuse', a green variety, also has a broccolilike flavor.

Cauliflower ...at a glance

Type of vegetable. Bud-forming; cool season.

Edible parts. Heads (flower buds).

Best soil. Fertile, well drained, pH 6.0 to 6.8.

When to plant. *Cold-winter climates:* Set out plants or sow seeds in early spring or midsummer. *Mild-winter climates:* Set out plants or sow seeds in autumn or winter. Sow seeds in flats 4 to 6 weeks before you intend to set out plants.

How to plant. Set out plants 15 to 24 inches apart in rows spaced 2 to 3 feet apart. Sow seeds ½ inch deep, 1 inch apart, in rows spaced as above. Thin seedlings to 15 to 24 inches apart.

Yield. 8 to 10 pounds per 10-foot row.

When to harvest. 55 to 100 days after setting out plants, after blanching 1 to 2 weeks, but before buds open.

Care. Keep soil moist. Weed regularly. Blanch heads as soon as they begin to develop.

Pests and diseases. See Cabbage, page 42.

How to harvest. Cut off heads.

Celery & Celeriac

Stately stalk & humble root, both crunch nicely in salads

Celery stalks—blanch for mild flavor

Gardeners living where summers stay cool often say that they can't really grow many edibles. Well, cool-summer gardeners, don't ignore celery and celeriac. These two vegetable relatives especially need a long (4-month), cool growing season.

Celery requires human help to turn into mild-tasting, crunchy, pale green stalks. But you don't have to fuss with celeriac's stalks—it's grown for its delicious knobby root.

To grow mild-tasting celery, you must use some sort of blanching technique. For example, 3 to 4 weeks before you're going to harvest celery, tie the tops of the stalks together and mound garden soil along the stalks to shut out sunlight. When you're ready to harvest, pull away the soil and cut off the celery plants.

Or you can place a 3-pound coffee can with both ends removed over the seedlings when you plant them, or make tarpaper cylinders or sleeves to slip over plants. The celery stalks will grow up inside the can or sleeve in a tight clump.

Chayote

On a warmth-loving vine, big mango-shaped fruits

Chayote: from a tender vine, a squashlike edible

What looks like a puckered pear or wizened avocado, has a single flat seed like a mango, and tastes like a mild squash? Give up? It's the chayote, also called mirliton, vegetable pear, or mango squash.

A Central American native, chayote prefers climates with long, warm, sunny days. It bears fruit in the shorter days of autumn. Chayote is popular in Louisiana and Florida. It can grow well—even rampantly—in the mild-winter regions along the Gulf Coast and in Southern California.

Since even a single vine climbs to 50 feet with clinging tendrils, the lush growth of chayote needs sturdy supports. In early autumn and through winter, in very mild regions, it will overwhelm you with 50 to 150 chayote, which you can bake, boil, or sauté.

Don't bother looking for chayote seeds. To produce a vine, you plant the entire fruit, fat end down. Frost kills plants to the ground, but chayote is a perennial and will come back year after year where there are only occasional light frosts.

Chicory

Garden-grown for its greens, its root is used in coffee

Chicory *leaves for salad greens*

Chicory's tousled and carefree appearance may remind you of dandelion leaves. Actually, different chicories are grown by gardeners for three purposes: for greens (small-rooted varieties), for roots to make a coffee substitute (large-rooted varieties), and for Belgian or French endive ('Witloof').

To create headlike clusters of leaves called Belgian or French endive, 'Witloof' chicory is grown from seed to mature by autumn. In the following winter, after the greens have been trimmed to an inch of stem, the roots are buried diagonally in moist sand and set in a dark, cool room. There, new growth is forced, its leaves pale and butter-tender.

For salad greens, sow the seeds of salad varieties in a sunny site.

As is true of lettuce or endive, chicory's immature greens taste delicious. To harvest, carefully cut off the outer leaves.

To grow roots for the coffee substitute, sow seeds as for salad greens. Harvest roots by digging them up, about 4 months after planting.

Collards

Southern cooking greens, steamy with nourishment

Collards *grow like headless cabbages*

"Cabbages that don't know where they're headed" is one way to describe lanky, open-growing collards.

Grown throughout the country for its succulent green leaves, this headless cabbage relative is most popular in the South, where it's planted in the summer for autumn and winter harvest. (The mature plants are frost hardy and yield sweeter leaves after light frosts.)

Collards also tolerate hot weather and are among the few greens that do well in gardens all summer long. Set out transplants in early spring for a spring-into-summer crop.

Collards are thirsty, hungry vegetables. Keep the stems and leaves tender by watering and fertilizing the plants frequently. A well-nourished plant will grow up to 3 feet tall and will yield many juicy, delicious leaves.

You can eat the thinnings—the young plants that you pull up to allow others more room to grow. Later, you can harvest the lower leaves from plants as they become large enough to eat.

Corn

Cook as soon as plucked for delicious sweet flavor

Tall corn stalks, their tassels waving in a summer breeze, are a vegetable garden's heraldic banners. Even though your garden space is limited, you may be tempted to plant corn—at the sacrifice of a square of lawn or a flower-growing space—when you read about all the wonderful varieties of sweet corn available to home gardeners.

By the way, it's neither pride nor your imagination that makes your home-grown corn taste better than store-bought. Corn plucked from the stalk at its prime and hustled into a pot of boiling water is indeed sweeter than corn bought at the store. The reason? The sugar within the kernels has not yet turned into starch.

The basic varieties

Corn varieties are so numerous that you can find at least one to fit the requirements of your garden wherever you live.

A long growing season means you can plant early, midseason, and late-maturing crops for a whole summer of sweet corn. A short growing season limits you to early-maturing or extra-early kinds—though there is still ample choice.

Here are some tried and true varieties. Early-maturing: 'Early Sunglow' (grows well in cool weather; plants only 4½ feet tall), 'Golden Beauty' (plants grow to 5½ feet), 'Morning Sun', 'Polar Vee', and 'Seneca 60'. Midseason-maturing: 'Butter and Sugar' (bicolor), 'FM Cross', 'Golden Cross Bantam', 'Golden Jubilee', and 'Honey and Cream' (bicolored). Late-maturing: 'Country Gentleman' (shoe-peg white kernels; good for canning and freezing) 'Io-chief' (large ears; wind resistant stalks), 'Silver Queen' (white kernels), and 'Stylepak' (good for canning and freezing).

As a rule, early varieties produce smaller and tougher ears, and later varieties have larger, longer ears with better flavor. Check with your county farm advisor for varieties adapted especially for your area.

You can wax nostalgic and grow an old-time (19th century) favorite such as 'Country Gentleman', a white corn with an irregular pattern of shoe-peg kernels.

Traditional, too, is multicolored Indian corn. Those handsome dried ears of bronze and red Indian corn that decorate your front door and table at Thanksgiving can be grown in your backyard garden.

Another possibility to consider is popcorn—either the common, yellow-kerneled popcorns or dark red, small-eared 'Strawberry Popcorn' (low yield, but decorative).

Supersweet corn

The latest developments in hybrid corn are the supersweet varieties. Not only are they remarkably higher in sugar content than regular corn, but they hold their sweetness longer—with these varieties you can stroll rather than run from corn patch to pot of boiling water.

You'll find three kinds of super-sweets: the extrasweets, (including 'Early Xtra-Sweet', 'Illini Xtra-Sweet', and 'Florida Stay-Sweet') which are twice as sweet as standard corn; synergistic hybrids that are up to 25 percent sweeter than standard corn (look for 'Sugarloaf' and 'Honeycomb'); and 'Everlasting Heritage' hybrids (designated 'EH' in seed catalogs).

Corn ears *of several types: white and yellow sweet corn, knobby red popcorn, multicolored Indian corn*

The 'Everlasting Heritage' hybrids also have a high sugar content that holds well. In addition, these varieties are not open to cross-pollination; you can plant them near other kinds of sweet corn without fear of harvesting an ear with sweet kernels, Indian corn kernels, and popcorn kernels within biting distance of each other. You'll see 'Mainliner EH', 'Kandy Korn EH' (with husks marked with burgundy red), and 'Golden Sweet EH' listed in many seed catalogs.

Success: The essentials

Whichever kind of corn you choose, you'll have the most success if you satisfy corn's three main requirements—ample space, warm weather, and generous amounts of fertilizer and water.

Adequate space. Unless you are growing just a few token stalks, you'll need a large area of soil to plant enough to feed your hungry hordes—those high-as-an-elephant's-eye stalks produce only one or two ears each, maybe three if you're lucky. There are some midget varieties, promoted as space savers and novelties, but they don't produce as heavily as full-size varieties.

The space you select for growing corn has to be in a block; you can't string a row of corn along the fence and expect the ears to develop. Since corn pollen from the tassels of one stalk is carried by the wind to the silks of a neighboring stalk, corn planted in adjacent rows has the best chance of being pollinated. The pollen from a single row of corn probably would not pollinate the ears completely. So plant at least two rows of corn together, or better, three or four rows.

Here are three other factors to keep in mind when choosing a site for corn. First, corn needs at least 8 hours of direct sunlight a day. Second, corn is tall and will cast shade over other plants, so it's best to plant it in the northern end of your garden plot. Third, if you want to grow more than one variety, you must make sure they can't cross-pollinate. You can do this by planting different varieties far enough apart so the wind will not carry pollen from one kind to another, by planting varieties that mature at different times, or by planting in succession to avoid different kinds maturing at the same time. If the garden is small, avoid unwanted cross-pollination by planting only one variety of corn.

Temperature. The proper soil and air temperature are important. Soil temperature should warm up to at least 50°F/10°C before you sow seeds. Planting early in cold soil won't give you a head start. In fact, you'll probably lose some seeds to decay and possibly some seedlings to frost. The warmer the weather, the faster corn grows: corn planted a week apart in May may ripen on the same day in August. (In hot areas of the Southwest, though, plant corn as early as possible to mature by June.)

Watering. Corn needs ample water; it won't produce if it's thirsty. Before planting, make sure the ground is thoroughly moist but not so wet you can squeeze water out of it. If the soil is moist enough when you plant seeds, you shouldn't have to water until they have sprouted and grown several inches. Seeds tend to rot if the soil is too wet. But once they are up, don't let the seedlings wilt.

In dry-summer climates, it's best to plan ahead for heavy watering by building irrigation ditches at planting time. Start by using strings to line up straight rows, about 30 to 36 inches apart. In moist, spaded or tilled soil, scoop out trenches and pile excavated soil along the rim of each trench. Plant seeds 1 to 2 inches deep and 4 to 6 inches apart in this shoulder of excavated soil.

Where summers are rainy or cool, you may have to water only once or twice during the season if at all. In such climates you can take care of watering with sprinklers.

Fertilizer. Corn needs a considerable amount of fertilizer. Mixing in compost, manure, or fertilizer before planting may be enough, but generally you should fertilize corn twice during the growing season. Apply a high-nitrogen fertilizer when plants are 12 to 15 inches tall and again when they are about 30 inches tall.

For vigorous growth, don't pull off the suckers (short side shoots) that grow from the main stalk.

Harvesting at the right time can make the difference between sweet, tender corn and tough, starchy corn. Read the directions on when to harvest in the checklist. Unless you've planted a variety that is extra-sweet, you'll get the best flavor from ripe corn if you can begin cooking it within a minute or two after harvesting.

Corn ...at a glance

Type of vegetable. Seed-bearing; warm season.

Edible parts. Seeds on ears.

Best soil. Rich, well drained, pH 5.8 to 6.8.

When to plant. In spring when danger of frost has passed and soil temperature is at least 50°F/10°C. Make successive sowings (give late crop time to ripen before first frost date in autumn). In Florida, also sow in autumn and winter in mildest areas.

How to plant. Sow seeds 1 to 2 inches deep, 4 to 6 inches apart, in rows spaced 2½ to 3 feet apart; thin seedlings 12 to 18 inches apart. Corn can also be planted in hills spaced 3 feet apart; sow seeds 1 to 2 inches deep, 5 or 6 seeds to a hill; thin seedlings to 3 plants per hill. Sow at least two rows of corn for pollination (three or four rows are better).

Yield. 10 to 12 ears each 10-foot row.

When to harvest. 60 to 100 days after sowing seeds, depending on variety. When silks turn brown on ears, pull back the outer husk on an ear or two. Ripe kernels will squirt a milky-white juice when pinched. If possible, harvest just before you are ready to cook.

Care. Keep soil moist (don't let soil dry out once ears start to form silks). Apply a high-nitrogen fertilizer when plants are 12 to 15 inches tall and again when they are 30 inches tall.

Pests and diseases. Aphids, army worms, corn borer, corn earworm, flea beetles; damping off. (For treatment, see pages 114–116.)

How to harvest. Twist ripe ears off stalks.

Cress

Bursts of zesty flavor from a dainty green garnish

Watercress thrives on this treatment

Watercress and garden cress have two things in common: a spicy, tingling flavor and their last names. Otherwise, these two salad garnishes are very different.

Watercress, a perennial, needs soaking wet soil. The best place to grow it is along the bank of an unpolluted stream. Practically speaking, you can grow watercress in a pot of sandy soil set in a basin of water. (Change the water weekly to keep it fresh.) Some gardeners also grow watercress in a coldframe or trench that's kept constantly wet under a dripping hose or spigot.

Start watercress from seeds. Sow the tiny seeds thickly, then thin out and transplant the seedlings when they are a few inches tall. You can also root sprigs of watercress in a glass of water.

Annual garden cress—also called curly cress and pepper grass—is a sprinter. You can sow its seeds indoors and harvest a crop in 10 to 14 days, or make repeated sowings outdoors to harvest every 2 to 3 weeks.

Cress ...at a glance

Type of vegetable. Leafy; cool season.

Edible parts. Leaves; stems.

Best soil. Watercress: Rich, sandy loam, pH 6.0 to 6.8. Cress: Rich, well drained, pH 6.0 to 6.8.

When to plant. Watercress: In spring. Garden cress: In spring.

How to plant. Watercress: Broadcast seeds in wide bands and cover with ⅛ inch of soil; thin seedlings to 2 to 4 inches apart. Garden cress: Sow seeds ¼ inch deep, 1 to 2 inches apart, in rows spaced 18 inches apart; thin seedlings to 6 to 8 inches apart.

When to harvest. Watercress: 50 days after sowing seeds. Garden cress: 10 to 14 days after sowing seeds.

Care. Keep soil moist. Weed regularly.

Pests and diseases. Cabbage maggot, flea beetles, harlequin bug, snails. (For treatment, see pages 114–115.)

Cucumbers

For teatime sandwiches & cool crunch in salads

Cucumbers are rich in variety. There are cukes for slicing and cukes for pickling; short, warty cukes and long, smooth cukes; dark green cukes and yellow cukes, to name just some of the possibilities.

Cucumbers can be divided into categories: the 8 to 15-inch slicers, the smaller 2 to 6-inch picklers, and a mixed group of novel cucumbers. All types will produce prolifically given rich soil, warm weather, sunshine, plenty of water—and enough room to grow. Greenhouse cucumbers, however, must be grown in greenhouses.

Among slicers and picklers, you'll find hybrid and standard varieties. Standards and many hybrids bear male and female flowers on the same vine. Vines first produce male flowers, then the female ones appear a little later. The female blossoms are identifiable by a swollen ovary just behind the flower that looks like a miniature cucumber. In the garden, insects, and the wind transfer pollen from male to female flowers. Fruits won't set without pollination, so go easy on insecticides that harm bees.

All-female hybrids. Some hybrids bear mostly female flowers and are called "gynoecious hybrids." Since every flower on a gynoecious hybrid vine has the potential to become a cucumber, the vine is far more productive. A few seeds of vines that contain male flowers for pollination are included in seed packages of gynoecious varieties and are often color coded, but most of the vines are all-female-flower ones. The pollinators look slightly different from the rest of the vines; be careful not to pull them up as weeds.

Hybrid cucumbers. Hybrids result from cross-pollinating flowers by hand. Hybrids are usually more robust and disease resistant than older, naturally pollinated standard varieties.

Slicing cucumbers

Slicing cucumbers, the kinds used for cool summer salads, are usually long, dark green, and fairly tough skinned. The tough skin makes mature slicing cucumbers undesirable for pickling,

Green cucumbers, ready for pickling

Lemon cucumbers—yellow, lemon-shaped, not tart

Cucumbers are extremely thirsty. They need long, deep drinks of water to grow fruit that is not bitter. Furrow irrigation works best; sprinkling is not recommended because it encourages mildew.

The vines of most varieties will spread over 6 feet before the plants stop bearing. You can curb their rambling nature by training vines up trellises or confining them in containers. You can also plant dwarf and compact varieties that take less space.

but you can pickle young slicing cukes. Harvest slicing cucumbers before they start to turn yellow. Keep the fruit picked to encourage more cucumbers to form.

Pickling cucumbers

Pickling varieties bear short, blocky fruits with tender skin. The fruits are compact in size, making them convenient for packing into jars. For making sweet pickles, harvest the cucumbers when they are 2 to 3 inches long; harvest cucumbers for dills when they are 5 to 6 inches long. The pickling varieties tend to be more prolific plants than the slicing kinds—pick fruit often so that vines will continue producing.

Novelty cucumbers

The lemon cucumber leads the novelty cucumbers in popularity. The tennis-ball-size fruit turns bright yellow and mild-flavored when ripe.

The Armenian cucumber—really a long, skinny melon—is another exotic variety. Once Armenian cukes

reach 18 to 20 inches, the sooner you harvest them the better they taste; left alone, the fruit will eventually grow to 2½ feet long.

Greenhouse owners can take advantage of a special group of cucumbers that were bred just for greenhouse growing. Self-pollinating, they must be grown indoors to avoid being pollinated by stray pollen from other cucumber varieties.

Other cucumber varieties worth trying include burpless types (for people who have trouble digesting cucumbers), space-saving bush varieties, and dual-purpose cucumbers—the latter make picklers when small, slicers when large.

Growing hints

All cucumbers love warm weather. The seeds need warm soil to sprout (for information about using hotcaps or other devices for an early start, see page 104). Warm weather also helps pollinating insects. (But temperatures above 100°F/38°C can cause bitterness or stop cucumber production.)

Currants

Britain's favorite berry for tea cakes & jelly

Lustrous red currants for future jam

Though prized in Europe for jams and jellies, currants are cultivated much less in the United States and Canada. Since they need a cold climate, currants are grown primarily in the Pacific Northwest and British Columbia, and in northern United States and adjacent southern Canada.

The small, tidy bushes offer striking beauty in spring and summer, their grapelike clusters of berries glistening amid the new foliage. Red currants are most common, but white and black varieties also exist.

Branches and spurs produce for 3 to 4 years, then should be pruned off during winter dormancy. If growth is dense, younger branches may need thinning to 6 or 8 per bush.

Used almost exclusively in jelly, currants really need to be cooked to be palatable. They ripen all at once, so harvesting can be a sizable job.

Caution: In some areas it is illegal to plant currants, which might be hosts to white pine blister rust. Check with your local agricultural advisor.

Eggplant

Let them sunbathe slowly to purple perfection

Eggplant—both elegant and edible

Purple, plump, and polished to an inky sheen, eggplant is as beautiful to behold in the garden as it is to taste in a cheesy moussaka.

Like its cousins, tomato and pepper, eggplant is an annual fruit commonly called a vegetable. Though the large, oval, purple-fruited variety is most familiar, yellow, green, and white varieties are available, as well as varieties with small eggplants in rounded or cylindrical shapes.

Eggplant requires a growing season of 60 to 95 warm days and nights (minimum night temperatures of 65°F/18°C) to produce its crop. Set out young plants in a sunny location in rich, well-drained soil. Where summers are short, choose fast-maturing varieties such as 'Dusky' and plant them in a warm, sheltered spot.

On large varieties, thin fruits to one per each main branch—three to six per plant. With small-fruited kinds, thinning isn't necessary. Use clippers or a knife to harvest eggplants individually as they ripen.

Endive

**A few frilly leaves
put zest in your salads**

Frilly endive adds tang to salads

What's in a name? *Endive* is a leafy vegetable with lacy or ruffled foliage. *Batavian endive,* or *escarole,* is a broad-leafed version with a creamy white center. (The expensive and elegant Belgian or French endive sold by gourmet grocers is really a blanched heart of *chicory.*) Whatever you call them, both Batavian endive and curly-leaf endive are worthy salad greens.

Though endive tolerates higher temperatures than lettuce, hot weather tends to make endive bitter.

Sow its tiny seeds in a sunny spot. As with lettuce and other greens, you can start cutting off outer leaves to eat while the plants are still young.

To tone down endive's strong flavor, it's a common practice to blanch the inner leaves. Draw up and loosely tie outer leaves together, forming shields around the interiors of the plants. Afterwards, water carefully to avoid wetting the leaves, or the insides may rot. Blanching should be complete in 2 or 3 weeks.

Garlic

**It bears a strong flavor
that good cooks treasure**

Garlic bulbs: elephant and regular

If you glory in garlic, why not grow it? It's practically foolproof when you start with pest-free bulbs from a nursery (some gardeners have luck with those from a grocery store).

Garlic needs a sunny spot with rich, well-drained soil. Select only the biggest cloves, ones with pieces of root attached, for planting.

Keep soil moist, weed regularly, and pinch off any blossoms that form. When leaf tips start to turn yellowish brown, stop watering and press foliage flat to ground. This prevents flowering and hastens maturation of the bulb. Harvest bulbs when leaves are mostly brown.

Be sure to harvest by lifting out bulbs with a garden fork—pulling plants by hand may crack bulbs and decrease storage life. Let bulbs dry outdoors in the sun until skins are papery (about 3 weeks); protect them from rain. Remove dirt and cut off most of roots, then store (braided or loose) in a cool, well-ventilated place away from direct sunlight.

Gooseberries

Close cousins of currants —but unrelated to geese

Gooseberries, *currant's larger cousin*

The elusive gooseberry almost never turns up in the grocery store, and the large, elongated type that's popular in Europe as a dessert won't grow here at all. So gooseberry gourmands, you'd better plan to grow your own.

Gooseberries are quite ornamental for a bush fruit. Some varieties have red berries, others have green. You can eat them fresh (they're tarter than other berries) or cooked in pie or jam.

Easy-going as long as your climate is cool enough, gooseberries are grown mostly in northern United States and in Canada, but also in some areas of the South. Plant against a north wall if your summer gets very hot.

Bearing for as long as 20 years, gooseberries produce at the base of previous season's stems and on spurs of two-year-old stems.

Caution: In some areas it is illegal to plant gooseberries, which might be hosts to white pine blister rust. Check with your local agricultural advisor.

Gooseberries ...at a glance

Growth habit. Berries borne in clusters on 1 to 4-year-old branches of bushes.

Climate preference. Best where winters are cold and summers are not hot and dry; hardy to about −40°F/−40°C.

Best soil. Fertile, well-drained, sandy loam or clay loam, pH 5.5 to 6.8.

When to plant. Spring or autumn.

How to plant. Set out bare-root plants 5 to 6 inches deep, 3 to 4 feet apart, in rows 6 to 10 feet apart. (See page 105.)

Yield. 4 to 6 quarts per plant.

When to harvest. In summer, when berries are soft, full-colored.

Care. Water and weed regularly. Fertilize yearly. Prune every year (after 4th year) in spring before growth starts. (See page 118.)

Pests and diseases. Aphids, mites. (See pages 114–115.)

Gourds

For crafts, decorations ... a fun crop for kids to grow

Whimsical gourds—*not for eating*

Mugs, jugs, masks, pipes, bowls, maracas, ladles, sponges—not to mention table decorations—all come from this hard-shelled and usually inedible cousin of squash. Fast-growing white or yellow-flowered vines, gourds bear fruits that come in a wide array of shapes, colors, and markings—round or cylindrical, solid or striped, smooth-surfaced or warty—in sizes from 3 inches to 3 feet.

Gourds need all the summer heat they can get to develop fruit before frost. Start seeds indoors where summers are short; elsewhere, sow seeds outdoors in full sun and well-drained soil. To keep individual gourds off the ground, give vines, which grow 10 to 15 feet long, a trellis support.

Let fruit ripen on the vine. When foliage withers, harvest gourds, leaving a little stem on each.

Wash with nonbleaching disinfectant (such as borax), dry, then hang up the gourds by their stems in a cool, dry, well-ventilated place away from sunlight, such as an attic, for 2 to 4 weeks. Preserve gourds with a coating of paste wax, lacquer, or shellac.

Gourds ...at a glance

Type of vegetable. Hard-shelled-fruit bearing; warm-season.

Edible parts. Inedible; ornamental.

Best soil. Fertile, pH 5.5 to 6.8.

When to plant. *Cold-winter climates:* Sow seeds, or set out plants in late spring. *Mild-winter climates:* Set out plants or sow seeds directly in garden in spring. For early start, sow seeds indoors in pots.

How to plant. Set out plants 2 to 4 feet apart (plants need room) in rows spaced 4 feet apart. Sow seeds 2 inches deep, 1 foot apart, in rows spaced as above; thin seedlings to 2 to 4 feet apart.

Yield. 6 to 12 gourds per vine.

When to harvest. 85 to 100 days after planting, when vines have withered, but before frost occurs.

Care. Keep soil moist. Set up trellis.

Pests and diseases. Cucumber beetle, mites, squash bug; powdery mildew. (For treatment, see page 114–116.)

Grapes

In luminous clusters, gems of glorious flavor

From the time that Noah planted a vineyard until today, viticulture—growing grapes—has flourished as one of mankind's few enduring traditions.

Though grapes have been and are much glorified as the source of wine, here we will discuss growing only those varieties called table or dessert grapes—the kinds used mainly for eating fresh or for making jellies.

Besides their sumptuous contribution to fruit bowls and jelly jars, grapes bring exceptional beauty to a garden. Vines create a fascinating filigree of heart-shaped leaves, twisting canes, and curling tendrils. Their glistening fruit comes in a color range from pale gold green through shades of red and purple to deep blue black. Extraordinarily long-lived, vines may endure for 100 years and more.

Grapes can be grown nearly everywhere in the United States—in many different types of soil and in widely varying climates—and in certain regions of western and eastern Canada (see map, page 25). Derived over the course of centuries from wild species of the Near East and our own continent, varieties grown today number roughly 8,000.

Three classes of grapes

Altogether, grape varieties fall into three major classes. Two of these classes encompass native North American vines: American grapes (*Vitis labrusca*) and muscadine grapes (*Vitis rotundifolia*). Both are also known as "slipskin" grapes because of the way their skins easily peel free. The third class is European grapes (*Vitis vinifera*).

In addition, numerous hybrids of European and American grapes have been bred over the years to bring out traits of hardiness or fruit quality.

American grapes. Also called "foxgrapes," American grapes adapt best to cold-winter areas. They are

Grape arbor *drips with season's bounty of fruit clusters; variety is 'Lady Finger'*

native to the eastern portion of our continent, from New York and adjacent Canada south to Georgia and west to the Mississippi valley. American grapes tend to be the most resistant to grape-marauding pests and diseases, many of which are indigenous to the plants' native soil. Their most famous representative is 'Concord', a blue black table grape (also used for wine, grape juice, jelly, and jam) that ripens in late autumn. Other

popular American varieties include 'Delaware' (red) and 'Niagara' (white).

As is true of the other two major classes, American grapes display the full color palette of blues, reds, purples, and pale green. Some seedless varieties are available. And to match your length of growing season, you can choose between early, midseason, and late-ripening vines. (For all grapes, this range lies between late summer and late autumn.)

(Continued on next page)

Muscadine grapes. This species originates and grows best in the southeastern United States. Muscadines are grown there by many home gardeners.

Muscadine vines, with few exceptions, bear only female flowers or only male flowers on one vine. To bring about fruiting, you must plant all-female vines near a vine with either male flowers or perfect flowers (male and female combined). One male vine can pollinate a dozen female vines.

The older they get, the more profusely muscadines produce. Clusters are relatively short, comprising as few as five large grapes. Grapes drop individually to the ground when ripe; the traditional harvest method is to shake them loose onto a tarpaulin.

The best-known and oldest muscadine variety is 'Scuppernong', originally found growing wild in Virginia; it ripens early, turning bronzy green. Other popular muscadines include 'Carlos' (bronze, self-fertile), 'Cowart' (black, self-fertile), and 'Fry' and 'Higgins' (both bronze, female vines).

European grapes. These account for the immense commercial crops of California, where the climate resembles that of their native Mediterranean-to-Middle Eastern habitat. They also grow in parts of Arizona and New Mexico. European grapes generally are not found east of the Rockies, for they're susceptible to freezing in the North and to Pierce's disease in the South.

Though more celebrated as wine-grapes, European varieties such as 'Red Malaga', 'Thompson Seedless' (pale green), 'Cardinal' (dark red), and 'Emperor' (red) make delicious table or canning grapes.

To guard against crop devastation by phylloxera (a root-attacking aphid), European vines are often grafted to the far more resistant American rootstocks. Hybridizing American and European varieties has been another approach to adapting European grapes to American climates and hazards.

Planting and care

Grapes prefer a well-drained soil. If you're planting a vulnerable European variety, avoid "old vineyard soil."

Pests or diseases may still contaminate the soil in which grapes were raised during the previous 3 years.

Consult your local county farm advisors to find varieties best suited to your local conditions. For example, early ripening American grapes would be grown in a cold-winter area where the growing season is quite short. (Earliest ripening grapes need at least 140 frost-free days; European varieties need many more.)

Vines need a full quota of sun and free air movement. It's better to plant them on a slope than in low-lying basins where trapped air will increase danger from frost or mildew.

In early spring, about 3 weeks before the last expected frost, set out year-old vines, after trimming their roots to 6 inches (this forces growth of feeder roots). Place them as deep in the soil as they grew in the nursery, spreading the roots in all directions. Cut top growth back to two buds. (In some areas, it's recommended that you plant grapes deeper than they grew in

Full cluster of 'Concord' grapes, an old favorite American variety

Ruddy 'Tokay' is popular table grape

the nursery, leaving just one bud exposed.)

If varieties are European or American, space the vines 8 to 10 feet apart in all directions. Rampant-growing muscadines need more room; place them 12 to 15 feet apart, in rows 20 feet apart.

Keep weeds and grass removed from the planting area. If you use a mulch, avoid using one rich in nutrients, such as compost. Keep vines irrigated regularly if rainfall is lacking.

After growth starts in the first spring, spread ½ cup of 10-10-10 fertilizer per vine in an encircling band 12 to 18 inches from trunk. In the second year apply 1 cup of fertilizer when buds swell in spring; in the third year, apply 1 to 1½ cups of fertilizer in spring. After the third year, apply 1 to 2 cups of fertilizer to each plant as the buds swell in spring. Spread the fertilizer in bands from 2 to 3 feet from the trunk of each plant.

Training and pruning

During the first few years of a grapevine's life, the object of training and pruning is to promote a thick, strong trunk that eventually divides into a branching framework to bear future crops.

There are many ways to train grapevines. We will discuss one of the most common: training grapes on a two-wire trellis (see drawing below). The technique can be used for American, European, and muscadine grapes and is essentially the same for these three classes of grapes during their first 2 years of growth.

For other training methods, consult

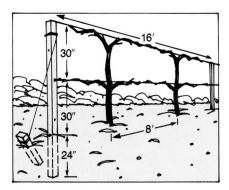

Sturdy posts *hold wires to support vines.*

a local county farm advisor or read a book on growing grapes.

In the first growing season, let vines sprawl undisturbed; in the first winter's dormancy, cut growth back to the single sturdiest cane. Tie this strongest cane as upright as possible to a stake or lower trellis wire; then cut the cane back to the bud that's closest to the lowest supporting wire (30 inches above ground). As these buds send forth shoots in the second year, pick the strongest upright shoot (removing all others) and tie it upright to the stake or to the top trellis wire. This creates a trunk. During the next dormant period, you generally begin to train the strongest new lateral canes produced from this trunk (pruning or pinching off all but two or four per season) to some kind of support.

Vines won't produce a full crop for 4 or 5 years. At that time, fruiting canes will develop from buds borne on canes that grew in the previous summer. The purpose of pruning is to remove old (or weak or extra) canes, creating space and ample nourishment for the new fruiting ones. By limiting the crop, you gain improved fruit quality, maximum size, and uniform clusters.

There are two basic approaches to pruning grapes: spur pruning and cane pruning. Spur pruning is used for most European grapes and muscadine grapes. Cane pruning is used for American grapes and some European grapes.

To spur prune, you select the strongest of the previous year's canes coming from each lateral branch. Thin out these year-old canes to space them 6 to 10 inches apart. Next, cut back each cane to its lowest two buds. The shortened cane is now called a spur. From each spur, two new fruiting canes will grow during the following summer.

In cane pruning, after the grape has been trained with four lateral branches (two growing in opposite directions from the main trunk along each of the two wires), new canes are produced each year to replace the lateral branches after they have borne fruit. (See "Pruning" on pages 120–121.)

Harvesting grapes

When ripe, grapes change color, sweeten to full flavor, and become slightly translucent. A good, healthy vine will put forth as many as 50 bunches per season.

For fresh eating, harvest grapes as soon as they are ripe, cutting clusters with shears to protect vines—or shaking grapes loose, if the vine is muscadine. Dry and sealed in plastic, they should keep for a month to 6 weeks in the refrigerator.

For preserving, harvest grapes while slightly underripe. They'll contain more pectin in this stage and will transform into crystal-clear jelly.

Herbs

*Fresh & aromatic,
they make cooking more fun*

A few garden herbs enrich even a simple dish immeasurably—some snips of parsley brighten potatoes; a bit of tarragon adds zip to a tossed salad; and a dash each of thyme and marjoram enhance a simple omelet. But before they get to the kitchen, herbs add fragrance and delicate color to the garden.

Most herbs are very easy to grow: they thrive with little care in soil that is not too rich. Whether they are annuals or perennials, spring is the usual time to plant herbs in most areas. (For growing information, see individual descriptions that follow.)

Harvest herb leaves for drying just as the first flower buds begin to open. Cut herbs early in the morning, after the dew has dried. Hang plants to dry in small bundles, or strip their leaves and place these in mesh-bottomed drying trays. Dry out of direct sunlight. Stir the leaves in trays every few days until they crumble easily. The leaves of the hanging plants are ready for use when they have dried completely.

Some herbs are grown for their seeds. Harvest seed heads or pods when they turn brown. Dry harvested seed heads or pods on trays until you can shake the seeds loose. Store thoroughly dried leaves and seeds in air-tight containers.

Basil

The rich, pungent flavor of freshly harvested basil leaves can be yours. Sow seeds or set out nursery plants directly in the garden from early spring to late spring. Available in both green or bronze purple ('Dark Opal') foliage, basil can be decorative when grown in containers.

Give this tender, bushy, annual herb full sun, moderate moisture, and light, well-drained soil. Pinch out tips and flowers to keep leaves coming; use leaves fresh or·dried.

Chervil

Chervil looks like tall (1 to 2 feet) parsley and tastes like mild anise. The French include this annual herb in their collection of *fines herbes,* along with basil, marjoram, thyme, rosemary, and tarragon.

Sow seeds in average, well-drained soil in partial shade; keep the soil moist.

Chives

Where would baked potatoes and sour cream be without chives? This onion-flavored herb is a perennial, so you can enjoy clipping its long, pointed leaves for several years.

Grow chives from seeds or from nursery plants. Give them fairly rich, moist soil in full sun, and fertilize regularly. Container-grown chives do well indoors when placed near a sunny window.

Coriander (Cilantro)

The seeds of this annual herb are called coriander, but its fresh leaves are most often called cilantro or Chinese parsley. The sharp, distinctive flavor of the fresh leaves is essential in many Mexican, Mediterranean, and Oriental dishes. The mature seeds have a mellower flavor that's good in bean dishes, stews, and sausage.

A sun lover, coriander prefers moderately rich soil that drains well. Sow seeds directly in the garden in early spring, or in containers. Harvest seeds as soon as they're ripe.

Dill

You can use either the fresh or dried leaves or the seeds of this versatile herb, to season many foods.

After danger of frost has passed, broadcast seeds of this annual in well-drained soil in full sun. Thin plants to 12 inches apart when 2 to 3 inches high.

Pinch off leaves to use any time after the plants are large enough to spare the foliage. Tie small plastic bags over the seed heads at maturity. When first seeds begin to drop into the bag, brush remaining seeds into the bag and store.

Mint

Peppermint, bergamot (orange) mint, pennyroyal, apple mint, spearmint—these are just a few of the refreshing mints that can thrive in your garden. In fact they will take over your garden if you don't contain their roots by planting them in containers.

They all like shade or semishade and light, moderately rich, moist soil. You can grow mint from seedlings or propagate it from cuttings or divisions. To encourage bushy growth, keep flowers pinched back.

Oregano

The pizza herb! But not just for pizza—oregano adds zip to tomato sauce, salads, and egg dishes.

This perennial herb thrives in well-drained soil in full sun. Given routine watering, seeds or cuttings will grow into bushy, 2 to 2½-foot-high plants. Oregano makes a good container plant

Array of herbs includes (left to right)—back row: basil, marjoram, summer savory,

until it becomes woody (in about 3 years). Keep the flowers cut back to encourage bushiness.

Parsley

Parsley comes with curly or straight leaves. The curly French parsley is popular because it is decorative both in the garden and on the dinner plate. The flat-leaved Italian parsley is favored by many cooks because it has a little more flavor.

The 6 to 12-inch plants are biennial—flowering the second year—but most gardeners treat them as annuals, starting anew from seeds or plants each year. Parsley likes partial shade and moderately rich, semi-moist soil. To speed seed germination, soak seeds in warm water for 24 hours before sowing.

Rosemary

Rosemary is a delight in any garden. You can find varieties to grow as ground covers, or upright varieties to clip into hedges. The dark, glossy green leaves look like short pine needles; flowers are delicate blue.

Rosemary prefers full sun and will thrive in dry, poor soil as long as it is well drained. Buy nursery plants or take stem cuttings. Rosemary does well in containers and can be grown indoors. Where winter temperatures seldom fall below 10°F/−12°C, it will survive winters outdoors.

Sage

When sage is mentioned, most gardeners think of gray green leaves on a shrubby, 2-foot-tall plant. But there are many varieties available, including golden, purple, and tricolor sage.

Sage likes poor but well-drained soil and full sun. Overwatering—especially from above—may cause mildew. You can grow all varieties from seeds or nursery plants; garden sage can be propagated from stem cuttings. Cut back stems after blooming occurs. Though plants are perennials, you may need to renew them every 3 to 4 years.

Summer savory

Summer savory adds a delicate peppery flavor to soups, salad dressings, meat, fish, and dishes featuring eggs and beans. An annual, summer savory grows about 18 inches tall in a loose, open fashion. The leaves appear in pairs along the stems, and its tiny flowers are a delicate pinkish white to rose.

Summer savory thrives in light, rich soil in full sun; it makes an excellent container plant. Sow seeds where they are to grow, and thin seedlings to about 18 inches apart. Water regularly.

Sweet marjoram

Marjoram tastes rather like a refined, sweet relative of oregano. Fresh or dried, the leaves are delicious in salads or casseroles, flavoring vinegar, and mixed with sweet butter and melted on steak.

In cold-winter climates, sweet marjoram, a tender perennial, can be grown outdoors as an annual or indoors in containers. It's a bushy little plant about 2 feet high with soft foliage and white flowers in knotted clusters.

You can propagate marjoram from seeds, cuttings, or root divisions. Plant it in full sun and keep the soil fairly moist. Cut off blossoms to encourage bushiness; regularly trim the plant to prevent woody growth.

Tarragon

The name tarragon comes from the French word for little dragon—referring, perhaps, to the aggressive, spreading root system. Be sure you're getting French tarragon, not the tasteless Russian tarragon. (Bruise a leaf to test for strong anise fragrance.)

A hardy perennial, French tarragon dies to the ground in winter but returns the following spring to grow into an attractive 2-foot-tall bush with slender dark green leaves. It thrives in full sun in poor soil—as long as the soil is well drained. French tarragon can be grown only from cuttings or divisions.

Thyme

Happiness, courage, and well-being are the pleasant historical associations with this herb. There are many varieties of thyme, all perennials are easy to grow. Some kinds grow 8 to 12 inches high; others form a mat that you can walk on.

Grow thyme from seeds or tip cuttings taken in spring. Plant in full sun, in light sandy soil that is moderately dry. Prune after flowering. Replant when it looks sparse, every few years.

Winter savory

Winter savory has a more pungent peppery flavor than summer savory. A perennial, it has a lower, more spreading growth than the annual species, which makes it a good edging for an herb garden or border for a flower garden. Bees love its white to lilac blossoms.

Winter savory prefers sandy, well-drained soil and average moisture. Seeds are very slow to germinate; buy seedlings or propagate from cuttings or divisions. Harvest stems from the start of the flowering period.

rosemary, oregano, chives, sage; front row: dill, thyme, chervil, mint, tarragon, parsley

Horseradish

From a funny-looking root, hot sauce for beef

Straggly root *is zingy horseradish*

To many lovers of roast beef, a slab of medium-rare is nothing without the bracing heat of horseradish sauce. Its unique flavor comes from a perennial root vegetable, as unpromising in appearance as a dog bone.

Horseradish is an unusual root crop—you plant it almost on its side. Plant roots in a shallow trench with the wide ends slightly higher in the soil.

Roots do most of their growing in late summer or early autumn. They're ready to harvest in late October or November, when they reach a good size—about 12 inches in length and 3 or 4 inches in diameter. You can dig them as soon as they're ready, or just leave them in the ground through the winter (where the ground does not freeze deeply), digging as needed. Once plants are established, they will probably grow back year after year from pieces of roots left in the ground.

For sauce, peel and grind the root, then mix three parts of minced horseradish with one part vinegar, adding a dash of salt.

Horseradish ...at a glance

Type of vegetable. Hardy perennial.
Edible parts. Roots.
Best soil. Rich, well-drained loam, pH 5.5 to 6.8.
When to plant. *Cold-winter and mild-winter climates:* For autumn crop, set out roots in spring.
How to plant. Set out 8 to 14-inch-long root cuttings at a slant, 18 to 24 inches apart, in 3 to 4-inch-deep furrows 30 to 36 inches apart. Cover with 2 inches of soil.
Yield. 3 to 7 pounds per 10-foot row.
When to harvest. In late autumn, before the ground freezes.
Care. Keep soil moist. Weed regularly.
Pests and diseases. Flea beetle, grasshopper, leafhopper. (For treatment, see page 115.)
How to harvest. Dig up roots with a spading fork.

Jerusalem artichokes

A tasty tuber whose cousin is a sunflower

Jerusalem artichokes *yield tasty tubers*

Jerusalem artichokes are knobby perennial tubers of a kind of sunflower. "Jerusalem" is just a misunderstanding of *girasole,* the Italian word for sunflower. Sometimes, they are also sold as "sun chokes."

Whatever you call them, these tubers are among the world's easiest crops. In fact, they may take off and spread like weeds. Given full sun, they'll grow almost anywhere, surviving poor soil, drought, and neglect.

In early spring, plant whole tubers or cut them into chunks with two or three eyes—growth buds—apiece. Grow them where you can keep plants from spreading uncontrollably, preferably surrounded by a foot-deep metal strip in the soil.

Plants shoot up to 6 feet or more, putting out yellow blooms (smaller than common garden sunflowers) in late summer. When leaves die in autumn, tubers are ready to dig up; those dug after light frosts taste sweeter. Refrigerate fragile tubers in airtight containers—or, better yet, dig only what you can eat very fresh. Raw or cooked, they taste rather like water chestnuts.

Jerusalem artichokes ...at a glance

Type of vegetable. Frost-hardy perennial.
Edible parts. Tubers.
Best soil. Fertile, well-drained, sandy loam.
When to plant. *Cold-winter and mild-winter climates:* For autumn crop, plant tubers in spring (4 to 6 weeks before the last frost date).
How to plant. Plant whole tubers, or cut them into 2-ounce pieces, each with 1 or 2 eyes (growth buds). Plant 4 to 6 inches deep, 24 inches apart, in rows 36 to 40 inches apart. Plant them where you can restrain their growth.
Yield. About ⅓ bushel per 10-foot row.
When to harvest. In autumn, after the tops die back.
Care. Keep soil moist. Weed regularly.
Pests and diseases. Mites. (For treatment, see page 115.)
How to harvest. Dig up tubers.

Jicama

Exotic, intriguing—the best part is hidden away

Jicama, *a crunchy tuber*

A familiar food in Mexico, jicama (pronounced *hee*-ca-mah) is almost as widely used in Hawaii, where it's known as "chop suey potato"—it develops underground like a potato. Sheathed in brown skin and weighing from 1 to 6 pounds, these white-fleshed tubers taste something like sweet water chestnuts. You can eat jicama either raw or cooked.

Jicama needs a long, warm growing-season and does well in areas such as southern California and southern Florida.

The vines grow 25 to 30 feet long and need the support of a trellis. To promote the best tuber development, pinch off any flowers that appear on the vine.

Tubers should be mature, plump, and ready to dig up by August or September. Or just leave the tubers in the ground until they're needed—but harvest them before the first frost hits, because they'll rot. Where there are no frosts, tubers can survive in the ground.

Jicama ...at a glance

Type of vegetable. Root; warm season.

Edible parts. Tubers.

Best soil. Fertile, well-drained, sandy loam.

When to plant. *Cold-winter and mild-winter climates: For autumn crop,* sow seeds in spring (about 4 weeks after last frost date).

How to plant. Sow seeds 2 inches deep, 4 inches apart, in rows along both edges of 24-inch-wide ridges; thin seedlings to 8 to 12 inches.

Yield. 1 tuber per plant.

When to harvest. In autumn before frost.

Care. Keep soil moist. Fertilize monthly with a high-nitrogen fertilizer. Train vines on a trellis; pinch off flowers.

Pests, diseases. None important.

How to harvest. Dig up carefully.

Kale

A touch of Jack Frost perks up its flavor

Kale *is a gussied-up cabbage relative*

Low in calories and loaded with vitamins and minerals, this frilly-leafed cabbage cousin is a dieter's delight. Use leaves as salad greens, chop them for garnishing soups and egg dishes, or steam them slightly and serve hot.

Kale is a cool-weather crop, hardy enough to survive moderately severe winters. A touch of frost sweetens kale's flavor; hot summer sun makes kale's natural sweetness turn bitter.

Grow ordinary varieties, or in a cramped garden, try compact, short-stemmed 'Dwarf Blue Curled Vates' and 'Dwarf Siberian' (a variety with plumelike foliage). As ornamental additions to flower beds, walkway borders, or window boxes, plant flowering kale—its "flowers" are brightly colored edible leaves.

When plants are a few inches high, thin to 12 to 18 inches apart. Don't discard thinned plants—they make delicious greens.

Plants can grow 2 feet high and equally wide, each plant producing prodigious crops of sweet leaves. Start harvesting outer leaves as soon as they grow large enough to use.

Kale ...at a glance

Type of vegetable. Leafy; cool season.

Edible parts. Leaves.

Best soil. Fertile, pH 5.5 to 6.8.

When to plant. *For summer crop,* sow seeds in early spring. *For autumn crop,* sow seeds in autumn (where winter temperatures remain above 0° to 10°F/−18° to −12°C).

How to plant. Sow seeds ¼ inch deep, 1 inch apart, in rows 18 to 24 inches apart; or broadcast seeds in wide bands. Thin seedlings to 12 to 18 inches apart.

Yield. 4 to 8 pounds per 10-foot row.

When to harvest. 55 to 75 days after sowing seeds. Harvest greens as you thin seedlings. Pick leaves as plants grow.

Care. Keep soil moist.

Pests and diseases. Aphids, cabbage worm; damping off; fusarium wilt. (For treatment, see pages 114–116.)

Kohlrabi

A cabbage curiosity, it looks like a flying turnip

Kohlrabi—*edible swollen stem, leaves*

Hovering just above the ground like a tiny space ship, kohlrabi's swollen stem resembles a small, airborne turnip. Kohlrobi offers a crisp texture and delicate flavor, but most gardeners are unaware of the culinary possibilities of this curious cabbage kin. The bulbous stems may look like turnips, but they are milder and less mealy. Also, kohlrabi's leaves and leaf stems taste like tangy cabbage leaves.

Kohlrabi tastes best when the stem is 2 to 2½ inches across; after it grows larger than 3 inches, it may taste hot and tough. Chill the stem until crisp, and serve raw slices with hors d'oeuvres or in salads as a substitute for water chestnuts. To cook kohlrabi, steam or sauté it.

Popular varieties include 'Early Purple Vienna', 'Early White Vienna', and 'Grand Duke hybrid'. Plant kohlrabi to harvest when weather is cool.

Kohlrabi ...at a glance

Type of vegetable. Stem and leaf; cool season.

Edible parts. Stem; leaves; leaf stems.

Best soil. Fertile, pH 5.5 to 6.8.

When to plant. *For summer crop,* sow seeds in early spring. *For autumn crop,* sow seeds in mid to late summer.

How to plant. Sow seeds ¼ to ½ inch deep, 1 inch apart, in rows 18 inches apart; thin to 4 to 8 inches apart.

Yield. 4 to 8 pounds per 10-foot row.

When to harvest. 45 to 60 days after sowing seeds.

Care. Keep soil moist. Weed regularly.

Pests and diseases. See Cabbage, page 42.

Leeks

Milder, fatter & slower than their onion cousins

Artistic leeks are mild-mannered onions

Long honored by French chefs, leeks are now acquiring admirers in this country as well. Since these mild-flavored onion relatives frequently fetch gourmet prices in the market, many cooks who use leeks grow their own.

Growing leeks takes patience—they spend 4 to 7 months fattening up to prime size. Though they prefer a mild, cool climate in full sun, leeks may do well in hotter climates if they're planted in partial shade.

As plants grow, mound up soil around stalks for blanching—a technique used to make stem bottoms white and mild. Keep heaped soil just short of leaf joints (where leaf joins stem), increasing the height of the mound as the plant grows. If soil is piled higher than the leaf joints, dirt will work its way into the bulbs.

To harvest leeks, lift clumps with a spading fork, then shake leeks to remove dirt. In cold-winter areas, harvest before the ground freezes. (If the ground doesn't freeze, you can leave leeks in place until needed.) To prepare leeks for use, remove most of the root, cut the leaves diagonally 6 to 8 inches above the stem to form a peaked cap of green, and wash leeks thoroughly, separating layers.

Leeks ...at a glance

Type of vegetable. Stem; cool season.

Edible parts. Stems.

Best soil. Rich, pH 6.0 to 6.8.

When to plant. *Cold-winter climates:* Set out plants in spring. *Mild-winter climates:* Set out plants in spring through autumn where summers are cool, in autumn where summers are hot. Sow seeds in containers 6 to 8 weeks before you intend to set out plants in garden.

How to plant. Set out plants 2 to 4 inches apart in 5-inch-deep furrows spaced 4 to 12 inches apart. Sow seeds ⅛ inch deep, 1 inch apart, in containers filled with 3 inches of potting soil.

Yield. 4 to 6 pounds per 10-foot row.

When to harvest. 4 to 7 months after setting out plants, when stems are ½ to 2 inches thick.

Care. Keep soil moist. Mound up soil along sides of stem as plants grow.

Pests and diseases. Thrips. (For treatment, see page 116.)

Lettuce

Bouquets of leafy loveliness for fresh, crisp salads

Nature smiles on the backyard lettuce gardener. It offers a choice of five types of lettuce—leaf lettuce (also called loosehead lettuce), butterhead lettuce (sometimes known as Bibb lettuce), romaine (cos), crisphead ('Iceberg') lettuce, and celtuce, which resembles a cross between celery and lettuce.

A short browse through a seed catalog or seed display rack reveals enough varieties of lettuce to keep your salad bowl crisp and colorful throughout the growing season. You can plant three or four varieties of quick-growing, easy-going leaf lettuce. Or try your hand at growing the slightly more difficult types: butterhead, romaine, crisphead, and celtuce.

Growing needs

The growing requirements for all the types are very much the same. Most of all, lettuce needs cool weather. In warm weather, lettuce turns bitter and quickly goes to seed (it "bolts").

Lettuce grows readily in cool soil, so you can start sowing seeds in very early spring and make repeat sowings at 2-week intervals until late spring. Then delay additional plantings until the weather cools off again in late summer or autumn.

Another precaution to take in warm weather is to plant lettuce in partially shaded areas that stay cool or in the shade of taller vegetables such as broccoli or corn. Check with your county farm advisor for varieties that do especially well in your particular location.

Lettuce has rather shallow roots and will grow well in containers—all you need is a soil depth of 9 to 12 inches. Container-grown lettuce has the same growing requirements as garden lettuce.

The best soil for lettuce growing is fertile and well-drained. Keep the soil moist, but not soggy. Leaf lettuce is the least fussy about soil and will perform well even in rather poor soil as long as it drains well. Give leaf lettuce only light fertilization at planting time; heading types will respond to a second light fertilizing when plants are half grown.

Healthy stand *of young lettuce plants—the butterhead (or Bibb) type*

Five classes

Taking a closer look at the five lettuce classes, you'll notice that the main differences in growing instructions concern how much space to allow between seedlings when you are thinning, and how to harvest the different kinds of lettuce.

Leaf lettuce has the most varieties and is the easiest to grow. As the name suggests, this type of lettuce produces loose bunches of leaves rather than a head. It comes in assorted colors (red, bronze, dark green, chartreuse) and in interesting textures (smooth, puckered, ruffly, frilled). The leaves on all varieties are exceptionally tender.

You can enjoy the home gardener's exclusive rights to red, ruffly 'Ruby' lettuce for color and sweet taste; super

Red variety *of loosehead or leaf lettuce*

Romaine, *or cos, has crisper, longer leaves*

Traditional *crisphead ('Iceberg') lettuce*

frilly 'Green Ice' lettuce, which is slow to go to seed; apple green 'Black Seeded Simpson' lettuce; dark green 'Oak Leaf' lettuce that has tender, thick midribs; 'Salad Bowl' lettuce with its deeply lobed bright green leaves; or 'Slo-bolt', a crisp leaf lettuce that tolerates warm lettuce.

Because of its rapid maturation (40 to 50 days), leaf lettuce is a favorite where hot humid summers follow closely on the heels of spring weather. Those who live where spring is long and cool can enjoy a longer leaf-lettuce season by planting a succession of crops. You can plant in rows or tuck seeds into any bare spot—different varieties in different spots for interesting salads.

Sow seeds according to checklist instructions. Thin to 4 to 8 inches apart, depending on the variety, to give the lettuce room to spread.

Harvest the thinnings for salads, then harvest more mature leaves by either picking just the outer leaves or by pulling up the whole plant. Some varieties, such as 'Grand Rapids' or 'Prizehead' can be cut off an inch or two above the ground and the plants will send out new leaves for a second crop.

Butterhead lettuce forms small, tender, rather open, (roselike) heads, that blanch to a creamy or butter yellow center. They mature in 65 to 80 days. Varieties include 'Bibb'; 'Buttercrunch' (heat-resistant); 'Butter King' (disease resistant; slow to bolt); 'Fordhook'; 'Great Lakes' (heat-resistant, very productive); and 'Tom Thumb' (miniature, good in containers).

Spring crops can be sown 4 to 6 weeks before the last frost date in spring. Autumn crops can be sown directly in the garden in late summer and early autumn.

Enjoy the thinnings, then pluck the leaves of maturing heads or pull up the whole head when it reaches full-size—or harvest when you can't wait any longer. Lettuce is delicious at all stages.

Romaine, also called cos, has upright clusters of big, crunchy leaves. The leaves are exceptionally crisp and flavorful. In fact, where would Caesar salad be without crunchy romaine? 'Parris Island' and 'Valmaine' are two

popular varieties.

Growing instructions for romaine lettuce are the same as for butterhead. However, they require 80 to 85 days to mature. The length of time required for romaine to reach maturity means you'll have to have a long stretch of cool to moderate weather to grow it. You can get a headstart by starting seedlings indoors in containers for early spring planting. Harvest by cutting off heads.

Crisphead lettuce, most familiarly marketed as 'Iceberg' lettuce, takes 80 to 90 days to mature. Crisphead lettuce can take a little more heat than butterhead lettuce but still prefers cool weather for the best growth and flavor. Try 'Iceberg' for vigorous growth or one of several warm-climate varieties: 'Imperial No. 44,' which forms good heads in warm weather; 'Premier Great Lakes', a variety resistant to tipburn and heat; 'Minetto', a small compact, heat-resistant variety; or 'Mirage', another good heading lettuce for warm climates.

Crisphead lettuce is ready for harvest when the heads are solid and the tops start to turn yellowish green. Heads should be cut off plants. When preparing them for eating, you'll want to trim the soiled leaves at the base before rinsing the heads in cool water.

Celtuce (*cele*ry and let*tuce*) is the fifth type of lettuce you might want to add to your salad bowl. This novelty looks and tastes like leaf lettuce when young, then sprouts stalks like celery as it matures. Like true lettuces, it loves cool weather and quickly bolts in hot spells.

Celtuce takes 90 days to mature. So, if you want to give it a try, start seedlings indoors for spring planting or wait for autumn planting. Sow seeds in moist, fertile, fast-draining soil. Keep the soil moist but not soggy. Thin seedlings to 8 to 12 inches apart.

You can use the thinnings as you would leaf lettuce. Also, the leaves of the plant, as it matures, can be eaten as salad greens. They taste like leaf lettuce. The mature stalks look and taste like celery and can be used raw or cooked as you would celery. Harvest by cutting individual stalks or pulling up the whole plant and cutting off the root.

Lettuce ...at a glance

Type of vegetable. Leafy; cool season.

Edible parts. Leaves; stems.

Best soil. Fertile, well drained, pH 6.0 to 6.8.

When to plant. *Cold-winter climates: For spring crop,* sow seeds or set out plants in spring (4 to 6 weeks before last frost date); make successive sowings or plantings until weather gets too warm (75 to 80°F/24 to 27°C). *For autumn crop,* make sowings or plantings again in late summer and early autumn (until 6 to 8 weeks before first frost). *Mild-winter climates: For autumn and winter and spring crops,* sow seeds or set out plants from autumn through midspring until weather gets too warm (75 to 80°F/24 to 27°C).

How to plant. Sow seeds of leaf lettuce ¼ inch deep, 1 to 2 inches apart, in rows spaced 12 to 24 inches apart; thin seedlings to 4 to 8 inches apart. Sow seeds of butterhead lettuce ¼ inch deep, 1 to 2 inches apart, in rows spaced 16 to 24 inches apart; thin seedlings to 6 to 8 inches apart. Sow seeds of romaine lettuce ¼ inch deep, 1 to 2 inches apart, in rows spaced 16 to 24 inches apart; thin seedlings to 6 to 8 inches apart. Sow seeds of crisphead lettuce ¼ inch deep, 1 to 2 inches apart, in rows spaced 16 to 24 inches apart; thin seedlings to 12 to 14 inches apart. Set out plants in rows as described and at spacing of thinning. Sow seeds of celtuce ¼ inch deep, 2 inches apart, in rows spaced 18 inches apart; thin seedlings to 8 to 12 inches apart.

Yield. 4 to 10 pounds per 10-foot row.

When to harvest. 40 to 90 days after sowing seeds. Harvest butterhead lettuce when loose head is formed; crisphead lettuce when heads are firm; and looseleaf and romaine lettuce any time after plants are large enough to use. Harvest celtuce when stem is formed, before it flowers.

Care. Keep soil moist. Weed regularly.

Pests and diseases. Aphid, cabbage looper, cutworm, flea beetle, leafhopper, leaf miner, slug, snail; downy mildew, fusarium wilt. (For treatment, see pages 114–116.)

How to harvest. Pull off leaves of loose leaf lettuce. Cut off heads of heading types just below bases of heads.

Melons

They like to spread out for a lazy summer sun bath

If you were voting for the most attractive and delightful "fruit" in the vegetable world, the palate-pleasing melon would probably receive top marks for aroma, flavor, texture, and juiciness.

But be prepared to pamper melons a bit—they can be temperamental if not given the proper attention. To mature to full sweetness, melons need a spacious garden site in full sun, 2½ to 4 months of warm weather, rich soil, and generous amounts of water.

If you live on or near the coast, where summer days are often cool or foggy, you can grow melons, but use some ingenuity to raise temperatures around the plants. Locating plants in hot pockets—near walls that reflect heat, in spots where breezes are blocked—will help raise the air temperature around them. You also may want to cover the growing area with black plastic, since warmth in the soil is as important as warmth in the air. Cut holes for four-leaf seedlings by slitting a 2-inch cross in the plastic for each plant.

Another approach is to plant seeds in your compost pile. Decomposition

Cantaloupe, *one of the many tasty melons*

of the vegetable refuse here creates heat that melon plants thrive on.

Container-gardening is another possibility for gardeners who need to create a hot-summer climate for their melon plants. Miniature and bush melons can be grown in large containers. To save space, train vines onto a welded-wire trellis. Fruit may need a cloth sling for support.

Melons grow best in rich soil with good drainage. To prepare your soil for melons, mix in bone meal, well-rotted (fine-textured) manure, and organic soil amendment (compost, ground bark, peat moss, or nitrogen-stabilized sawdust) with average garden soil, in the ratio of one part amendment to three parts soil. In soils that are almost pure clay or sand, the ratio should be about half and half.

Plant melons in hills or rows. To plant in hills, form the tilled soil into flat-topped mounds 1 inch high and 2 to 3 feet in diameter, with irrigation ditches encircling them. Sow four or five seeds 1 inch deep, in the hill. When seedlings begin to grow, thin out all but two.

To plant in rows, mound the tilled soil to a height of 3 to 4 inches above the soil surface and to a width of 12 to 15 inches. Make irrigation ditches along each side of the row.

When seedlings are small, apply water near enough to them that its moisture reaches the tiny roots. When plants are established, fill ditches with water, keeping foliage and fruit dry to prevent mildew and rot. Plants may wilt slightly on hot days. If they wilt badly, water deeply when the temperature drops.

To make melons taste sweeter, hold off watering a week or so before you expect to harvest the ripe fruit. This gives melons time to develop flavor. But don't let the vines wilt; resume watering after the first harvest so the next crop will continue to put on size.

The cantaloupe is fully ripe when it pulls off the stem easily. With other kinds of melon, a strong, pleasant aroma at the blossom (not stem) end is the best indicator of ripeness.

For sweetness and flavor, cantaloupes (muskmelons) are second only to watermelons (see listing on page 96). For cool-summer areas, choose varieties that mature quickly. Popular

varieties include 'Honey Rock', 'Sweet 'n' Early', 'Sugar Salmon', 'Saticoy Hybrid', and 'Minnesota Midget'.

Long-season melons—such as the greenskinned 'Persian', the pink-fleshed 'Crenshaw', the yellow-skinned 'Casaba' and the lime green 'Honeydew'——require up to 115 days of 75°F/24°C temperatures to mature. Since these late melons also dislike high humidity, they grow best in the warm interior valleys of the West and Southwest.

Other melon varieties worth trying include hybrids developed in Europe and the Middle East: 'Charentais', 'Chaca', and 'Haogen'.

Melons ...at a glance

Type of vegetable. Fleshy fruited; warm season.

Edible parts. Fruit.

Best soil. Rich, well drained, with high organic content, pH 6.0–6.8.

When to plant. Set out plants or sow seeds directly in garden in spring (when danger of frost has passed and day temperatures are 60° to 75°F/16° to 24°C). Sow seeds in peat pots 3 to 4 weeks before you intend to set out plants. Set out plants in peat pots to protect sensitive roots.

How to plant. Set out two plants per hill (2 to 3-foot mounds spaced 4 to 6 feet apart); or set out plants 2 feet apart in rows spaced 5 feet apart. Sow seeds 1 inch deep, 4 to 5 per hill, or 1 inch deep, 12 inches apart, in rows spaced as above; thin seedlings to two plants per hill.

Yield. 2 to 3 melons per vine.

When to harvest. 70 to 115 days after sowing seeds. Cantaloupes: when fruit slips easily off stem. Other melons: when they have a strong, pleasant aroma at the blossom end.

Care. Keep soil moist. Avoid getting leaves and fruit wet (especially if vines sprawl on ground).

Pests and diseases. Cucumber beetles, mites, squash vine borer; downy mildew, powdery mildew. (For treatment, see pages 114–116.)

Mustard greens

This cool-weather garnish puts extra bite in salads

Mustard greens, *a tangy winter crop*

Need some quick-growing greens to lift you out of those winter doldrums? Try mustard. The tender young leaves of mustard greens have a watercress-like tang. Use them minced like parsley as a garnish for soups, fish dishes, and casseroles; add whole young leaves to lettuce and other greens for zesty salads; or cook them southern-style with fat back.

Mustard greens thrive in cool weather; too much heat makes leaves tough and strong flavored.

In well-moistened soil, greens spring up in about a week after sowing seeds. When plants are 4 to 5 inches high, it's time to thin—and consume the discards. Harvest mature mustard leaves when the lower leaves reach the size of your outstretched hand. (You can use larger leaves than these for cooking.) Continue harvesting leaves until hot weather.

Curly-leaf varieties such as 'Southern Giant Curled' make attractive additions to flower beds and deck or patio containers. 'Florida Broad Leaf' has smooth, easy-to-wash leaves; 'Tendergreen' is a mustard with a spinach flavor.

Okra

Southerners like it in gumbo

Okra *pods, a hot-summer crop*

The slippery texture of stewed okra takes some getting used to. But when it is quickly fried, sautéed, or steamed, a crisper texture emerges. Or flavor and thicken soups and gumbo with pretty rounds of sliced okra.

Like corn, okra thrives on midsummer heat and tolerates almost any soil condition except poor drainage. Seeds should be planted only after the soil is warm (over 70°F/21°C) and the danger of frost has passed.

Okra's large, erect plants with tropical-looking leaves may grow to 6 feet. Apply a complete fertilizer when first pods set and when plants are shoulder high. The prickly pods appear where leaf stems join the main stem.

To avoid the necessity of wearing gloves when harvesting pods, plant 'Clemson Spineless'. If you have a small garden space, plant a dwarf variety such as 2½-foot-tall 'Dwarf Green Long Pod' or decorate a warm patio with one 'Red River' (red-podded) plant potted in a large tub.

Onions

This versatile bulb works hard in the kitchen

Raw or cooked, mild-tasting or pungent, onions greet our palates just about daily—from the merest hint in a soup or stew to the bold, tingling burst of flavor in a dressed-up hamburger. With such culinary demand awaiting them, it's not surprising that onions appear in so many home vegetable gardens.

Almost as if aware of their premium value to the cook, onions are quite tempermental about their cultural requirements. On the other hand, these needs can be met in either a city-balcony or a suburban garden plot, since bulbs don't need much space.

Kinds of onions

Members of the lily family, most onions grow into flattish or spherical globes, but some are elongated, with tapering ends. Common kinds of onions include storage, bunching, sweet Spanish, and torpedo onions. Onions may be sheathed in white, red, yellow, or russet skins.

Most of the small green onions, or scallions, that we put in salads are simply immature onions. Some fastidious gardeners insist that only white varieties are suitable for scallions, but red, yellow, and russet onions taste just as exhilarating when young, crisp, and raw. If you should pull up an overmature scallion (one past its youthful delicacy and too strong to eat raw), simply use it in cooking as if it were a leek.

Growing onions

Onions need fairly cool conditions to get off to a good start. Cultivated almost everywhere in the United States, onions tolerate frost well and, where winters are mild, they're frequently started in autumn for a spring harvest. If your winter's temperatures drop below freezing, plant onions in spring, as soon as the ground can be worked.

Onions are finicky about soil, wanting it fine-textured, loose, and rich in organic matter. Before planting, rake the soil free of stones, clods, and sticks. Work in soil amendments and a complete fertilizer, such as 10-10-10, then rake soil fine and smooth.

Three ways to start

You can start onions from seeds, nursery plants, and sets.

Sets. These are miniature, dormant onions (red, white, yellow, or brown)

Indispensable onions *come in variety of types and colors*

raised specifically for propagation. Easiest to manage, sets also produce quick results. You can have green onions on hand as early as 3 weeks after planting.

But, unless you want an entire crop of green onions, plant only the smallest of the sets available. Large ones often grow too fast, bolting into flower as soon as the weather warms up and before bulbs have had much chance to develop. (As soon as you notice bolting, pull up the onion; flowering drains away nourishment and causes the bulb to shrivel and toughen.)

Onion sets planted in October, where winters are mild, aren't so likely to bolt, since their growth during the cool winter months will be slower.

For green onions, place sets in 1 to 2-inch-deep furrows, 1 to 2 inches apart. For big bulbs, simply push sets under the surface, aligning their pointed ends with the soil level, and space them 3 to 4 inches apart to allow for expansion.

Transplants. The main advantage of using transplants instead of sets is there's less chance of the onions' bolting before they're well fattened. After preparing the soil as you would for sets, set out onion plants about 1½ inches deep and 4 inches apart, in furrows spaced 18 to 24 inches apart. At planting time it's a good idea to apply a mild dose of fertilizer—1 tablespoon of water-soluble fertilizer, such as 10-50-10, dissolved in a gallon of water; apply 1 cup of the solution per plant. (You'll need to feed again, later, as explained further along.)

Seeds. Seeds are a slower way to grow onions than sets and transplants; they require more care initially, but you'll find more varieties available as seeds than as sets or transplants. After preparing the soil as for transplants in furrows of similar spacing, sow one to five seeds per inch, burying them about ½ inch deep. Seeds germinate best at temperatures close to 65°F/18°C. After young plants are established, thin to an inch apart for scallions or to 3 or 4 inches apart for large bulbs.

Continuing care

No matter how you may start your onions, follow up with loving care for good results. Keep young plants weed-free; shallow-rooted, they can't reach far for nourishment to successfully compete with weeds. Cultivate carefully with a hoe, never working it deep enough to damage bulbs or roots. Keep the soil constantly moist especially during the onions' early, fast-growing phase in the cool months. Your object is to prevent any disturbance of even, rapid growth, so you'll have big, well-formed bulbs by the time warmer days roll along, when the bulbs will swell and ripen.

Onions appreciate, sometimes require, a great deal of fertilizer. Give rows a second feeding of 10-10-10 (one pound per 30 feet of row) as a side-dressing, 40 to 60 days after planting.

Harvesting

The yellowing and drying up of onion tops signals the approach of harvest time. At this time, you should push the foliage flat to the ground (a procedure called "lodging," also recommended for garlic) with the back of a rake. Lodging forces the bulbs into their final maturing stage and ensures longer-lasting storage after harvest.

Roughly 3 weeks later, fully withered tops will indicate that ripened bulbs are ready to harvest. Use a spade or fork to dig up the onions. Just leave them in the ground until needed—but be sure to use them before any new growth starts, such as a flowering stalk; like bolting, this new growth will starve the onion, causing it to toughen and shrivel.

Lay harvested onions on newspapers outdoors in a dry, shady spot protected from dew or rain for about 10 days. Then brush off dirt, and trim away most of the stems and roots.

Some varieties (some of the Spanish and Bermudas) don't store well, but most onions will keep several months or all winter long if stored under the proper conditions. Hang cleaned bulbs in mesh bags in a dark, indoor place (such as the garage) where temperatures remain 35° to 50°F/2° to 10°C. If roots appear, the air is too humid; if onions sprout, the temperature is too warm. In either case, rotting will probably ensue, so use up the onions quickly.

Onions ...at a glance

Type of vegetable. Bulb; cool season.

Edible parts. Bulbs; leaves.

Best soil. Rich, well drained, loose, pH 6.0 to 6.8.

When to plant. *Cold-winter climates: For spring and summer crop,* plant sets or transplants in spring (4 to 6 weeks before last frost date). Sow seeds later (when soil temperature has warmed to at least 35°F/2°C, but preferably 50°F/10°C). In some areas, perennial onions (multiplier and Egyptian) can be planted in autumn. *Mild-winter climates: For late spring crop,* plant sets or transplants in spring (4 to 6 weeks before last frost date). Sow seeds when soil temperature has warmed to at least 35°F/2°C. *For winter-into-spring crop,* plant sets or transplants in autumn. Sow seeds when soil temperature has cooled below 95°F/35°C.

How to plant. Plant sets ¾ to 2 inches deep, 2 to 4 inches apart, in rows spaced 18 to 24 inches apart. Plant transplants 1 to 2 inches deep, 3 to 4 inches apart in rows spaced 18 to 24 inches apart. Sow seeds ½ inch deep, ½ inch apart, in rows spaced 18 to 24 inches apart; thin seedlings to 3 to 4 inches apart. Apply liquid fertilizer.

Yield. 7 to 10 pounds per 10-foot row.

When to harvest. 80 to 150 days after planting. Harvest green onions (scallions) whenever they are large enough to use. For mature onions, push leaves flat to ground when tops turn yellow. Harvest onions when tops have fully turned brown.

Care. Keep soil moist. Weed regularly. Apply fertilizer when plants have grown 4 to 6 leaves.

Pests and diseases. Thrips, wireworms; downy mildew. (For treatment, see pages 115–116.)

How to harvest. For green onions, pull up plants. For dry onions, pull up bulbs, remove roots and stems, and dry in a cool, dark room.

Oriental vegetables

Travelers from abroad, welcome garden additions

Chinese broccoli *has mustard-broccoli taste*

Large-leafed *bok choy is still young, hasn't yet reached full size*

Oriental garden *features well-prepared planting beds, space-saving trellises*

Special cabbage—*seeds came from friend*

Bitter melon *has lumpy skin, unusual taste*

"We loved cooking with them. I bought an Oriental cook book and learned to prepare different dishes all summer. We raised the vegetables just like our regular crops and gave them the same treatment, but they are different—like people from far-away lands." That's one reaction to a season's experiment growing Oriental versions of greens, broccoli, melons, squash, and radishes.

Though the flavor may be exotic, Oriental vegetables are as easy to grow as their Western relatives. Growing information for most are listed below. For directions on growing snow peas, see page 73; for sprouting bean sprouts, see page 85; for Chinese parsley and chives, see Herbs, page 58.

Oriental greens

The mainstays of most stir-fry dishes are greens. By themselves, with other vegetables, or with meat, chicken, or seafood, thin slices of real Oriental greens will make your Far Eastern recipes authentic.

Leafy Oriental greens are all quick-maturing, cool-season vegetables. As long as the weather is cool, you can continue to sow seeds or set out plants for successive crops in spring or autumn.

Greens related to broccoli have a longer growing season than other Oriental greens. Like Western broccoli, they do best in cool weather. Care is the same for both types of greens.

Sow seeds ¼ to ½ inch deep, 2 to 4 inches apart, directly in the ground or in containers for transplanting. When seedlings are 2 to 3 inches tall, transplant or thin as indicated for each vegetable. Water and fertilize amply, and keep soil loose and weed-free for fast, tender growth.

Sample leaves and flowers at various stages of growth to use the crop fully and to discover which stage you like best. Even Oriental gardeners debate whether peak flavor and tenderness are reached when the first flower buds open, or slightly before.

To harvest, pull up the whole plant, trim off the root end, and discard tough stalks and leaves. Cut the tender portion in slices or chunks for stir-frying, steaming, or soups.

• Broadleaf mustard (*dai gai choy*)

has large green leaves with a pungent, somewhat bitter, mustard flavor that gets stronger as the plant matures. Hot weather or lack of adequate water also makes it more pungent. It's best diluted in soup.

Thin or transplant seedlings to 10 inches apart. Harvest the plants when they are loosely headed and 10 to 14 inches tall, about 65 days after sowing seeds.

• The mild member of the Chinese mustard family is *gai choy*, Chinese mustard greens. It is excellent in soups or with other vegetables in stir-fry dishes.

Thin or transplant seedlings to 10 inches apart. Harvest first greens when the plants are 2 inches tall; continue harvesting until the greens are tough or bitter. It takes about 45 days after sowing seeds for plants to reach the size of 6 to 8 inches.

• Chinese white cabbage (*bok choy*) is one of the more familiar Oriental greens. It's a tender-crisp, sweet, very mild vegetable that's good alone, with meat, and in soup.

Thin or transplant seedlings to 6 to 12 inches apart. Harvest Chinese cabbage approximately 50 days after sowing seeds, when loosely headed and 10 to 12 inches tall.

• Flowering cabbage, called *yao choy, choy sum,* or *ching soy sum,* is a tender, delicate, broccoli-type vegetable, tasty when served alone or in recipes that require greens.

Thin or transplant seedlings to about 6 inches apart. Harvest when the plants are 8 to 12 inches tall. It takes flowering cabbage about 60 days to reach maturity after seeds are sown.

• Chinese broccoli (*gai lohn*) is similar in flavor and texture to Western broccoli but with a slight mustardy pungency and less cabbage flavor. Flower heads are much smaller than Western broccoli. It is good served by itself or in recipes that call for an assertive green.

Thin or transplant seedlings to 10 inches apart. Harvest central stalk and side shoots when the plant is 8 to 10 inches tall, or when flower buds just begin to form. Chinese broccoli needs about 70 days after seeds are sown to reach maturity.

Oriental melons

Oriental melons are like squash in the way they taste and the way you use them. Their requirements are similar to those of their cousins, Western melons and winter squash.

Members of the curcurbit (melon-squash) family, they love a long, sunny, warm growing-season and rich well-drained soil supplied with abundant water. Like most melons and trailing squash, the vines are ramblers and need space to grow. It is a good idea to train them up a trellis to keep the vines from taking over the yard. A trellis helps fruits stay clean and dry, too.

Plant seeds 1 inch deep in soil that has warmed to 70° to 75°F/21° to 24°C. Sow seeds 2 inches apart in rows spaced 48 inches apart; thin to 12 to 24 inches apart. Or plant in hills (5 seeds per hill) spaced 2 feet apart; thin seedlings to 3 seedlings per hill. To get an early start, you can sow seeds in peat pots indoors 2 to 3 weeks before you intend to set out plants. Plant the whole pot so you disturb the roots as little as possible. Space plants about 2 feet apart.

• Winter melon (*doong gwah*) looks like watermelon, but has white, firm flesh. It is the base for the famous winter melon soup. Its name comes from the fact that you can store and use it through the winter (or for as long as a year).

Use slings to support the heavy melons if you trellis the vines. For immediate use, harvest melons when they reach pumpkin size (about 120 days from seed). For long storage, wait until stem of fruit is hard and dry; keep in a cool, dry place. To use, peel and cube flesh to cook in any broth soup. For classic winter melon soup, the hollowed-out melon is used as the steaming vessel and serving bowl.

• Fuzzy melon (*moh gwah*) is a faster-maturing version of winter melon. Immature fuzzy melons, about the size of zucchini, are delicious peeled, sliced, and quickly cooked tender-firm in a little butter (or oil) and water; or stuff and bake as you would zucchini. When melons mature to around 1 foot in diameter, use them like winter melon.

• Bitter melon (*foo gwah*) is definitely an acquired taste. You may want to grow it just for its unusual lobed leaves (which can be cooked like spinach) and unusual bright green, lumpy, long fruit.

Harvest when melons are 4 to 8 inches long, about 75 days after sowing seeds. Plumper ridges and warts indicate milder flavor. To eat, cut in half lengthwise, scrape out and discard seedy pulp, then immerse halves in boiling water one or more times, discarding water each time to reduce bitterness. Chop into chunks to simmer in soup, or cut in slices for stir-fry dishes.

If you leave the fruit on the vine, it will turn golden yellow and split up the sides to reveal showy red seeds. In India, mature bitter melon is sliced and used for curries. The red seed coat is edible, but the seed itself acts as a purgative.

Sponge gourd (*see gwah*) is also known as Chinese okra or luffa. You can use the dried gourd as a bathing sponge, or eat the immature gourd as you would cucumber or summer squash. Vines are very vigorous.

To eat, harvest before the seeds develop (about 90 days), when gourds are between 6 and 12 inches long. Peel off ridges. Cut into slices to use raw in salads or stir-fried with meat and vegetables. Cut into chunks, sponge gourd is simmered in soup or deep-fried for tempura.

For sponges, leave gourds on vine until they're all completely brown, then pick and dry completely. Crush the skin lightly and soak in boiling water until soft enough to peel off easily. Soak in bleach if fiber is discolored.

More Oriental vegetables

Japanese radish (*daikon*) is a large—sometimes gargantuan—version of our little radish. Oriental chefs use daikon cooked, in soup, pickled, and as a condiment—grated or sliced raw, sometimes mixed with vinegar and hot mustard.

The very largest, the 'Sakurajima' radish, is the size of a pumpkin and takes up to 5 months to mature. Medium-size varieties like 'Miyashige' take only 50 days to produce roots. The smaller varieties, still gigantic in comparison with Western radishes, take 6 to 8 weeks to mature.

Soil preparation is crucial; there should be no hard lumps or debris in the rich, well-drained soil. Soil should be dug and mixed with amendments as deep as roots grow, or the big roots will be distorted. Be sure to give these large radishes plenty of water. The less water they receive, the stronger their flavor; more water, milder flavor.

Asparagus bean or yardlong bean (*dow gauk*) is actually a variety of cowpea or field pea. (For growing instructions, see Southern Peas, page 83.) The bean pods grow 25 to 30 inches long and are stringless. They can be cut and cooked like other kinds of snap beans. Grow these beans on a trellis. They are ready for harvest about 65 days after sowing seeds.

Parsnips

A touch of frost brings out their best flavor

Parsnips are cool-season carrot kin

Parsnips were popular in the bygone era of root cellars because they stored so well. Modern storage methods have made these delicately sweet, creamy white carrot cousins less well known. Why not revive the past with a few garden-fresh specimens in a savory stew?

Like carrots, parsnips need a deep, light, loose soil to develop straight, slender roots. Adding sand and well-rotted compost to the soil helps parsnips to grow and you to dig them up later. Till the soil to a depth of 18 inches because parsnips grow to lengths as long as 15 inches. Usually parsnips are planted in early spring and harvested in autumn and winter. Apply a fertilizer 4 to 6 weeks after sowing seeds.

Cold increases the sugar in mature parsnips, so leave them in the ground until the first frost. If you prefer to leave them in place through winter, digging them up as needed, mound up soil over crowns in autumn. Dig up roots before they sprout in the spring because overmature parsnips become woody.

Parsnips ...at a glance

Type of vegetable. Root; cool season.

Edible parts. Root.

Best soil. Fertile, pH 6.0 to 6.8.

When to plant. *Cold-winter and mild-winter climates: For autumn crop,* sow seeds in spring as soon as soil temperature has reached 50°F/10°C.

How to plant. Sow seeds ½ inch deep, 1 inch apart in rows 18 to 36 inches apart; thin seedlings to 2 to 4 inches apart.

Yield. 10 pounds per 10-foot row.

When to harvest. 100 to 130 days after sowing seeds. To develop sweetest flavor, leave in ground until light frosts occur or all winter where winters are cold.

Care. Keep soil moist. Weed regularly.

Pests and diseases. Army worms, cabbage root maggot, flea beetles, leafhoppers, nematodes. (For treatment, see pages 114, 115.)

Peas

In the pod or out, glorious when garden-fresh

So delightful is the taste of fresh garden or English peas that two out of five gardeners find room for peas in their gardens. Some kinds are for shelling, some have edible pods, and some can be relished either way. (For the vegetables known as Southern, or field, peas, see page 83.)

A cool weather crop, garden peas will even withstand light frosts. Where winters are cold, plant peas in early spring as soon as you can work the soil. Where winters are mild, you can sow a crop of peas in early spring for a spring crop and again in the autumn for a winter or early spring harvest.

Garden peas grow on a vine. Dwarf varieties range in height from 18 to 24 inches and will stand best with some support. The tall varieties grow 6 to 8 feet high and need poles, or string, or chickenwire trellises to climb. Tall varieties give harvest of longer duration than dwarf kinds.

Shelling peas are old-time favorites of gardeners. Besides dwarf and tall, they come in early, midseason, and late-ripening varieties. Edible-pod peas, also known as sugar peas, are available in dwarf and tall varieties. 'Sugar Snap' (and other varieties of this type) combines the qualities of shelling peas and edible-pod peas: you can eat the immature pods, or eat pods and peas together as you would string beans (the most widely used way), or wait for the peas to mature and harvest them for shelling.

Peas like well-drained soil that is rich in organic matter but limited in nitrogen. (Too much nitrogen will produce mostly foliage.) If your soil is lacking organic matter, prepare the soil by digging a trench 1 or 2 feet deep and mixing in large amounts of compost, leaf mold, bone meal, and manure.

Before sowing seeds, soak them overnight in water. Keep the soil moist, but avoid overwatering while the seeds are germinating. (Overwatering pea seeds in cold soil will result in their rotting.) Put up poles or trellises at planting time.

Begin harvesting peas for shelling when pods have swelled to almost a round shape. Harvest edible pods when the pods are 2 to 3 inches long, before the seeds begin to swell. For the freshest taste, harvest peas every 2 days.

Pea pod shows bumps of developing peas

Peas ...at a glance

Type of vegetable. Seed-bearing; cool season.

Edible parts. Harvested seeds; pods of some varieties.

Best soil. Rich, pH 5.5 to 6.8.

When to plant. *Cold-winter climates: For spring crop,* sow seeds in spring (6 to 8 weeks before last frost date). *For autumn crop,* sow seeds about 90 days before first frost date in autumn. *Mild-winter climates: For spring crop,* sow seeds in spring (6 to 8 weeks before last frost date). *For autumn and winter crops,* sow seeds from late summer through autumn.

How to plant. Sow seeds 1 to 2 inches deep, 1 inch apart, in single rows spaced 24 to 48 inches apart, or in double rows spaced 6 inches apart with 30 to 36 inches between double rows. Thin seedlings to 3 to 4 inches apart. Set up stakes or trellises for vines at planting time.

Yield. 2 to 6 pounds per 10-foot row.

When to harvest. 55 to 70 days after sowing.

Care. Keep soil moist. Weed regularly.

Pests and diseases. Aphids, cucumber beetles; powdery mildew. (For treatment, see pages 114–116.)

Pea vines offer plentiful picking

Peanuts

They have the curious habit of "hatching" underground

Familiar peanuts are legumes

You won't find peanuts growing on trees like other nuts but, instead, hidden underground. Peanuts flower aboveground, but produce seed pods underground from pegs, stemlike appendages from the flowers, that burrow down into the soil.

The four basic classes of peanuts are Virginia and Runner types with two large seeds per pod, Spanish with two or three small seeds per pod, and Valencia with three to six small seeds per pod. Order seeds from a mail-order catalog or nursery, or use unroasted peanuts from the grocery store.

Peanuts need a long, warm growing-season; coarse, reasonably fertile soil; and ample moisture. Sow peanut seeds with shells removed but with skins intact.

Peanuts are ready to harvest when the plants' leaves turn yellow—in late summer or early autumn. With a spading fork, dig up and turn over entire plants. After several days, hang plants to cure in a warm, dry, well-ventilated dark place. Pull peanuts from the plants in 2 to 3 weeks.

Peanuts ...at a glance

Type of vegetable. Seed bearing; warm season.

Edible parts. Harvested seeds.

Best soil. Fertile, well-drained, coarse sandy loam, pH 5.8 to 6.2.

When to plant. *Cold-winter and mild-winter climates: For late summer crop,* sow seeds in spring after last frost date.

How to plant. Sow shelled seeds of Virginia and Runner peanuts 1½ to 2 inches deep, 6 to 8 inches apart, in rows spaced 3 feet apart. Sow seeds of Spanish and Valencia peanuts 1½ to 2 inches deep, 4 to 6 inches apart, in rows 2 feet apart.

Yield. 1½ to 3 pounds of nuts in shells per 10-foot row.

When to harvest. 110 to 150 days after sowing seeds, when leaves turn yellow.

Care. Keep soil moist. Weed regularly.

Pests and diseases. Armyworms, cutworms. (For treatment, see page 114.)

Peppers

A little touchy to grow, they're sweet or fiery

Peter Piper once picked a peck of popular peppers. Frankly, that task wouldn't be too difficult even now, considering all the sizes, shapes, colors, and flavors of peppers that are available to home gardeners.

There are short chunky peppers, long skinny peppers, cone-shaped peppers, round peppers, and crumpled peppers—in shades of green, yellow, and red. Their flavors range from mild and sweet to sizzling hot and pungent. They have all sorts of uses, from cooking by themselves and with other foods, to making salads and appetizers.

As garden plants, peppers are somewhat demanding about conditions but well worth the effort it takes to get them to produce. Besides a sunny location, fertile soil, ample moisture, and protection from strong winds, peppers also need warm days and slightly cooler nights.

Sweet peppers grow best when daytime temperatures range between 70° and 75°F/21° and 24°C. Hot peppers prefer slightly warmer temperatures. They thrive when daytime temperatures are between 70° and 85°F/21° and 29°C. For sweet and hot peppers, if night temperatures fall below 60°F/16°C or stay above 75°F/24°C, blossoms often

Green bell pepper tastes mild, sweet

'Gypsy' offers colorful bell pepper

fall off and fruit set is poor.

Sweet peppers grow on stiff, rather compact, large-leafed bushes, mature in 60 to 80 days, and can be grown almost anywhere except at high elevations and in extreme northern areas. Taller, more spreading hot pepper plants have smaller and narrower leaves than sweet pepper varieties. Hot peppers ripen later and are best suited to areas with long, warm growing seasons, but they can be grown in northern states. Other than liking slightly warmer weather, hot peppers require the same care as sweet peppers.

Sweet peppers

The best-known sweet peppers are bell peppers, so named because of their bell shape. Frequently these peppers are harvested when green in order to make the plants more productive. When left on the plants to mature, bell peppers turn red or yellow, depending on the variety. Varieties of bell peppers differ from each other in the size and color of the fruit at maturity, resistance to disease, and earliness of ripening.

A quartet of non-bell peppers with names and flavors that delight diners may be scarcely known to most gardeners. Worth seeking out and growing, these peppers are thinner fleshed and less watery and are packed with a more concentrated sweet-pepper

flavor than big bell peppers. They are also strong garden plants that produce heavily and continuously from the start of harvest until the first heavy frost of autumn. (Don't give up on plants that stop bearing during hot weather. Keep plants alive and they should produce again when the weather cools.)

Pimiento peppers, relatively small peppers with thick, sweet flesh, are used for flavoring sauces and dips and in salads and appetizers.

Pointed Italian frying peppers are 4 to 7 inches long and yellow green to red when mature. As the name implies, they are used for frying or cooking with various meats.

Sweet Hungarian yellow peppers are slender, pointed, and 4 to 6 inches long. In some areas they produce more reliably in hot weather than bell peppers do. They are usually harvested when yellow, but turn red when mature. Only fully red-ripe peppers are used for drying, whether dried in the sun or in a dehydrator.

Cherry peppers are globe-shaped, about 1½ inches wide, and sweet. They can be harvested when green or when they turn red at maturity to be used whole for pickling.

Hot peppers

Ranging in flavor from mild to searing hot, hot peppers range in size from 1¼-inch-long 'Tabasco' peppers to 7-inch-long 'Pasilla' peppers. Their colors include green, red, and shades of brown. Hot peppers are used for making sauces, for pickling, and for making dried seasonings. You can select some varieties by degrees of hotness; for example, there are 'Anaheim Mild' and 'Anaheim Hot' varieties.

Some hot peppers, such as 'Hungarian Wax Hot' and hot cherry peppers, look just like their sweet counterparts. Read labels carefully at planting time to avoid confusing hot and sweet peppers, or you'll be in for a surprise at harvest time.

To harvest all kinds of peppers, cut them carefully from the plants with pruning shears.

Peppers ...at a glance

Type of vegetable. Fleshy-fruited; warm season.

Edible parts. Fruits.

Best soil. Fertile, well-drained, pH 5.5 to 6.8.

When to plant. *Cold-winter and mild-winter climates: For summer crop,* set out plants in spring (1 week or more after last frost date when temperature has warmed up to at least 65°F/18°C). Sow seeds in flats indoors 6 to 8 weeks before you intend to set out plants in garden.

How to plant. Set out plants 18 to 24 inches apart in rows spaced 30 to 36 inches apart.

Yield. 5 to 18 pounds per 10-foot row.

When to harvest. 60 to 95 days after setting out plants. Sweet peppers: when they are full size. Allow pimientos to turn fully red on plants; harvest other kinds at any color stage. Hot peppers: when they reach full size and turn yellow or red; harvest jalapeños when they are dark green.

Care. Keep soil moist, especially during flowering and fruiting. Weed regularly.

Pests and diseases. Aphids, armyworms, Colorado potato beetle, corn borer, mites. (For treatment, see pages 114, 115.)

'Patio Bell', a dwarf sweet pepper

Yellow banana peppers—sweet ones

Potatoes

Packages of nourishment plucked from the soil

Nowadays we think of potatoes as commonplace. But the food that we often take for granted has come a long, roundabout way to our gardens. Carried by Spanish explorers to Europe from South America, potatoes were received as a curiosity. However, Irish farmers discovered their food value and made potatoes popular, so popular that we call this crop that was native to South America "Irish potatoes." Irish settlers brought potatoes to the colony of New Hampshire in the early 1700s, and eventually farmers in the United States grew and developed many varieties.

It's a food with all the virtues one could ask: easy to grow, long-lasting if properly stored, thrifty, nutritious, heartily satisfying, and wonderful to eat, especially with butter or sour cream.

Like its relative, the tomato, the potato produces an abundance of sprawling, bushy vines above the ground. But, unlike tomatoes, the potatoes that we eat fatten up under the soil as tubers (swollen underground stems).

In a home garden, potatoes aren't likely to trouble you with the many pests and diseases that beset a commercial grower—as long as you start with certified disease-free seed potatoes. Available from some nurseries, from farm supply stores, from seed and feed stores, and from mail-order sources in numerous varieties, they come with red, brown, or "white" (actually pale yellow) skins. Some kinds mature faster than others; most take

Colorful potatoes, *fresh from digging*

Potatoes ...at a glance

Type of vegetable. Tuber; cool season.

Edible parts. Tubers (thickened underground stems).

Best soil. Fertile, well drained, sandy loam, pH 4.8 to 5.4 (will grow in higher pH, but may become scabby).

When to plant. *Cold winter climates: For summer crop,* plant cuttings of early-maturing varieties in spring (4 to 6 weeks before last frost date). *For autumn crop,* plant late-maturing varieties in late spring. *Mild-winter climates: For summer crop,* plant in early spring (4 to 6 weeks before the last frost date). *For winter-into-spring crop,* plant in late summer or early autumn.

How to plant. Use certified seed potatoes (specially grown disease-free potatoes). Cut seed potatoes into blocky chunks, each with 2 eyes (growth buds). Plant in furrows 4 inches deep, 12 to 18 inches apart, in rows spaced 30 to 36 inches apart; cover potatoes with 2 inches of soil; add 2 more inches of soil when sprouts emerge.

Yield. 10 to 20 pounds per 10-foot row.

When to harvest. 90 to 120 days after planting. Harvest tender "new" potatoes when vines start to flower. Harvest mature potatoes (for storage) when tops die.

Care. Keep soil uniformly moist. Weed regularly. Mound up soil around vines as vines grow to keep growing tubers protected from sunburn.

Pests and diseases. Aphids, Colorado potato beetle, flea beetles, leafhoppers, wireworms. (For treatment, see pages 114–116.)

How to harvest. Dig beneath plants with spading fork or shovel. Keep tool 8 to 10 inches from plants to avoid injuring potatoes. Lift plant gently, shake off loose soil, and pull potatoes from vines.

about 3 months.

Just prior to planting, cut the seed potatoes into chunks, each about 1½ inches square and having at least two "eyes," from which sprouts will emerge.

Plant in spring as soon as the ground can be worked—or in midwinter if frosts aren't too severe. Potatoes need plenty of growing room compared to most backyard crops. They want full sun and fertile, sandy, fast-draining soil. If the soil is heavy or waterlogged, tubers may become deformed or rot.

Set chunks 12 to 18 inches apart in 6 to 8-inch-wide, 4-inch-deep furrows, that are spaced 30 to 36 inches apart. (Closer spacing will result in higher yields of smaller potatoes.) Cover chunks with 2 inches of soil.

At planting time, fertilize in bands along both sides of each furrow, keeping fertilizer about 2 inches away from seed potatoes but at the same soil level. Use a 10-10-10 fertilizer at about 8 to 12 pounds per 100 feet of row—half

this amount if manure was previously tilled into the soil. Too much nitrogen will encourage excessive above-ground vegetation and poor tuber development.

After sprouts emerge, add another 2 inches of soil to the furrow. As potato vines grow, continue adding soil, mounding a ridge of soil up and over each row, until ridges are about 4 inches high and 18 inches wide. Keep ridges formed as plants mature, since the soil cover helps ensure the best temperature and moisture for the tubers developing below. It also keeps tubers protected from the sun, which would turn them green and inedible on exposed areas.

When most of the potato foliage has turned yellow to brown, harvest time is at hand. Water plants for the last time, then wait a week to 10 days and cut away vines. This sets or hardens the skins, so they won't peel or bruise too easily.

In another 5 to 7 days preferably when it's cool and overcast, dig up the potatoes with a spading fork. Gather the harvest in burlap bags or baskets. To heal any injuries, store potatoes for 2 weeks in a dark place with high humidity and a 50° to 60°F/10° to 16°C temperature. Loosely cover stacked bags or baskets with burlap.

Keep only healed specimens for further storage; unblemished potatoes are best for long storage. Don't expose them to light for any length of time. Further storage should be in a well-ventilated, dark, and dry location, such as a basement, where the temperature is about 40°F/4°C. (If much warmer than that, potatoes are likely to sprout; if much cooler, their starch may turn to sugar, sweetening the flavor.) In these conditions, potatoes should keep well for 3 to 6 months.

Before cooking, cut off and discard any green portions, since these are poisonous.

Pumpkins

For jack-o-lanterns & holiday pies galore

Pumpkins—*both decoration and food for holidays*

Carve its shell, cook its flesh, and snack on its seeds—versatile pumpkins can be enjoyed by the whole family.

Depending on the variety grown, the fruits range in size from tiny jack-o'-lanterns to giants weighing more than 100 pounds. You can eat the seeds of all kinds, but the easiest to prepare are ones without hulls; get them by planting 'Lady Godiva' or 'Triple Treat' pumpkin.

Pumpkin vines need lots of room to grow. Even the bush types can spread over 20 square feet.

In most areas, sow seeds outdoors in late spring (when soil has warmed to 65°F/18°C). In areas with a short growing season, give plants a 2 to 3-week headstart by starting pumpkins indoors in peat pots. Water plants generously, but keep the leaves dry to prevent leaf diseases.

For a monogrammed jack-o'-lantern, scratch a name onto the fruit in late August or early September, before the shell is hardened. As the pumpkin matures, the inscription will callus over and become easily readable. Harvest pumpkins when they are ripe, usually after the first autumn frost.

Radishes

From seed to salad in a few short weeks

Up and away before their slower-growing garden mates have even gotten started, radishes are a sure-fire success for children. They're hardy, they take up little space, and they offer bright, crunchy bouquets for the kitchen in as little as three weeks after seeds are sown.

Most people limit their mind's-eye picture of a radish to the typical supermarket variety—small, round, and rosy to deep red. But you'll also find radish varieties in a parade of different colors, shapes, and sizes.

Some radish surprises include colors of burnished gold, deep purple, white, and even black. Besides forming bite-size nuggets, roots may stretch to the size of foot-long carrots, or resemble miniature turnips or cucumbers. Flavors vary widely, too, from delicate and mild to sizzling hot. Don't expect the large varieties—especially winter radishes—to grow as fast as the small round ones. Many medium and long varieties take 50 to 70 days to mature. (For *Daikon,* see "More Oriental vegetables," page 72.)

Appreciative of cool weather, radishes sown in autumn will thrive through winter if your climate is mild. Otherwise, plant in early spring, leaving space for successive sowings until summer (don't expect most varieties to do well in really hot weather).

Give radishes a sunny spot and a well-pulverized soil. Till the soil several inches deeper than the expected length of the radishes you're planting,

so they can fatten up to size without interference from clods or stones and can be harvested easily. The soil should be loose, light, and rich in organic matter. Rake the soil smooth and form it into ridges 4 to 6 inches high and 8 to 18 inches apart. Ridges aid drainage and let air enter soil easily.

Sow seeds ½ inch deep and 1 inch apart down the center of each ridge. Cover the seeds lightly, and keep the soil reasonably moist throughout the season. Seedlings will appear in 4 to 6 days. After their roots begin to swell, thin out every other plant, eating thinnings that are large enough. Begin checking the root development shortly before the expected harvest date. Harvest radishes as soon as they're mature; if left to overripen, they'll become pithy and perhaps hollow inside.

Successive sowings every 7 to 10 days should keep your salads amply supplied during spring and fall and, where it's possible, during winter.

Colorful radishes—mild to hot-tasting

Radishes ...at a glance

Type of vegetable. Root, cool season.

Edible parts. Roots.

Best soil. Fertile, well drained, pH 5.5 to 6.8.

When to plant. *Cold-winter climates: For spring crop,* sow seeds during spring. *For autumn crop,* sow seeds in autumn. *Mild-winter climates: For spring crop,* sow seeds in spring. *For autumn crop,* sow seeds in autumn. *For winter crop,* sow seeds in autumn and winter.

How to plant. Sow seeds ½ inch deep, 1 inch apart, in mounded rows (4 to 6 inches high) spaced 8 to 18 inches apart (depending on the size of the variety). Thin seedlings to 1 to 4 inches apart.

When to harvest. 22 to 70 days after sowing, before roots get tough and woody.

Yield. 2 to 5 pounds per 10-foot row.

Care. Keep soil moist. Weed regularly.

Pests and diseases. Cabbage root maggot, flea beetles. (For treatment, see pages 114, 115.)

How to harvest. Pull up small radishes. Pull or dig up large radishes.

Raspberries

Velvety morsels of mouth-watering sweetness

A soft blushing red is the color we usually associate with raspberries, but the juicy little nuggets also come in purple, black, and even yellow.

The parent shrubs, which may bear as long as a dozen years, have perennial roots and biennial stems, called "canes." The canes grow up to full size one year—called the "primocane phase"—and bear fruit the second year—called the "floricane phase." Canes that have borne their fruit then die; in the meantime, new primocanes have appeared to produce next year's crop. Ordinarily, raspberries bear their fruit in summer.

One group of raspberries, the fall-bearing (or ever-bearing) kinds, has a pattern of growth and fruit-bearing that differs from the usual. These plants bear a crop of fruit in the autumn of their first year of growth. The fruit is borne on the upper third of the new canes, the primocanes. The summer of the second year, these canes bear a second crop of fruit on the lower part of the canes (now called floricanes). After this second crop, the canes die.

Raspberries thrive where the climate is fairly cool in summer and where there is adequate rainfall during the growing season. (Irrigation can take the place of summer rainfall.) For regions where raspberries are best adapted, see the climate map on page 24.

Planting raspberries

The planting site for raspberries should be sunny, with good air circulation and rich, well-drained soil. Avoid planting raspberries where you have previously raised tomatoes, potatoes, peppers, or eggplants, for they may have tainted the soil with a potentially harmful fungus.

Since raspberries differ widely in their adaptability to local conditions, check with your local county farm advisors for the best varieties for your climate. Buy only certified virus-free plants from a reputable nursery, or you may face disease problems. Plant red and yellow raspberries in rows; purple and black raspberries should be planted 2 to 3 feet apart and allowed to develop into clumps of canes or hills. (See "How to plant" in the checklist and the drawings on page 105.)

Once raspberries are established, caring for them is fairly simple. Twice a month during the growing season, cultivate around the plants (but no deeper than 2 inches) to remove weeds. Putting down a layer of mulch will discourage weeds and also help keep the soil moist. If the soil is rich or has been enriched before planting, you probably won't need to fertilize plants. But if plants grow poorly, apply a complete fertilizer the next spring before the start of growth.

The main care that you will give raspberries is pruning. To learn how to prune raspberries, read the following instructions and look at the drawings on pages 118, 119.

The dormant pruning takes place in early spring—after frost danger is past, but before buds start to swell. For all raspberries, cut down any canes that are weak or diseased; leave 6 to 8 sturdy canes in a hill, or leave canes spaced 6 to 8 inches apart in a row.

During the first summer's growth, "top" black and purple raspberries (remove the tops of the stems) to force the plant to grow lateral branches. Top black raspberries when they are 24 inches tall, purple raspberries when they are 30 inches tall. During the following spring, before growth starts, cut back lateral branches on the year-old canes to 12 to 15 inches long.

After summer harvest, cut out all canes that bore fruit. (For fall-bearing varieties, cut off only the tops, after the autumn harvest, of all canes that bore fruit.) Burn all removed canes to prevent the spread of disease.

Raspberries—*easily grown delicacies*

Raspberries ...at a glance

Growth habit. Berries borne in clusters on 1-year-old canes.

Climate preference. Plants do best where winters are cold and summers are not too hot and dry; hardy from 0° to −35°F/−18° to −37°C.

Best soil. Rich, well-drained, sandy loam, pH 5.5 to 6.8.

When to plant. In early spring.

How to plant. *Red and yellow raspberries:* Set out bare-root plants 24 to 30 inches apart, in rows spaced 6 to 10 feet apart. *Black and purple raspberries:* Set out bare-root plants 2 to 3 feet apart, in rows spaced 6 to 8 feet apart. *Note:* Set all raspberry plants 1 to 2 inches deeper in soil than they were in nurseries. Cut back all newly planted canes to 5 to 6 inches above the ground. Cut back all newly planted black raspberry canes to the ground.

Yield. 1 quart or more per plant.

When to harvest. In summer or autumn, depending on variety. Pick berries when they easily slip off their stems.

Care. Keep soil moist. Weed regularly. Prune yearly. (For pruning information, see pages 118, 119.)

Pests and diseases. Borers, rose chafer; verticillium wilt. (For treatment, see pages 114–116.)

How to harvest. Gently pull ripe berries from their short stems.

Rhubarb

**For pie lovers
with patience**

Succulent stalks, *rhubarb's edible part*

Does your mouth water at the thought of rhubarb pie? If you'd like to grow some of your own rhubarb, plant and plan to be patient—it can take 3 to 4 years to get the first full harvest.

In the meantime, however, you can enjoy the color and shape of the developing plants: broad, pink-veined leaves on tall, smooth red or green stalks. Rhubarb is so attractive that you may decide to plant some in flower beds.

A perennial, rhubarb shoots up new leaves in spring and dies back each autumn. It does best in areas where the ground freezes in winter. Planting time is usually in spring when the dormant crowns (clumps of roots with growth buds attached) are available.

You may be able to harvest a few stalks during the second year after planting, but bigger harvests will come in the third and fourth years. Using a sideways twist, snap off leaf stems at their base when they reach 10 to 15 inches long. Let some leaves remain on each plant to make food to replenish the crowns.

Roquette

**A salad green of Europe
seldom discovered here**

Roquette *adds zest to salads*

Whether you call it *roquette* (French), *arugula* (Italian), or *rocket* (English), it's a salad green with a spicy tang somewhere between that of cress and horseradish. If you want to try it, you'll have to grow your own.

Fortunately, no spring or autumn crop could be easier to grow. In a sunny garden spot, either sow seeds thinly in a row, or scatter them in a patch.

When seedlings have four or five leaves, thin them and eat the surplus plants. Harvest entire plants when they are young and tender. Unharvested plants will eventually shoot up and bloom, producing tender flower buds and white flowers. At this time, harvest only the flower buds and flowers. (The leaves turn sour and tough with age.) The flower buds and flowers taste just like the leaves.

Because the leaves of roquette have considerable bite, mix your first harvest with more bland lettuce leaves. If you like the tang, eat roquette straight with a dressing of vinegar or lemon juice and oil.

Rutabaga

Like its turnip "twin," a winter stewpot favorite

Rutabagas yield edible roots, leaves

The big, yellow "superturnip" your gardening neighbor boasted about last autumn was most likely a rutabaga, not a turnip. These cool-season, frost-hardy cousins are a lot alike, except for color.

Hardy, slow-growing rutabagas are almost always planted in early summer to midsummer for an autumn harvest. These large plants need plenty of space to allow their roots to reach their full weight of 3 to 5 pounds each.

Sow seeds in rows about 18 inches apart. Water generously and thin several times. Main harvest begins about 90 days after sowing seeds, when roots are 3 inches thick. After roots reach full size, they can stay in the ground; dig them as needed. Rutabaga greens are edible, but you may prefer to use only the tender thinnings. Older leaves tend to become coarse.

Cook and serve the roots as you would turnips. Sliced, rutabagas make tasty additions to soups and, when cooked and served as a side dish, a spirited complement to pork or beef.

Recommended varieties of rutabagas include 'Altasweet', 'American Purple Top Yellow', and 'Laurentian'.

Rutabaga ...at a glance

Type of vegetable. Root; cool season.

Edible parts. Roots; young leaves.

Best soil. Fertile, well drained, pH 6.0 to 6.8.

When to plant. *Cold-winter climates: For summer crop,* sow seeds in early spring. *For autumn crop,* sow seeds in early summer to midsummer. *Mild-winter climates: For winter-into-spring crop,* sow seeds in early autumn.

How to plant. Sow seeds ½ inch deep, 1 inch apart, in rows spaced 18 to 36 inches apart; thin seedlings to 5 to 8 inches apart.

Yield. 8 to 12 pounds per 10-foot row.

When to harvest. 90 to 120 days after sowing, when roots are about 3 inches wide.

Care. Keep soil moist. Weed regularly.

Pests and diseases. Armyworms, cabbage root maggot, flea beetles. (For treatment, see pages 114, 115.)

Salsify

Surprising oyster flavor from young & tender roots

Salsify, the oyster-flavored root

If it looks like a parsnip and tastes like an oyster, it has to be a salsify root. Reactions to the "oyster plant" are as strong and varied as the food for which it's nicknamed. For fanciers of oyster who enjoy growing root vegetables, salsify is worth trying.

Plants are slow-growing (up to 150 days) but undemanding. If you start seeds in the spring as soon as the soil is workable, small roots should be ready to pull by midsummer; or they can be left in the ground to be harvested when needed.

When left in the ground through the winter months, the roots will produce large, purple, dandelionlike flowers in spring and, in moist soil, lots of volunteer salsify plants for the second year's crop.

Grown well, young salsify roots are delicate in flavor and very tender. As they age, lengthening to 10 inches or so, their flavor gradually becomes quite strong and their texture somewhat fibrous. 'Sandwich Island Mammoth' is a popular variety.

Salsify ...at a glance

Type of vegetable. Root; cool season.

Edible parts. Root.

Best soil. Rich, well-drained, sandy loam, pH 6.0 to 6.8.

When to plant. *Cold-winter and mild-winter climates: For summer or autumn crop,* sow seeds in spring (2 to 4 weeks before the last frost date).

How to plant. Sow seeds ¼ to ½ inch deep, ½ inch apart, in rows spaced 18 to 30 inches apart; thin seedlings to 2 to 4 inches apart.

Yield. 3 to 7 pounds per 10-foot row.

When to harvest. 140 to 150 days after sowing seeds.

Care. Keep soil moist. Weed regularly.

Pests and diseases. Armyworms, flea beetles, leafhoppers. (For treatment, see pages 114, 115.)

Shallots

They look like green onions, but lend a hint of garlic

***Shallots**—flavors of onion, garlic*

Prized for their flavor—a combination of mild onion and pungent garlic—shallots are grown for their dry bulbs and young green shoots. Shallots are divided into cloves that grow on a common base.

In mild-climate areas shallots are often planted in the autumn, harvested during the winter, and raised primarily for the green portion. In colder zones, shallots are planted as early as possible in the spring and grown for both green shoots (summer) and dry bulbs (autumn).

Use cloves purchased by mail order or from seed stores, or bulbs you can buy in a grocery store. Place the cloves (small bulb divisions) in the ground with fat base downward and tips just covered with soil. You'll have bulbs in 90 to 120 days.

At bulb maturity, tops yellow and die. Harvest by pulling up clumps and separating the bulbs. Let outer skin dry for about a month before using. You can store shallots for as long as 6 months in a cool, dry place.

Shallots ...at a glance

Type of vegetable. Onion family; cool season.

Edible parts. Bulbs; young green shoots.

Best soil. Fertile, pH 5.0 to 6.8.

When to plant. *Cold-winter and mild-winter climates: For summer crop*, plant in early spring (2 to 4 weeks before last frost date). *Mild-winter climates: For winter crop*, plant in autumn (at least 6 weeks before first frost date).

How to plant. Plant cloves (sections of bulb) ½ inch deep, 4 to 8 inches apart, in rows spaced 24 to 48 inches apart.

Yield. Each clove produces a cluster of several cloves.

When to harvest. 60 to 120 days after planting.

Care. Keep soil moist. Weed regularly.

Pests and diseases. Thrips. (For treatment, see page 116.)

Sorrel

Hardier than spinach with a similar sprightly flavor

***Enjoy sorrel** leaves raw or cooked*

Scarcely known in this country, sorrel is a staple in French cuisine, where it is known as *oseille,* and in eastern European and Jewish cuisines, where it's called *schav.*

A hardy perennial, sorrel tastes like a sharp, sprightly spinach but is a much better garden performer. Indifferent to heat and mild winters, it produces leaves all year. (Plants go dormant in winter where the ground freezes, but revive earlier in spring than other vegetables.)

Sorrel plants and seeds are not easy to find. Search herb sections of nurseries for young plants, and explore seed racks and catalogs for the seeds. Set out nursery plants when they are available. Sow seeds early in the spring. The following spring, divide plants to increase your supply. A dozen plants supply plenty of sorrel for a family of four.

With its lemony tang, sorrel is good raw or cooked. You can use the tender leaves in place of lettuce in sandwiches or hamburgers. Cook it in an omelet, sauté it with mushrooms, or blend it into gazpacho.

Sorrel ...at a glance

Type of vegetable. Leafy; hardy perennial.

Edible parts. Leaves.

Best soil. Fertile, well drained, pH 5.0 to 6.8.

When to plant. *Cold-winter and mild-winter climates: For spring to autumn crops,* plant in spring (about 2 weeks after the last frost date).

How to plant. Set out plants 8 inches apart in rows 18 inches apart. Sow seeds ¼ inch deep, 1 inch apart, in rows spaced 18 inches apart; thin seedlings to 8 inches apart.

When to harvest. 60 days after sowing seeds, or when leaves are big enough to use.

Care. Keep soil moist. Weed regularly. Cut off flower stalks in summer.

Pests and diseases. None of importance.

Southern peas

A "down home" staple with delicious variety

Southern peas and the common varieties—cowpeas, crowder, blackeye, cream, and purple hull—come in an array of shapes, sizes, and colors. They can be long or round, smooth or wrinkled, solid or speckled. And they are packed with vitamins and protein.

Originally brought to the United States from Africa as part of the slave trading in the early 1700s, Southern peas flourished in the long sweltering summers in much of the Deep South. Soon these peas became a delicious staple in Southern cuisine.

Although referred to as "peas," these plants grow and look much like string beans. Southern peas prefer a long warm season, but you can grow them in cooler regions of the country. Where the growing season is short, you'll have the best chance of success with early-bearing dwarf or bush varieties—but the yield may still be paltry.

Wait until early summer nights are warm before sowing seeds. For Southern peas the soil needn't be as rich as for most vegetables; a few varieties can even grow in poor soil.

When planting, a Southern space-saving trick is to intersperse peas with corn. The cornstalks provide a natural trellis for vining kinds of Southern peas to climb.

Water these plants by soaking the soil—sprinkling may encourage mildew.

After young pea plants are fairly well established, fertilize them once only with a 5-10-10 side dressing, at 3 pounds per 100 feet of row. Giving too much nitrogen will hinder good seed pod development. (Southern peas are leguminous plants and have nitrogen-fixing bacteria on their roots.)

Peas are most flavorful if they are picked when the pods are still green, their seeds fully grown but soft to the touch. Enjoy these soft peas fresh, or freeze or can them for future use. The pods will shell more easily if they are left to ripen fully. At this stage the pods turn yellow, tan, or purple. Let the peas dry or harden on the vine, then shell and store them dry in jars.

To cook dried Southern peas, simmer them, with a slab of bacon, in three times their volume of water until they are tender (1 to 1¼ hours). They are delicious served with rice or ham. Or top each portion with a sweet tomato and green pepper salsa.

Long-podded Southern peas like warm weather

Southern peas ...at a glance

Type of vegetable. Seed-bearing; warm season.

Edible parts. Seeds.

Best soil. Average, well drained, pH 5.5 to 6.8.

When to plant. *Cold-winter and mild-winter climates: For summer crop,* sow seeds in spring (2 to 4 weeks after last frost date). Make successive sowings in summer until 11 weeks before first frost date in autumn.

How to plant. Sow seeds 1 inch deep, 1 inch apart, in rows spaced 24 to 42 inches apart; thin seedlings to 3 to 6 inches apart.

Yield. 5 to 8 pounds per 10-foot row.

When to harvest. 50 to 120 days after sowing. Harvest for fresh peas when pods are plump and firm. Harvest for dry peas when pods turn yellow.

Care. Water soil regularly but don't overwater. Weed regularly. Avoid applying too much nitrogen-rich fertilizer.

Pests and diseases. Aphids, nematodes, thrips. (For treatment, see pages 114–116.)

Spinach

Make sure it keeps its cool —or it may bolt overnight

Two thousand years before Popeye, spinach grew in the gardens of ancient Persia. Definitely the gourmet's choice today among greens, it lends its leaves to everything from soup to quiche, tasting wonderful whether raw or cooked. And it offers not only flavor, but a wealth of vitamins and minerals as well.

For the gardener, spinach has only one irksome tendency—it bolts quickly into flower if the weather gets too warm or if days lengthen too much before harvest. To pursue just the right pace of rapid, steady growth, spinach needs the cool of spring or autumn—or even winter, where the climate is mild and frost-free. Temperatures should average about 60° to 65°F/16° to 18°C, never rising above 75°F/24°C. If you live in a hot region, or want to grow a summertime crop, try instead one of the taste-alike alternatives, New Zealand or Malabar spinach, described further along. (The hot-weather spinach substitute, tampala, is described under "Amaranth" on page 34.) None of these are true spinaches, but they have the flavor of spinach.

Spinach does best in rich soil and full sun. To prolong the harvest, plan to make successive sowings at 2 to 3-week intervals. Thin seedlings to 3 to 4 inches apart when they are well established. As plants grow larger and begin touching, thin out every other plant and eat the thinnings.

When spinach has put out 6 to 8 leaves, it's ready for harvest. Either cut off the entire plant at its base, or pinch (don't pull) just enough of the outer leaves for one meal. Wash thoroughly, because the leaves are probably sandy or gritty.

Spinach is a versatile cool-season crop; use it raw or cooked

New Zealand spinach

New Zealand spinach, a native of New Zealand, was discovered in the 18th century by British explorers. A spreading, low-growing, and vigorous annual, it tolerates some cool weather but can't survive frost. It can even grow as a perennial in regions of the Deep South.

Soil for New Zealand spinach should be rich. Though it can stand poorer conditions, this kind of spinach won't produce really succulent leaves unless it's well cared for.

Presoak the seeds overnight in cool water to speed germination. In late spring, sow seeds in the garden, thinning the seedlings to 12 inches apart when they are established. Pinch back runners to encourage leafy growth.

When leaves reach 3 to 4 inches long, begin harvesting them by plucking off the last 3 inches of stem tips. To promote growth and prolong the harvest until frost, pick leaves at least once a week while the leaves are young and tender. Overmature leaves may taste tough and bitter.

Malabar spinach

Similar to New Zealand spinach, but a native of India, Malabar spinach is a tender perennial vine. It won't survive frost, and to thrive it requires night temperatures that stay above 58° F/ 14° C.

Malabar spinach prefers rich soil. Sow seeds in early summer; thin established seedlings to a foot apart. When the young vines are about a foot tall, train them on wires or a trellis. After vines reach a height of 2 feet, pinch out a few inches of stem tip (harvesting any young, tender leaves) to encourage the plants to branch and form more stems (vines reach a maximum height of about 4 feet).

As they reach full, succulent size, leaves are ready to be picked individually. Since they're bigger and thicker than leaves of true spinach, you'll need fewer per serving.

Sprouts

Quick & easy crop for salads, stir-fry, sandwiches

Growing sprouts is truly gardening without tears—no mucking about in the dirt and no worries about weather, weeds, and insects. And you'll be enjoying your crop within days instead of weeks.

Grow alfalfa, cress, chia, mustard, or radish seeds for their tiny sprouts that form green leaves—great for salads and sandwiches. For a more substantial crunch that's delicious in breads, entrées, or salads, try lentils, mung beans (used in Oriental cooking), or fenugreek seeds; you harvest these "crops" before the leaves open or turn green. For variety, sprout a mixture of similar-size seeds. Cress, mustard, or radish sprouts add peppery bite to alfalfa, for instance.

When you shop for seeds to sprout, be certain to buy seeds that are for sprouting and not for planting. Seeds for planting in gardens are often treated with poisonous chemicals to prevent them from rotting in the soil.

A 1 or 2-quart glass jar with a screen lid or cheesecloth cover is a good container for sprouts. (Cress seeds do better in a shallow container.) Use 1 tablespoon of alfalfa seeds to fill a quart jar. For others, plan on using a total of two to three tablespoons of seeds per quart jar. Discard any broken seeds of large-seeded sprouting vegetables, such as beans. Don't bother for small-seeded sprouts. Discard any unhealthy looking seeds.

Soak seeds overnight in two to three times their volume of water. The next day drain the water through the screen or cheesecloth, and place the jar on its side, out of direct sunlight. Rinse and drain two or three times a day for about a week.

Give alfalfa, mustard, chia, and radish sprouts indirect sun to turn leaves green; harvest when their leaves open. Keep fenugreek and mung bean sprouts in the dark to prevent them from developing a strong flavor. Lentil sprouts can grow in the light or dark. Harvest fenugreek, lentil, and mung when sprouts are ½ to 1 inch long. Cover and refrigerate sprouts until you are ready to use them (up to 2 weeks).

Another way to sprout seeds is to line any shallow non-metallic container with cheesecloth or white paper towels and sprinkle seeds in a solid layer over the surface. Cover the seeds with water overnight; the next morning drain and cover the container with clear plastic wrap. Add water as necessary to keep sprouts moist. Snip off or pull sprouts when you're ready to use them.

***Sprouts**—instant vegetables all year*

Squash

Thin-skinned or hard-shelled for summer & winter meals

Squash is a rewarding crop for novice and experienced gardeners. Few other vegetables can produce such a bountiful harvest for so little effort. There are summer squash and winter squash. Basically the difference between them is in the stage at which the fruits are harvested and in their ability to last well in storage.

Summer squash is planted for a warm-weather harvest and eaten when its fruit is small and tender—skins, immature seeds, and all.

Winter squash, with slower-to-mature and usually bigger fruits, is grown for late summer harvest and winter storage. The skin is hard and inedible. Ordinarily, you scoop out seeds and pulp before baking. Seeds may be saved, dried, and roasted.

Summer squash: *vigorous zucchini, patty pan, scallop squash*

Summer squash

Summer squash yields prodigious crops from just a few plants and continues bearing for several weeks. The vines are large—2½ to 4 feet across at maturity—and need plenty of room. If space is limited, look for "bush" varieties—they have short vines but are still big plants.

Summer squash used to mean slender green zucchini, pale green scallop squash, and yellow crookneck and straightneck squash. But in the last few years, plant breeders and seed companies have expanded this popular group of vegetables by developing several new types.

Zucchini now comes in a variety of shapes and colors: baseball-shaped with light green stripes; top-shaped and dark green (a cross between scallop squash and zucchini); and cylindrical and golden.

You won't have much problem finding golden zucchini's beacon-yellow fruits under its foliage. Even after cooking, the skin retains its deep yellow color. Golden zucchini has a distinct zucchini flavor with slightly less bite than the green-skinned kinds.

Harvest the ordinary and golden zucchini fruits when they are 4 to 6 inches long. Harvest round zucchini when it's 3 to 4 inches in diameter, the zucchini-scallop squash hybrid when it's 2 to 3 inches across.

Other kinds of summer squash include straightneck, crookneck, and scallop varieties. Straightneck squashes are yellow and smooth-skinned; crookneck squashes are yellow and warty; scallop squashes are white, light or dark green, flat and smooth-skinned, with scalloped edges.

Though they can grow larger, it's usually best to harvest crookneck squashes when they are 4 to 6 inches long, straightneck squashes when they are 5 to 6 inches long, and scallop squashes when they are 2 to 3 inches wide. If you allow summer squashes to grow larger than the recommended harvest size, test them for tenderness with your thumbnail (it should pierce the skin easily). When summer squashes have become large and tough, hollow them out and cook them stuffed.

Winter squash

Winter squash is planted and grown just like pumpkins, which it resembles both in the size of its vine and in its fruiting characteristics. It comes in a wide array of colors, shapes, and sizes.

Acorn squash looks like an oversize acorn with fluted sides. Dark green or golden yellow, acorn squash ranges in size from 5 to 7½ inches long and from 4 to 6 inches wide.

Butternut squash looks like a fat zucchini with a stubbed toe. The tan-skinned fruit is 8 to 10 inches long and 4 to 5 inches wide.

Resembling an oversize banana with

Winter squashes *come in variety of sizes, colors, and flavors*

Growing squash

Few vegetables are easier to grow than squash. With plenty of organic material added to the soil (squash will happily grow on a compost pile), regular watering, and occasional fertilizing, they'll fruit with reckless abandon. Your biggest job, especially for zucchini, will be keeping them picked.

One word of caution about watering. Avoid splashing water on the leaves, stems, and flowers. Squash plants are susceptible to mildew. Water them by flooding or soaking the soil after its surface has dried out.

Squash ...at a glance

Type of vegetable. Fleshy-fruited; warm season.

Edible parts. Fruits.

Best soil. Rich, well-drained, sandy or clay loam, pH 5.5 to 6.8.

When to plant. *Cold-winter and mild-winter climates: For summer and autumn crops,* sow seeds in spring (when soil temperature has warmed to at least 60°F/16°C).

How to plant. Sow seeds of vining squash 2 to 3 inches deep, 12 to 18 inches apart, in rows spaced 6 to 8 feet apart; thin seedlings to 3 to 8 feet apart. Or plant seeds of vining squash in hills (groups of 4 or 5 seeds), 5 to 6 feet apart, in rows 7 to 12 feet apart; thin established seedlings to 2 per hill. Sow seeds of bush squash 2 to 3 inches deep, 12 inches apart, in rows spaced 3 to 5 feet apart, thin seedlings to 2 to 4 feet apart.

Yield. 10 to 80 pounds per 10-foot row, depending on variety.

When to harvest. 50 to 65 days after sowing summer squash, when skins are still tender (poke with a fingernail). 60 to 110 days after sowing winter squash, when skins are hard (not scratchable).

Care. Water deeply to keep soil moist; avoid overhead watering, which can encourage leaf diseases. Weed regularly.

Pests and diseases. Aphids, cucumber beetles, mites, nematodes, squash bug, squash vine borer; powdery mildew. (For treatment, see pages 114–116.)

pink or gray skin, banana squash can grow up to 20 inches long and 5½ inches wide.

Hubbard squash is roughly pear-shaped, sometimes with a pointed rather than rounded narrow end. The fruit grows from 10 to 15 inches long and 8 to 10 inches wide. The skin is warty and can be dark green, blue gray, or red orange.

Buttercup squash's "turbans" are 4 to 5 inches long, 6 to 8 inches wide, and dark green, gray green, or orange in color.

Delicious squash looks like a gigantic acorn. The fruit is 6 to 10 inches long and 6 to 8 inches wide. Skin colors can be green, blue gray, or gold.

Also included among the winter squash are novelties such as 'Turk's Turban', spaghetti squash, and melon-squash. Large (8 to 12 inches wide), turban-shaped 'Turk's Turban' squash comes in an array of colors—orange, red, brown, white, and dark green. You can either eat this squash or use the fruit for autumn decorations indoors.

Though spaghetti squash looks like just a fat, yellow-skinned zucchini, once baked and cut open, this 10 to 12-inch-long squash offers a surprise. Its unusual flesh is made up of long, spaghettilike strands.

Melon squash looks like an extra-large butternut squash; it grows 24 to 30 inches long and sports an orange skin when ripe. The flavor is sweeter than that of most winter squash, more yamlike than melonlike. It takes a long time to mature and will grow best where watermelons do well.

Harvest winter squash in late autumn after the vines have dried but before the first heavy frost. The skins of the fruits should be hard and unscratchable when tested with your thumbnail. Stems are thick; cut them with a sharp knife, leaving a 2-inch stub on the fruit.

Strawberries

When the sun smiles down, they grow big and sweet

Since tiny *fraises des bois* were first found carpeting their native woodlands of southern and central Europe, strawberries have enraptured artists and epicures alike. In illuminated manuscripts of the 15th century, strawberries shown with the Madonna and Child symbolized Christ's wounds and the promise of eternal life. Today, strawberries are one of the most widely cultivated small fruits, with a botanical history that goes back to the writings of ancient Rome.

But strictly speaking, strawberries aren't really fruits at all: the juicy red flesh is actually the swollen tip of the flower stalk. The true fruits of this popular perennial are those tiny seed capsules that stud the flesh like pins in a pincushion.

Because strawberries are very sensitive to subtle shifts of environment, such as the length of daily exposure to sunlight, it has been necessary to develop a seemingly endless procession of varieties. A variety that produces copiously in one state may prove disappointing in its neighboring state, even when the general climate appears to vary only slightly. For reliable choices, you need to consult local agricultural authorities.

Varieties also offer a range of sweet-to-tart flavors, susceptibility to freezing, berry sizes and shapes, and rosy to deep-red colors. Some, called "everbearing," have been especially developed to bear fruit twice or more in one year, giving an extended harvest.

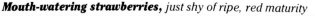

Mouth-watering strawberries, *just shy of ripe, red maturity*

Choosing a location

Most varieties will thrive in any good garden soil; some are more robust than others in adverse conditions. Strawberries prefer a rich, well-drained soil, one that never becomes water-logged, yet retains enough moisture to supply constant growth.

Avoid planting at sites where you have raised potatoes, eggplants, tomatoes, peppers, or raspberries in the previous 3 years—any of these may have infected the soil with verticillium wilt. To guard against invasion by weeds or white grubs, don't plant strawberries where a lawn has grown recently.

If you live in a cold-winter climate, or wherever late frosts are likely, try to plant strawberries on relatively high or gently sloping land. Because their blossoms are vulnerable to frost damage, it is important to plant strawberries where cold air will drain away.

Select a site that receives full sun all day in the growing season.

Growth cycle of strawberries

Strawberries begin to grow and bloom early in spring, fruiting later in spring or early summer. Their harvest duration depends both on variety and climate. Being perennial, they go dormant in winter and grow back the following spring to bloom and fruit again. Usually blossoms are removed by gardeners in the first year so that plants will build strength for a heavy first harvest in the second year of growth. Though plants repeat the cycle of dormancy, growth, and bearing each year, the harvests in the second and third years may not be as good as the first. You may want to replant strawberries every 3 years, or even as often as every year.

Everbearing varieties fruit in summer, then produce a second crop in autumn that may extend until the first frost. Though they bear fruit for a longer time, everbearing varieties tend to be less vigorous than short-season varieties and may produce fewer fruits.

Preparing the soil and planting

In most parts of the country, strawberries are planted in early spring, 3 to 4 weeks before the last expected frost. Where winters are mild, you can also plant strawberries in early summer, early autumn, and winter.

Thoroughly till or spade the soil until it is loose and free of rocks and lumps. If the soil contains a generous amount of organic matter, you should need no fertilizer. But if a soil analysis indicates the need, spread and mix in 1 pound of 10-10-10 fertilizer per 100 feet of row prior to planting.

Your success is best assured by planting certified disease-free strawberries from a reliable nursery. These will probably be year-old plants that have been kept in cold storage. Keep their roots moist and, just before planting, trim the roots to 6 inches for easier management. In setting plants into the ground, it's essential to have the base of the crown at soil level; roots, gently fanned out and the soil firmed around them, must be completely buried.

Methods of growing

Spreading by runners, strawberry "mother" plants produce a number of "daughters." Depending on which planting system you follow among the three explained later, daughter plants are either left alone, trained, or thinned out to coax a lusher growth of the mother.

There are three common arrangements for strawberry plants: in hills, in an intensive spacing called "matted rows," and in a modification of this latter system, called "spaced matted rows."

The hill system is popular west of the Rockies. Compared to the matted row system, the hill system results in a relatively smaller yield of big, beautiful berries from large and vigorous mother plants. Though more costly, the harvest may seem well worth the price of extra plants involved. Hills are the preferred arrangement, too, for any everbearing variety.

Set plants 12 to 14 inches apart on long mounds spaced 28 inches apart; the mounds, or hills, are 5 or 6 inches in height and width and are irrigated from the furrows that separate them. All runners are removed as soon as they appear; this encourages more vigorous growth of the crown of each mother plant.

In matted rows, runners are allowed to set roots freely in all directions. Mother plants are placed 18 to 24 inches apart, in rows spaced about 4 feet apart. Beds are kept to a width of 18 to 24 inches by trimming off any runners that extend beyond this limit. Obviously, fewer plants are needed initially.

Spaced matted rows differ only in that each mother is allowed only a few runners, usually six. Daughter plants are carefully placed by hand to root so that the resulting plants are spaced 6 to 8 inches apart in rows 18 to 24

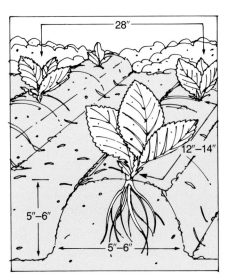

Hill planting for strawberries— plants grow on long, low mounds, produce very large berries.

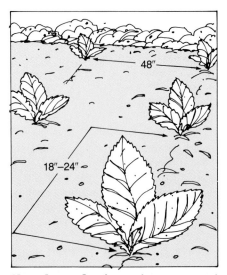

Matted-row planting—plants start out far apart on level ground (left), but are allowed to spread out to make dense mats of plants (right). Trim off any runners that grow beyond the boundaries shown.

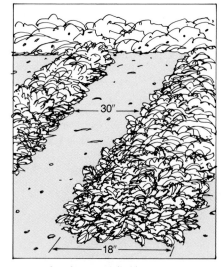

Strawberries *bear well in containers*

...Strawberries (cont'd.)

inches apart. This method requires a bit more work, but the result is usually a higher yield of larger and lovelier berries, with few disease problems.

Care

During the first year, no matter how plants are arranged, remove all their blossoms. (If you grow an everbearing variety, remove blooms only until plants are well established, usually by midsummer.) This practice ensures that ample nourishment will strengthen mother plants, fostering the early production of vigorous runners. Early runners of the first year will bear the best fruit the following year.

Since strawberries have shallow roots, weed control and adequate irrigation during dry spells are important. For most varieties, cultivate frequently (about once a week) for the first 6 weeks. Cultivation keeps the soil loose to allow the easy rooting of

daughter plants and to uproot competing weeds. Avoid cultivating so deeply as to endanger roots.

Though many strawberry varieties can survive drought, it takes plenty of water to produce prime fruit. Allow at least an inch of water per week (rainfall included), more in dry weather.

Cultivate everbearing varieties for only 10 days to 2 weeks after planting, then mulch with sawdust, taking care not to mix it with the soil. Pay special attention to irrigation, because the berries develop during the months when the soil may be at its driest.

Mulching strawberries to prevent winter damage is vital in areas with very cold winters. Alternating periods of freezing and thawing can cause the ground to heave, uprooting plants. In late November, when temperatures have dropped to freezing several times, loosely sift mulch to cover plants completely. Straw is a commonly used material (hay, unless threshed, may contain weed seeds).

In the following spring, as new growth starts, brush the straw into the alleys between rows (be absolutely sure to clear mulch off leaves). The mulch will help keep the fruit clean and hold down weeds; also, you can heap it over plants again whenever a late frost threatens—but remember to clear it away again the next day.

Another precaution against late spring frost damage is to turn on sprinklers whenever the ground-level temperature drops to 32°F/0°C. A protective layer of ice will form on the plants, usually preventing excessive frost damage.

If birds frequent your garden, you'll probably have to protect emerging berries with plastic netting—or scare away the feathered marauders with suspended aluminum pie pans.

Let strawberries ripen to a full red color before you harvest them; then pick immediately. You'll probably have to do this every day during the season's peak. Harvest carefully by cutting stems to avoid bruises. Ripe fruit will keep for a day or two in the refrigerator.

After the harvest, you can choose whether to renovate the bed for another season's crop, or simply to dig under the plants. Before renovating, remove all mulch still clinging to the

foliage, then mow or clip the leaves to within an inch of the crowns. Remove and burn any plants that show signs of insect infestation or disease. Using a cultivator, narrow row widths to 10 or 12 inches.

To stimulate a renewal of top growth, apply ½ to ¾ pound of a high-nitrogen fertilizer per 100 feet of row. If plants are too crowded, thin after new growth starts, to space the plants 6 to 8 inches apart. Keep soil weed free and adequately wet. Fertilize in autumn and mulch at the onset of winter just as in the first year. A new crop will develop in the following spring or summer, perhaps somewhat less grand and abundant than the first.

Strawberries ...at a glance

Growth habit. *Berries borne on fruiting stems of clumping leafy perennials.*

Climate preference. *Different varieties are adapted to almost every climate in United States.*

Best soil. *Rich, well-drained, sandy loam, pH 5.8 to 6.5.*

When to plant. *Cold-winter climates:* Set out plants in early spring (3 to 4 weeks before last frost date). *Mild-winter climates:* Set out plants any time of year, except when soil is too wet to work.

How to plant. *For hills, set out plants 12 to 14 inches apart on mounds 5 to 6 inches high and 5 to 6 inches wide; mounds should be spaced 28 inches apart at centers (see illustration). For matted rows, set out plants 18 to 24 inches apart in rows spaced 48 inches apart.*

Yield. *5 to 10 quarts of berries per 10 feet of matted row.*

When to harvest. *Most varieties:* In spring, a year after planting. *Everbearing varieties:* In autumn, when planted in early spring or summer; in spring, when planted in previous autumn. Harvest all berries when fully red and ripe.

Care. *Water and weed regularly. Keep matted rows trimmed back.*

Pests and diseases. *Mites, rose chafer, strawberry root weevil; verticillium wilt. (For treatment, see pages 115, 116.)*

Sunflower

A "flower" too big to believe, with delicious seeds inside

Dramatic sunflower—edible seeds

Health stores stock them, birds fight over them, and Kansas sings about them. What are they? Sunflowers.

Though many people use seeds from these towering plants for nutritious snacks, some grow them to provide winter feed for birds or just enjoy their decorative golden blooms.

Probably the most common sunflower variety grown is 'Mammoth'. Living up to its name, this variety's 8 to 10-inch flower heads peer down from giant stalks, which often reach more than 10 feet high. Shorter varieties bear similar-size flowers on 5 to 6-foot stalks.

Easy-to-raise sunflowers grow wild in some areas of the country. Sow seeds in a sunny location when the soil and weather are warm.

When seeds are mature and fairly hard, cut off the flower heads with a foot of stem attached and spread them to dry in a warm, well-ventilated spot. When the seeds are thoroughly dry, remove them from the heads and store in a cool, dry place.

Sunflower ...at a glance

Type of vegetable. Seed-bearing; warm season.

Edible parts. Harvested seeds.

Best soil. Rich, well drained, pH 5.8 to 6.2.

When to plant. *Cold-winter and mild-winter climates: For summer crop,* sow seeds in spring (4 weeks after last frost date).

How to plant. Sow seeds ½ inch deep, 6 to 12 inches apart, in rows spaced 30 to 36 inches apart; thin seedlings to 12 to 18 inches apart.

When to harvest. 68 to 80 days after sowing seeds, when seeds are full-size.

Care. Give lots of water. Cover seedheads with cheesecloth or paper bag to protect ripening seeds from birds.

Pests and diseases. Aphids, cucumber beetles, mites. (For treatment, see pages 114, 115.)

Sweet potatoes

Easy to grow from cuttings for a butter-tender treat

Sweet potatoes—for warm climates

It's fun to start a sweet potato in a jar of water on a windowsill. It's almost as easy to grow sweet potatoes in your garden if you live where summers are long and hot.

You can buy slips (rooted cuttings) from some nurseries and by mail order, or you can start your own cuttings indoors or in a hotbed. To start cuttings, place sweet potatoes in a container and cover them with 4 inches of moist sand. For the first 3 to 4 weeks, keep them at 80° to 85°F/27° to 29°C. When sprouts appear, reduce the temperature to 70°F/21°C until sprouts are several inches long and ready to transplant.

Carefully pull or cut the rooted sprouts from the starter potatoes when it's time to set them out. Plant the slips in the garden in ridges in late spring when the soil temperature has warmed to 70°F/21°C.

There are two classes of sweet potatoes—those with soft, sugary yellow orange flesh ('Centennial', 'Gold Rush', 'Vineless Puerto Rico') and those with firm, dry whitish flesh ('Yellow Jersey', 'Nemagold').

Sweet potatoes ...at a glance

Type of vegetable. Root; warm season.

Best soil. Fertile, pH 5.0 to 6.5.

When to plant. *Cold-winter and mild-winter climates: For summer crop,* plant rooted cuttings in spring when soil temperature has warmed to 70°F/21°C. Start cuttings indoors or in hotbed 4 to 6 weeks before planting time.

How to plant. Set out rooted cuttings 2 to 3 inches deep, 10 to 18 inches apart, on ridges 8 to 15 inches high spaced 3 to 4 feet apart.

Yield. 8 to 12 pounds per 10-foot row.

When to harvest. 110 to 120 days after setting out sprouts; harvest immediately if tops are killed by autumn frost.

Care. Allow soil to dry slightly between waterings. Let vines sprawl.

Pests and diseases. Aphids, flea beetles, leafhoppers, nematodes, wireworms. (For treatment, see pages 114–116.)

Swiss chard

For hesitant gardeners, almost foolproof success

***Obliging Swiss chard** gives leaves all season*

Swiss chard is easy to grow and virtually indestructible. Though it's closely related to beets, this plant is grown not for its root but for its succulent stalks and tangy leaves.

Sow seeds early in spring in most climates and start harvesting overcrowded seedlings soon after. Stalks mature in about 8 weeks and keep shooting up until the ground freezes in autumn. In mild-winter climates, plants produce up to a year if you remove bloom stalks as they form.

To harvest, tear off outer stalks near the base, allowing central stalks and leaves to grow. If you want to use the whole plant, slice it off a couple of inches above the ground; new leaves will eventually sprout.

Some Swiss chard varieties include 'Lucullus' with yellowish green leaves and broad yellowish white stalks, decorative 'Rhubarb' with bright crimson stalks and red-veined leaves, 'Fordhook Giant' with broad, pearl white stalks, and 'Perpetual' with smooth, dark green leaves.

Swiss chard ...at a glance

Type of vegetable. Leafy; cool season.

Edible parts. Leaves; stalks.

Best soil. Fertile, well-drained, sandy or clay loam, pH 6.0 to 6.8.

When to plant. *Cold-winter and mild-winter climates: For summer and autumn crops,* sow seeds in spring (2 to 4 weeks before the last frost date).

How to plant. Sow seeds ½ inch deep, 2 inches apart, in rows spaced 18 to 30 inches apart; thin seedlings to 12 inches apart.

Yield. 8 to 12 pounds per 10-foot row.

When to harvest. 50 to 60 days after sowing seeds. Harvest first greens as you thin seedlings.

Care. Keep soil moist. Weed regularly.

Pests and diseases. Aphids, cabbage worm, flea beetles, leaf miners, nematodes. (For treatment, see pages 114, 115.)

Tomatillo

The tomato's baby brother —small, green, tasty

***Tomatillos**—tomatolike fruits in jackets*

A tomatillo is a large green cherry tomato with a husk. These tough, prolific tomato relatives are easy to grow, but there are only two ways to get seeds: scrape them out of fresh fruit when available at grocery stores, or order them from seed specialists.

Sow tomatillo seeds directly into the ground, or start seeds in containers. Most seeds germinate in warm, moist soil in about 5 days.

Seedlings are ready to transplant in about 3 to 4 weeks. Space plants about 10 inches apart in fertile soil with full sun. Bury the stem almost up to the bottom leaves to encourage rooting, and water well.

Tomatillos sprawl all over the ground unless you stake or trellis them. Once mature, plants need infrequent watering—every 5 to 10 days.

Harvest fruits when fully grown—usually walnut-size, sometimes smaller. For best piquant flavor, pick while the fruit is deep green and after the husks turn dry and brown. You can use raw tomatillos in salads, and cooked tomatillos as ingredients for green taco sauce and for preserves.

Tomatillo ...at a glance

Type of vegetable. Fleshy-fruited; warm season.

Edible parts. Fruit.

Best soil. Fertile, well drained.

When to plant. *Cold-winter and mild-winter climates. For summer crop,* sow seeds in spring (4 to 6 weeks after last frost date when soil has warmed up).

How to plant. Sow seeds ⅛ inch deep, 2 inches apart, in rows spaced 2 feet apart; thin seedlings to 10 inches apart. Set up supports for vines at planting time.

Yield. 1 to 2 pounds per plant.

When to harvest. 120 days after sowing seeds, when husks around fruits turn tan and split.

Care. Water every 5 to 10 days. Weed regularly.

Pests and diseases. See Tomato, page 95.

How to harvest. Pull fruit from plant. To store, leave papery husks on fruit.

Tomatoes

A flavorful, juicy joy when you grow your own

What makes home-grown tomatoes so great? Taste and texture are surely at the top of the list. Commercially grown tomatoes that are picked green before flavor develops often consist of a bland mealy flesh encased in a tough skin. They've been bred for long storage and easy shipping at the expense of zesty-sweet taste and smooth fleshy texture.

Home gardeners, however, can choose from among dozens of varieties with real, old-fashioned tomato flavor. What's more, home gardeners can pick vine-ripened tomatoes at the peak of their flavor. No tomato tastes better than a juicy one plucked from the vine, rinsed with the garden hose, and eaten right on the spot.

Sizes, shapes, and colors

A wide choice of sizes, shapes, and colors awaits the adventuresome home tomato-gardener.

Tomatoes range in size from the pop-in-the-mouth cherry type, such as 'Sweet 100', 'Tiny Tim', 'Toy Boy', 'Pixie', 'Small Fry', and 'Sugar Lump', to the 1 to 2-pound giants, such as 'Big Boy', 'Beefeater', and 'Beefmaster'. In between these extremes are medium-size tomatoes such as 'Early Girl', 'Pearson', 'Rutgers', and 'Floramerica'.

Besides the usual round, red tomatoes, you can grow yellow types shaped like pears or plums. These have mild, sweet flavor, and some have low acid content. Or you can grow orange-colored tomatoes, such as 'Caro-red' or 'Burpee's Jubilee'. There are even pink tomatoes: 'Oxheart' produces large fruit that can weigh 1 pound each, and 'Ponderosa' has mild-tasting, 1½-pound fruit.

If you want to grow special tomatoes for canning or to make your own tomato sauce or paste, you'll find types available for processing such as 'Heinz 1350', 'Roma' (plum-shaped), 'Royal Chico' and 'San Marzano' (oblong), and

Most popular home-grown vegetable, the tomato comes in many colors, sizes

versatile hybrids such as 'Freedom'. These have a high amount of solid matter and ripen over a short period for early harvest.

Determinate and indeterminate plants

The number of tomatoes a plant produces is often (though not always) related to whether it's an indeterminate or determinate tomato. Determinate tomatoes are bush types that stop growing when they reach 3 to 5 feet; their crop tends to ripen over a shorter period than the crop of indeterminate tomatoes.

The vines of indeterminate tomatoes keep on growing until frost kills them; some varieties like 'Better Boy' and 'Big Boy' can reach 12 to 14 feet in height. Indeterminate vines tend to produce larger crops over a longer period than the bush determinate types. Those extra-large tomato plants such as 'Big Boy', however, make you wait an extra-long time—so long that they really can't be grown where the summer growing season is short.

Other factors

Earliness of ripening is an important characteristic to consider for garden-

Examples *of tomato range—cherry to giant*

Cherry tomatoes *produce lavish crop when grown in large containers*

ers living in areas with short growing seasons or chilly summers. As one gardener from the cool Northwest exclaimed, "Any slow-bearing plant is a loser for me—I want action out there!"

Seed packets, catalog descriptions, and tags on packs of seedlings give the maturity dates. Keep in mind that the dates are only rough averages of the time that will elapse between transplanting and the first ripe fruit under good growing conditions.

Disease resistance is another element to look for when searching for the great garden tomato. Seed packets and pack tags bear initials to tell you if the plants have some inbred resistance to one or more of the big three tomato troublemakers: "V" for verticillium wilt; "F" for fusarium wilt; "N" for nematodes.

We wish we could give you a failproof list of tomatoes that taste great, ripen early, produce reliably and bountifully, and resist diseases. But climate and soil differences make it impossible to list even one or two varieties in each size, shape, and color of tomato available that will do well everywhere. For instance, beefsteaktype tomatoes—the gorgeous behemoths—usually thrive in the South, Midwest, and East but flop in the West because they need long, humid summers and warm (65° to 70°F/18° to 21°C) night temperatures. Your local garden center and cooperative extension service agents—not to mention neighborhood gardeners willing to share their expertise—are the best guides to selecting great garden tomatoes for your area.

Getting started

You can start your own tomatoes from seeds, or plant seedlings purchased from a nursery or garden center. Purchased seedlings should be sturdy—not weak, spindly, or overmature. If you grow your own seedlings, start them indoors 5 to 7 weeks before you plan to set them out (at least 10 days after the last frost date in spring). Expose tender seedlings, including purchased tomato plants, to cool outdoor air gradually. This is called "hardening off" the plants before setting them out in the garden, and it will decrease transplant shock.

If you have heavy clay soil or very sandy soil, it's a good idea to dig in ample organic matter before planting. Add compost, peat moss, or ground bark at the rate of one part organic matter to two parts soil.

Unlike most other plants, tomato seedlings prefer being planted deep. You can bury as much as half to three-quarters of the stem after removing the leaflets. Roots will form along the buried part of the stem and make the plants grow strong.

Space the seedlings 2 to 4 feet apart, depending on the variety. Remember that indeterminate vine types will need the greatest amount of space. Cut off the suckers that form at the notch between the branches and main stem to get earlier ripening and larger tomatoes. Let suckers remain to get more fruit and for protection against sunscald.

Gardeners in cool-weather zones (where summers are cool or short) can give their plants a faster start by covering the soil with black plastic sheeting or by planting tomatoes in bottomless containers made of old automobile tires. These devices can help speed the growth of roots by raising the soil temperature.

If you set out plants early in the season, be prepared to cover them with hotcaps or other protective devices (see page 104) to give them protection from frost.

Continued care

Watering tomatoes is relatively simple: water often enough to keep the soil in the root zone damp but not soggy. This may mean watering seedlings every day or two until they become established. During dry spells you should water well-established plants deeply about every 10 days.

It's wise to support tomatoes on stakes or in wire cages. This practice keeps plants neat and avoids fruit rot by keeping the fruit from touching the soil. In extremely hot areas, avoid using metal supports, for they may burn plants.

If you use stakes, choose sturdy ones at least 1 inch thick and 6 feet tall. Hammer stakes into the ground 1 foot from the plant at the time of planting. To avoid any damage to stems, tie the tomato vines to stakes or other supports with strips of cloth or other soft ties. (For ideas for tomato supports, see page 110.)

If the soil is well prepared, you probably won't have to fertilize tomatoes until the fruit starts to develop. At that time, you can apply a low-nitrogen fertilizer that is high in potassium and phosphorus. Avoid giving a high-nitrogen fertilizer which would encourage lush foliage at the expense of fruit production.

Dealing with problems

Hot weather can cause plants to stop setting fruits, especially when temperatures go above 100°F/38°C. If you live where the temperature sometimes goes above that mark, you can decrease the temperature around your plants a few degrees with a protective cover. Use nursery shadecloth draped over stakes, or construct a simple wooden framework to support a lath or bamboo shade. These devices also prevent sunscald on fruit.

On the other hand, tomatoes do need warm temperatures to pollinate reliably: 65°F/18°C for late varieties; 60°F/16°C for early varieties. Fruit-setting hormones that you apply to the flowers are worth the expense where summer nights are cool. You can encourage pollination by tickling the blossoms once or twice a day.

Blossom-end rot, which looks just like its name—a hard brown rotten spot on the blossom end of the fruit—is another common problem. Though this malady is still somewhat of a mystery, it tends to be associated with wide fluctuation in soil moisture and perhaps a calcium deficiency. Try to maintain even soil moisture, and apply a fertilizer with calcium as a precaution if you've had a problem with blossom-end rot in previous years in the same garden soil.

Tomato hornworms are disgustingly fat 4-inch worms that are the exact color of tomato foliage with a reddish horn on the hind end and a few inconspicuous white stripes. They love tomato leaves but will also eat green and ripe fruit; you can hear them munching if you listen closely. Control is simple, if brutal: pick them off and stomp on them.

Tomatoes in containers

Though any tomato plant can grow in a container that's large enough, the dwarf and miniature varieties are best suited for pots with a soil capacity of 1 cubic foot. Try varieties such as 'Patio', 'Sweet 100', 'Small Fry' (grows like a small tree, needs to be caged), 'Pixie', 'Presto', 'Early Salad' (hanging basket or trellis), 'Tumblin' Tom' (hanging basket), dwarf 'Champion'. Put a stake in each pot at time of planting and tie the stem to the stake as the plant grows.

Standard-size tomatoes need a container with a capacity of 3 cubic feet.

Tomatoes ...at a glance

Type of fruit. Fleshy-fruited; warm season.

Edible parts. Fruits.

Best soil. Fertile, well-drained, pH 5.5 to 6.8.

When to plant. *Cold-winter and mild-winter climates: For a summer crop,* set out plants in spring (10 days to 7 weeks after the last frost date). Sow seeds in flats 5 to 7 weeks before you intend to set out plants.

How to plant. Set out plants that will be staked 12 to 24 inches apart in rows spaced 36 to 48 inches apart. Set out plants that will not be staked 18 to 48 inches apart in rows spaced 36 to 60 inches apart. Cover ½ to ¾ of leafless stem with soil.

Yield. 15 to 45 pounds per 10-foot row.

When to harvest. 50 to 90 days after setting out plants, when tomatoes have reached desired size and color. Harvest before first frost in autumn.

Care. Water and weed regularly. Stake large, sprawling varieties. Give frost protection to plants set out early.

Pests and diseases. Aphids, cutworms, flea beetles, leaf miners, nematodes, tomato hornworm, whitefly; fusarium wilt, verticillium wilt. (For treatment, see pages 114–116.)

Turnips

Pleasurably edible, from leafy top to bulging root

Eat turnip's *leaves as well as roots*

There are no wasted frills on turnips. They're edible from top to bottom, offering good nutrition in a package of very few calories. With most kinds, you can eat the leaves when they're young and tender and the roots when they reach maturity. With some varieties you eat only the leaves.

Turnips are frost-hardy and like cool weather. You can sow seeds in early spring for a harvest before the weather gets hot, and sow again in late summer and autumn for a harvest when the weather cools down again.

Some people prefer the roots from the autumn harvest because they are most flavorful and tender then. Also, turnips protected from frost by a straw mulch can stay in the ground in autumn until you're ready to dig the roots. (Dig them up before the ground freezes solid.)

Turnips aren't fussy about care. Grow the ones you want for leaves closer together than the ones you want for roots.

As greens grow, pick the outer leaves. Harvest roots when they're 2 to 3 inches wide; they become tougher and more pungent as they grow fatter.

Watermelon

For barbecues, picnics— the summertime supermelon

Watermelon, *the summer-sweet favorite*

Gardeners with plenty of space and a hot summer in store should take the opportunity to grow this big, jolly blimp of a melon with its sweet siren-pink (or bright golden) flesh. It's a delightful treat, especially for children.

A favorite of the South, watermelons need plenty of summertime heat to reach their full, sweet potential. Large varieties may require as many as 95 days of sun-drenching, but you can also buy smaller, earlier-ripening "icebox" types.

Sow five or six seeds per hill; later, thin to one to two seedlings per hill. Keep the soil moist, but avoid overhead watering. Feed with a complete fertilizer every 4 to 6 weeks. A mulching of straw prevents soil from drying out too fast, reduces chances of rotting, and helps keep soil warm. For fatter melons, thin to three or four fruits per vine when they're small.

A watermelon is probably ripe if it makes a dull "thunk" when thumped, when its underside has turned from white to pale yellow, and the tendril opposite the stem of the melon has withered.

Loving Care—Detail Work That Counts

*U*nderstanding general gardening procedure is important to anyone planning a food garden. The dual purpose of this section is to present the basics as concisely as possible, and to serve as a handy reference throughout the growing season.

• Because any garden begins with the soil, the first pages (98–101) discuss the various soil types and how each may be modified or improved so roots will have the conditions they need to produce good plants and crops. Garden soils are notoriously individualistic, but this section will help you to understand your particular soil and its needs, so you can grow the crops you want.

• After the soil is prepared, your next step is planting. On pages 102–105, we tell you about planting from seeds, setting out young plants, and dormant-season planting of perennials and shrubby plants.

• Knowing when, how, and how much to water your vegetables or berries is important if you are to achieve maximum success with them. On pages 106 and 107 we show a number of ways in which water can be delivered to plants. How you choose to do it will depend on your water availability, size of garden, climate—and personal preference.

• Nutrients are vital to the growth of your crop plants. On pages 108–109 we give you the basics of fertilizer knowledge: what nutrients are needed and when, and the kinds of fertilizers and methods of application you choose.

• As your garden grows, two maintenance jobs may emerge: 1) management of plant growth, and 2) elimination of the ubiquitous garden interlopers—weeds. We show you various ideas for supporting the vining crops (pages 109 and 110) and give you advice and cautions on various types of weed control (page 111).

• The harvest and storage section (pages 112 and 113) explains what to do with the rewards of your efforts: how to handle the produce in excess of what you can consume immediately.

• Pests and diseases aren't universal problems, but should you find a chewed leaf, a wilted branch, or a strange "bug," check our illustrations, descriptions, and control suggestions (pages 114–117).

• Pruning treatment for berries and grapes is described on pages 118–121. This information is vital for getting best crops from these garden "sweets."

• Finally, we offer suggestions for special garden methods (pages 122–125) for the more adventuresome—methods that can increase yields from a given area and ideas to help give you a jump on the season or let you defy the weather conditions outside.

Preparing the soil

Visions of vegetables and berries may be foremost in your mind, but you must first think deeper, to the soil that will support the plants' growth. For just as a well-constructed house depends on a solid foundation, a successful garden starts with a fertile, well-prepared soil.

What's your soil type? Can it be improved? Should you fertilize? What type of fertilizer should be used? The answers to these questions follow.

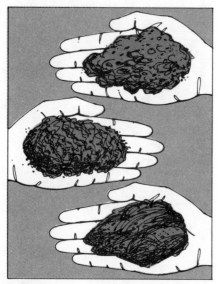

Soil is ready for tilling (top) when it crumbles easily from ball. It's too dry (middle) if it's powdery, too wet (bottom) if it forms a gummy ball.

Soil structure

Soil is a mass of mineral particles, living and dead organic matter, air, and water. The size and shape of a soil's mineral particles determine its characteristics. The smallest mineral particles are clay particles ($\frac{1}{12,500}$ of an inch in diameter); the largest, sand particles ($\frac{1}{25}$ to $\frac{1}{50}$ of an inch). Silt particles are intermediate in size ($\frac{1}{500}$ of an inch). The four basic soil types are clay, silt, sand, and loam—a soil composed of all three particle types.

Clay soil probably causes more consternation among gardeners than any other soil type. When wet, it's gummy and unworkable; when dry, it cracks apart. Because it's composed of many tightly packed particles with great surface area for holding, clay soil holds water and nutrients well. But there's little room for air in this soil and drainage is poor, making it difficult for you to grow plants in it.

Sandy soil, at its worst, is the exact opposite of clay. Large particles and large spaces between them make for well-aerated soil, but water pours through, taking the nutrients with it.

Silt soil drains better than clay and holds more nutrients than sand.

Loam, a mixture of clay, silt, and sandy soils, preserves the best characteristics of each and is considered the ideal soil. It drains well, holds ample nutrients, retains moisture, and provides enough air for root growth.

Soil pH

A soil's acidity or alkalinity is expressed in terms of pH, on a scale of 1 to 14. A pH of 7 is neutral; any pH less than 7 is acid and any pH greater than 7 is alkaline. The ideal vegetable and berry garden soil is slightly acid to neutral (pH 6 to 7), but you can grow excellent crops in slightly alkaline soil (pH 7 to 8).

Acid soil is most common in areas of heavy rainfall. If soil pH is less than 5.5, you can add ground limestone (lime) to counteract the acidity—the calcium in the limestone neutralizes acids. If you can find it, add dolomitic lime, which contains both calcium and magnesium. Check with your local cooperative extension service agent or nurseryman for the amounts of lime necessary to correct your area's soil.

Alkaline soil is common in areas with low rainfall, poor drainage, and natural limestone deposits. Often alkaline soils are also too salty. To reduce mild alkalinity, fertilize with an acid-type fertilizer. To reduce salinity on well-drained soil, irrigate the land for 24 to 48 hours to wash excess mineral salts down below the root zone.

If moderate alkalinity remains after leaching and applying an acid-type

1) Organic amendments help improve any soil. Spread amendment layer evenly over surface of soil.

2) Incorporate organic amendments into soil, using either a rotary tiller or spade to mix amendments in.

3) Rake the tilled soil smooth to break up clods, remove stones, level surface.

fertilizer, you may need to add sulfur to neutralize the soil. The large-scale chemical treatment of extremely alkaline soils is expensive and complex; it may be best to garden in raised beds (see "Raised beds," page 101).

Nutrients in the soil

Because plants get many essential nutrients for growth from the soil, it is a good idea to have your soil tested (see below) before you prepare it for planting. The test will tell you whether your soil will provide the nitrogen, phosphorus, and potassium that plants must have in order to thrive.

If the soil lacks one or more of these nutrients or if they are present only in small amounts, you'd be wise to add fertilizer (see pages 108–109) as well as soil amendments.

Nitrogen. Plants use large quantities of this element. The nitrogen that isn't used by the plants is easily lost through the leaching action of rainfall and irrigation or is quickly used up by microscopic soil organisms.

Because nitrogen promotes rapid growth of plant stems and leaves and gives plants a deep green color, it is especially needed by leaf crops. Signs of nitrogen deficiency are a yellowing and falling off of older leaves and stunted growth (smaller leaves, fewer flowers, and smaller fruits).

If plants have too much nitrogen, they grow so fast that they may become weak and spindly and produce leaves and stems instead of flowers and fruit.

Chemical sources of nitrogen include ammonium nitrate, ammonium sulfate, calcium nitrate, and urea. Organic sources of nitrogen are blood meal, hoof and horn meal, cottonseed meal, fish meal, fish emulsion, animal manures, and bone meal.

Phosphorus. To get plants off to a fast start, work a fertilizer high in phosphorus into the soil as you prepare it. Phosphorus encourages root formation, flowering, and fruiting but doesn't move very far in the soil. When you set out transplants, water them with a high-phosphate solution.

Dull green leaves with purple tints are the visible signs that a plant is deficient in phosphorus. In general, when this nutrient is lacking, plant growth is stunted. There is little or no danger of too much phosphorus in the soil.

Chemical sources of phosphorus include phosphoric acid and superphosphate. Bone meal is a good organic source of phosphorus.

Potassium. Essential to all plant processes, this vital nutrient promotes root growth and seed production.

Potassium deficiency results in slow overall plant growth. Leaves may have mottled yellow tips and edges; older leaves may look scorched at the edges. Like phosphorus, an excess of potassium presents little danger.

Chemical sources of potassium include potassium chloride, potassium nitrate, and potassium sulfate. Organic sources of potassium are granite dust, pulverized granite, potash rock, and wood ashes.

Soil testing

Prior to tilling or amending the soil, you should consider what soil problems you may face and how to correct them. A soil test will show you if you have problems such as alkalinity, acidity, and nutrient deficiency.

A quick, dependable method for testing is to use an inexpensive soil test kit, available at a garden supply store or through a mail-order catalog. Check with your cooperative extension service agent or state university for other sources of soil testing.

Soil amendments

A few gardeners are fortunate enough to have ideal loam soil, but most must improve the texture of their soil with organic soil amendments. Organic matter changes the physical structure of the soil to allow a healthy balance of air and water to enter. Also, it increases the moisture-holding capacity of sandy soils and acts as a buffering agent to prevent rapid changes in the soil pH. In addition, the decomposition of organic matter releases some nutrients, increasing soil fertility.

In adding an amendment, you should mix in a quantity that is 25 to 50 percent of the final volume of soil. For an even, deep mixture of amendments and soil, try to work in 3 to 4 inches of amendment at a time to a depth of 9 to 12 inches. Double digging (see page 100) will greatly improve poor soil. If your soil is so poor that it will need extensive (and expensive) amending, consider bringing in new soil and planting in raised beds (see page 101).

Descriptions of some common soil amendments and their uses in various soil types follow. Keep in mind that organic amendments don't work forever. Because the material is constantly decomposing, you'll need to replenish the soil before every planting.

Wood products. Sawdust and bark work well in clay soils because they physically separate the fine clay particles without holding moisture. Wood products quickly use up nitrogen as they decompose, so if you're using *raw* wood products, you must add nitrogen to the soil. If you don't plants won't have enough nitrogen for growth.

Manure. In all its varieties, manure improves most soils and acts as a mild fertilizer. Fresh manure must be aged before using or it will burn plants; composting is a good way to age it. Some manures, especially steer manure, may have high concentration of soluble salts. It's important not to add too much steer manure to the soil, because excess salts can harm seedlings and transplants.

Peat moss. This fairly expensive but excellent soil amendment is ideally suited for sandy soils because it holds water and nutrients well. Most peat moss sold in bales is air dried; wet it thoroughly before mixing it into the soil.

Compost. One of the best soil amendments, compost is also one of the least expensive. Directions on page 101 tell you how to build a compost pile.

(Continued on next page)

Green manure. This term is used by agriculturalists to describe a cover crop that usually is grown during the winter to be tilled into the ground in the spring. In autumn, plant any of the fast-growing members of the grass family (annual rye grass, barley, or oats) or the legume family (clover, vetch, lespedeza, broad beans, or peas). In the spring, about a month before planting time, till the crop into the ground. Though the top growth may be sparse, the well-developed root system will add organic matter to the soil as it decays.

Spading and tilling

Turning up the soil helps prepare it for planting by separating and aerating the tiny soil particles. If your soil has not been worked recently, it's best to turn up the soil thoroughly and then, well ahead of planting time, blend in amendments and fertilizers. However, if your soil has good texture and has been gardened before, you can apply amendments and fertilizers and mix them into the soil without prior tilling.

Working and conditioning the soil—whether done in one or two steps—can be accomplished by hand or with a power tiller.

Turning up the soil by hand is hard work (you may get in shape as well), but the task will seem easier if you use the proper tool. A spade—square bladed, sharp, and straight in the shank—is the ideal tool for breaking up the soil (see drawing below). A shovel, with its rounded blade, is the best tool for mixing or turning materials once you've loosened the soil. The point of the shovel helps you to slide it into the material, and the concave blade keeps the material from falling off as you lift and turn the shovel.

In spading up small areas, many gardeners make the mistake of turning each spadeful of earth completely over. If you do this, any weeds, leaves, or other debris in the soil may form a one-spade-deep barrier that cuts off air and water. Instead, you should lay the dirt on its side (against the previous shovelful) so the original surface is vertical to the ground.

For really big jobs, rent or buy a power tiller. If the soil is firmly packed, you may have to start tilling at a shallow depth, then go over the area a second time, even a third, with the tiller at a deeper setting each time.

Timing is critical in successful soil preparation. If the soil is gummy wet, wait until it dries out enough to crumble when you squeeze it into a handful (see drawing, page 98). If it's brick hard, water deeply and wait until it dries to the moist-but-crumbly stage. If your spade slides in easily, you know it's time to work the soil.

Raking and leveling

Smoothing out the soil and forming beds are the final steps in soil preparation. Your soil will probably still contain lumps and debris, even after spading and tilling. Using a metal bow rake (the bow gives the rake springy, resilient action), break up any large clods and remove stones and other materials. After one last levelling with either a metal bow rake or level-head rake, you're ready to plant.

Double digging

If your soil is extremely poor or has never been worked, double digging—digging down two spade depths into the soil—will improve its condition. Double digging is hard work, but the improved soil will produce plants that make your efforts worthwhile.

Double digging has a two-fold purpose: to amend the soil on the upper level and to break up the soil on the lower level to allow roots to grow deeper. With double digging, you should be able to space plants closer than usual. This approach is the basis of French intensive gardening, which calls for closely spaced plantings in richly amended beds (page 125).

The steps shown at the right explain how to double dig. Once done, let the bed settle; After a few days, rake the soil to remove any large clods and work the soil into a fine even texture.

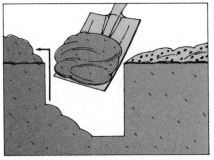

1) Dig trench *for planting bed one spade deep; set soil alongside trench. (Soil amendments at right.)*

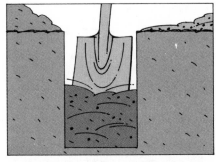

2) Dig down *one spade's depth further in same trench, mixing some amendments with soil in lower level.*

3) Dig second trench *alongside first one. Mix in soil amendments and move amended soil to first trench.*

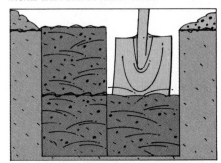

4) In second trench, *dig one spade's depth more; mix in amendments. Continue to dig trenches.*

Raised beds

Gardening in raised beds is one way to overcome the problem of poor soil. Rather than endlessly fighting to improve hard, infertile soil, you can start out fresh with a light, rich soil mix in a raised, enclosed bed. You'll do less stooping as you water, weed, and cultivate; as a bonus, the raised soil tends to warm up faster in the spring, resulting in earlier crops.

A good width for a raised bed is 4 or 5 feet; the length can vary to fit the garden. Soil depth should be from 12 inches to 18 inches. If you build several beds, be sure to leave room for a wheelbarrow to pass between them. The drawings at the right illustrate simple raised beds, with helpful hints for better drainage.

Fill the bed with a rich, light soil mix, such as equal parts peat moss, compost, and topsoil. First, though, you should till the existing topsoil a bit. Then, as you begin to add the new soil, you can mix it with the existing soil in

the bottom of the bed. Soak the bed before planting so the soil will settle to about 2 or 3 inches below the top of the bed. (If you wait until after

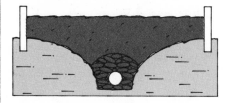

Poorly drained soil may require raised bed and drain tile. Drain tile (center circle), covered by rock, aids water runoff.

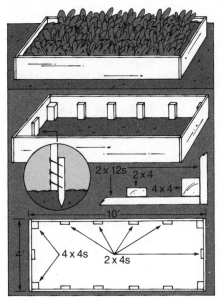

Large planter box makes good raised-bed garden. Use decay-resistant wood for construction, anchor sides firmly.

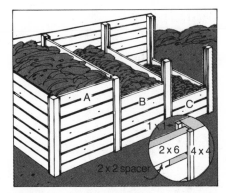

Railroad ties or old construction timbers make sturdy raised bed. Overlap ends for greater stability.

planting to soak the soil, many plants will sink.) Remember to replenish organic soil amendments (see pages 99–100) at replanting time.

How to make compost

A compost pile can turn waste materials from your garden and kitchen into a rich, organic soil amendment. Below are a few basic composting guidelines:

• Spread a layer of plant debris (leaves, weeds, or grass clippings) on the ground or in a bin. Follow with shallow layers of manure (or a few handfuls of nitrogen-rich fertilizer), topsoil, and kitchen scraps (except meat, fat, and bones). Continue adding layers, but don't put too much of one material in one layer.

• Chop or grind large materials such as big stems into small pieces; fine materials such as grass clippings should be mixed with coarser pieces.

• A pile 4 to 6 feet high will hold the heat necessary to promote decomposition while allowing sufficient air to enter the pile and minimize odor; see the drawings above for ideas on

Compost bin is made of four wood frames covered with chickenwire. Frames unlatch to remove compost.

compost enclosures.

• Keep the compost moist but not soggy; it should be about as wet as a squeezed-out sponge. During heavy rainfall, cover the pile with a plastic sheet or a tarp.

• Turn the pile every three to four weeks to discourage odor and flies and to help the compost decompose evenly.

• Periodically you may need to add

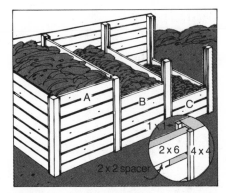

Three-stage compost bin has removable sides. "A" holds raw materials; "B," partly decomposed matter; "C," compost.

small amounts of nitrogen, such as fresh manure, blood meal, or commercial fertilizers, to the layers to keep the decomposition process going.

• Compost is ready to use when it is very crumbly and the starting materials have decomposed beyond recognition—usually about 3 months. Before using, sift the compost through a coarse, 1-inch-mesh screen to remove large, undecomposed pieces.

Planting a garden

*I*t's early spring; you have your vegetable seeds, and your soil is ready. To schedule your planting, you'll want to consider two factors: the best method of planting and the best time.

Crops that are easy to germinate and don't require an early start can be sown outdoors directly in the ground. Crops that are difficult to sprout outdoors or that require a long growing season should be started indoors. Crops that are tricky for home gardeners to start can be purchased as transplants at nurseries. Individual descriptions will give you the recommended method for planting each vegetable.

To determine when to plant each vegetable, check the last frost date of spring for your area (see the map on page 22) and then refer to the individual descriptions.

To start seeds indoors

You'll find the materials for starting seeds indoors at nurseries or garden centers, in seed catalogs, or in your home. Seed starting kits include all the materials in one package. Here are the basics:
- Sterilized potting soil
- Milled sphagnum moss or vermiculite
- Containers with drain holes (clean used containers with a dilute solution of bleach)
- Peat pots (2½ to 3 inches in diameter), peat pellets, growing cubes, paper or plastic cups with drain holes
- Plastic bags

Sow seeds in flats or trays or, if you are not sowing a large quantity, in peat pots or paper cups. The steps for planting the seeds are as follows:
1) Fill the containers with soil mix, leveling and firming the soil to ½ inch from the top of the container.
2) Sow seeds at the depth and spacing given on the seed packet.
3) Cover the soil with a thin layer of moistened sphagnum moss or vermiculite.

Starting seeds indoors

Peat pots, cubes, pellets: *sow seeds in them, plant container and all when seedlings are big enough.*

Shallow clay pot, *foil tray with drain holes are starting chambers. Clear plastic keeps soil moist.*

Separate seedlings *are easy to transplant from egg carton, plastic or paper cups. Add drain holes.*

Fluorescent lights *on adjustable stand help get seedlings started for earliest planting date.*

Sowing seeds outdoors

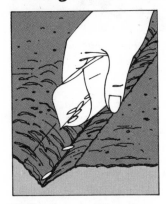

Furrows *are used to sow seeds in rows. Make as deep as seeds need, sow evenly, cover with soil.*

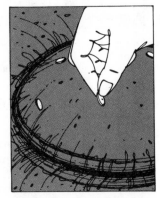

Hills—*seeds sown in small clusters—are used for vining vegetables. Basin directs water to roots.*

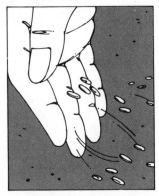

Broadcasting seeds *takes a steady hand. Use to sow wide bands of one vegetable. Cover seeds with soil.*

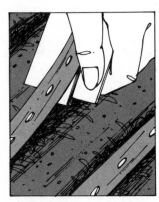

Seed tape *spaces seeds at proper distance apart. Lay tape in furrow, cover with soil. Tape soon decomposes.*

4) Set the containers in an inch or two of water and allow the water to move slowly upward until the soil surface is moist.

5) Drain the containers, and place them in clear plastic bags. Either make small holes in the tops of the bags for ventilation, or open the bags for 15 minutes each day.

6) Place containers out of direct sunlight but where the temperature is 70° to 75°F/21° to 24°C. If the seeds you are starting require soil temperatures over 75°F/24°C, use a starting tray with an electric heating cable or a hotbed (see page 123) to provide the extra warmth needed for germination.

7) As soon as the seeds have sprouted, remove the plastic bags and set the containers beside a sunny window or under a seed-starting light fixture. If nights become very cold, move containers away from the window glass. Keep the soil moist, but not soggy.

If you have planted seeds in a tray or flat, the seedlings can be transplanted to individual containers after the second set of leaves appears. Set each transplant in a pot at the same depth it was grown in the tray. By giving each seedling room to develop its own roots freely, you save plants considerable shock later when you set them out in the garden.

Artificial light. Before seeds sprout, light from the sun or from artificial lights provide the heat necessary for germination. As soon as the first sprout shows above the soil, light is needed for photosynthesis and growth.

To germinate seeds under fluorescent lights, position the seed containers just 3 to 4 inches below the tubes. Keep the lights on constantly until the sprouts have emerged.

Once seeds have germinated, they will grow into compact seedlings when temperatures are 60° to 65°F/16° to 18°C. Under fluorescent lights, place seedlings no more than 12 inches below the tubes, and then give them 12 to 16 hours of light daily. At greater distances from the light source, light intensity falls off drastically and the seedlings become leggy.

To start seeds outdoors

Getting seeds sown outdoors to germinate depends on the following four factors about the soil:

• Soil condition. Soil should be thoroughly tilled or spaded (see pages 98–100) and raked fine (free of lumps or clods) so seeds will germinate easily. Rake it level so water won't run off. It is a good idea to add a high-phosphate fertilizer at this time, to aid in root formation later.

• Soil temperature. Seeds planted too early, when soil is too cold for germination, may rot. The suggested planting times in the plant descriptions are designed to allow enough time for the soil to warm up adequately.

• Planting depth. Seeds planted too deep will not sprout. Examine the checklist in each description or the instructions on the seed packet for proper depth—usually about twice the thickness of the seed.

• Soil moisture. The right amount of water keeps the soil moist but not soggy and prevents crusts from forming on the soil's surface. Use a fine mist spray or perforated soaker to water so seeds aren't washed away. For tiny seeds that are barely covered with soil, blanket the seed row with clear plastic sheeting to keep moisture in. Allow ventilation and remove the sheeting as soon as seeds sprout.

For large vegetables such as corn, squash, or tomatoes that you may want to water by soaking, make furrows or basins before you plant (see illustrations on page 106). Smaller vegetables that can be watered by sprinkler do not need basins or furrows.

What's a hill?

You may encounter a term that causes a lot of misunderstanding: "hill." A "hill" in gardening refers to the grouping of seeds or plants in clusters, not necessarily on mounds. A "hill" of squash or corn can consist of two or three plants growing together on a level with the rest of the garden. "Hills," or clusters, are usually contrasted with rows in which plants are spaced equal distances apart.

Transplanting

When transplanting, try to make the transition to the out-of-doors an easy one for seedlings. Any sudden change in environment can cause a slowing or stunting of growth from which the

(Continued on next page)

Sets, roots, and cuttings

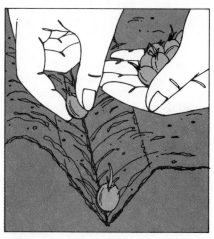

Sets, *small onion-family bulbs, will grow full-size in a season. Plant sets in furrows 1½ to 2 inches deep.*

Roots, or divisions, *are used to start perennial vegetables such as asparagus. Planting depth depends on crop.*

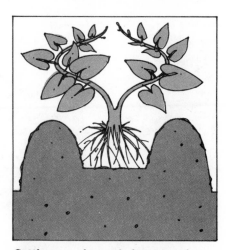

Cuttings *can be made from tips of sweet potato sprouts. These rooted cuttings are being planted in mound.*

plant may not fully recover.

For the best chance at success, start with healthy plants. If you are purchasing plants from a nursery, shop for plants that are compact and bushy (if it's a branching plant), with leaves of a good green color and free of obvious insect damage. Roots should not be sticking out through the drain holes. Avoid plants that are spindly or leggy.

Plants that you have raised indoors and some plants from the nursery come from greenhouselike conditions. To prevent undue stress to these tender plants, you should gradually accustom them to the out-of-doors. This acclimation process, called hardening-off, involves setting plants out on a warm day and gradually extending their time outdoors until they are left out overnight. After several nights outdoors in their containers, plants should be ready.

When transplanting to the garden, try to disturb the roots as little as possible. (Peat pots involve no disturbance; you plant the entire pot.) Follow these steps for setting out purchased or home-grown plants:

1) Dig holes for receiving the plants and fill the holes with water.

2) Water plants thoroughly before setting them out.

3) If the plants are not in individual pots, carefully separate the root ball of each plant from the larger mass of soil, preserving as much soil around the roots as possible. If a plant in an individual pot is rootbound, loosen the surface of the root ball with your fingers before planting. Trim off any roots that are very long.

4) Until young plants are planted, keep roots from drying out.

5) Set out the plants so that the root mass of each is just slightly covered. Planting too deep can slow or stop plant growth (tomatoes are an exception; see page 95). Cover each root ball with loose soil and gently firm it down; then water each plant.

6) If you didn't add a high-phosphate fertilizer to the soil during preparation (see pages 108–109), apply a high-phosphate starter solution.

7) Protect transplants from hot weather or frost and from pests (such as cutworms and snails) by using one of the illustrated protective devices. Open plastic coverings during the day.

Though most vegetables are started from seeds, some perennial vegetables are grown by other methods.

Eight ideas for protecting transplants

Piece of board or shingle shades seedling from hot sun. Prop up board immediately after setting out plant.

Cloche to protect seedlings from cold is made of clear plastic sheeting over wire wickets. Rocks anchor it.

Tarpaper collar slips around stem of seedling to foil damage by cabbage root maggots and cutworms.

Paper or plastic caps over tender seedlings prevent late frost damage. Smaller kinds cover just one plant.

Cardboard box, upside down, keeps out cold, heat, bugs, birds. Cut out bottom to make lid.

Plastic sheeting over wood frame covers seedlings. Lower flap on cold night for frost protection.

Paper bags anchored by four stakes block wind, cold, heat. Plant will grow up center stake.

Bottomless plastic milk containers held up by stakes protect seedlings from cold, wind, birds.

Planting cane & bush berries

Usually you plant cane and bush berries during the dormant season. Depending on where you live, that means planting could occur at any time from January through April.

Because these berries live and bear for many years, it's important to choose a location with full sunlight, free air circulation, and a good soil, especially one that drains well. Note also that blueberries require a very acidic soil.

Try to plant these berries where perennial weeds have been eliminated. If you plant where you have had a garden, avoid soil where tomatoes, potatoes, peppers, or eggplants have grown in the past 3 years. These vegetables encourage a fungus disease—verticillium wilt—to build up in the soil; it can kill most cane and bush berries.

When you buy plants, get ones that are certified nursery stock, free of diseases. Most often they'll be bare-root plants, and their main stems or canes will show a mark indicating the depth at which they were planted in the nursery. When you plant them, set them 1 to 2 inches deeper in the soil than they had been as nursery plants.

The canes or stems of most berry plants are cut back right after planting. Approximate lengths are shown in the drawings.

Blackberries

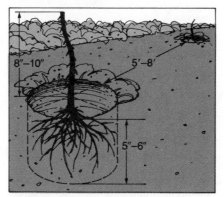

Plant trailing blackberries in separate holes. After planting, cut back canes to 8 to 10 inches long. Leave 9 to 10 feet between rows of plants.

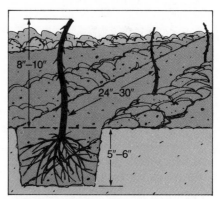

Plant upright blackberries in trenches. After planting, cut back canes to 8 to 10 inches long. Leave 6 to 10 feet between rows of plants.

Raspberries

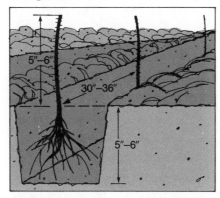

Plant red and yellow raspberries in trenches. Cut back canes to 5 to 6 inches long. Plants will spread; leave 6 to 10 feet between rows.

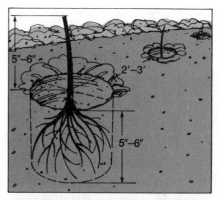

Plant black and purple raspberries in holes. Cut back canes to 5 to 6 inches long. Plants do not spread; leave 6 to 8 feet between rows.

Currants

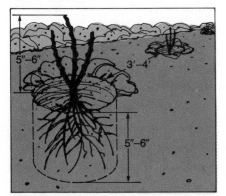

Plant currants in holes. Leave 6 to 10 feet between rows. Cut back plants to three strongest stems; make pruning cuts just above outward-facing buds.

Gooseberries

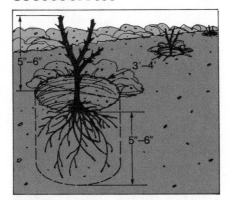

Plant gooseberries in holes. Leave 6 to 10 feet between rows. Cut back plants to three strongest stems; make pruning cuts above outward-facing buds.

Blueberries

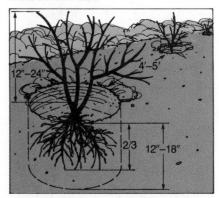

Plant blueberries in holes that are 1/3 deeper than roots. Leave 8 to 10 feet between rows of highbush varieties, 10 to 12 feet between rabbiteye kinds.

Watering techniques

Food crops need a steady supply of water from the time of planting until harvest. Giving plants *too little* water in their root zones will result in wilting and, if not remedied, eventual death. Giving plants *too much* water may drown roots, causing plants to stop growing or die. Proper watering is something of an art—how often and how much to water your crops is best learned through experience.

Watering ... how often

How often you water depends on the kinds of crops you are growing, the age and size of the plants, the kind of soil you have, and the weather.

Different crops need different amounts of water. For example, leafy crops require more than root crops.

Young vegetable seedlings with small, shallow roots that lie in the top layer of soil will need to be watered frequently—sometimes as often as two or three times a day—to keep their root zone moist. However, a mature grape vine with roots that extend deep into the soil may need watering only once a month.

The proportion of clay, sand, and silt in the planting soil also determines how often you will have to water. Clay soils hold lots of water and release it slowly; sandy soils hold less water and release it quickly. Silty soils are intermediate in character, holding less water than clay and more water than sandy soils. Clay soils can be watered less often than silty soils which, in turn, can be watered less often than sandy soils.

Weather also affects how often you'll need to water. Cool, cloudy weather allows any soil to stay moist longer than does hot, dry weather. In some areas, rainfall during the growing season supplies all of the water needs.

...and how much

You need to apply enough water to reach the root zone of the plants. How deep a given amount of water will penetrate depends upon the soil type. On the average, 1 inch of water applied at the surface will wet sandy soil 12 inches deep, and clay soil 4 to 5 inches deep.

If you are using a sprinkler, you can determine how much water you have applied by setting a coffee can out in the garden and, after watering, measuring the amount of water in the can.

The only precise way to determine how deeply water has penetrated in your soil is to dig down.

Six ways to water

Hand-watering with hose and sprinkler nozzle. Advantage: Control when you are watering seedbeds, transplants.

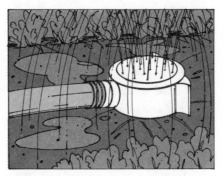

Hose-end sprinkler delivers gentle "rainfall." Area covered is determined by water pressure, spray pattern.

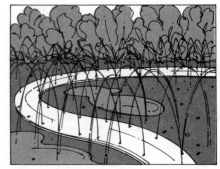

Soaker hose delivers thin jets of water from pinprick-size holes. It's good for slow soaking with no runoff.

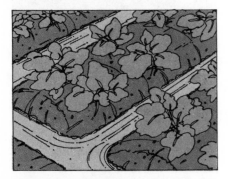

Furrow irrigation is good for crops that don't appreciate overhead watering. Ground must be level.

Drip irrigation soaks soil for individual plants. It's useful where water is scarce, pressure low, land sloping.

Watering can is good for watering containers, patches of seedlings, transplants; applying liquid fertilizer.

Some ways of watering

Several methods of applying water are shown on these pages, but in principle they are variations of two approaches: soaking and sprinkling.

Soaking. The slow soaking of water into the soil will wet the soil evenly to the depth you want. Watering basins around plants—often used with shrubby plants and large vegetables—will work in nearly any situation and soil. Furrow irrigation is most successful on level ground and with soil that is not very sandy.

Furrow watering works best where plants are no more than 3 to 4 inches in from the shoulder of the furrow, since lateral wetting of soil doesn't go much beyond this. Dig the furrows before planting, making them up to a foot wide and 6 inches deep. Be sure they're as level as possible.

Send water into the furrows slowly so that soil won't wash away. Furrow watering will be more effective in sandy soils if you divide long furrows into 6-foot segments. On less permeable soils, such as clay, increase furrow length to 12 feet. To hold the water in a section of furrow until the soil is soaked, use a dam made of a board, a piece of metal, or a wide shovel placed upright across the furrow.

Occasionally you will need to do some furrow repair: dredging out the bottom or replacing soil that has eroded from the sides.

Drip irrigation. Another method of soaking the soil is to irrigate with a drip system. Plastic tubing on the soil surface carries water to individual plants, and special emitters release water slowly to each plant.

Drip systems require very little water pressure to deliver the water. By leaving the water on for a few hours, you can thoroughly moisten each plant's root zone. Drip irrigation is also very economical because water is directed only to the soil that needs it.

Drip irrigation is most useful on plants that have deep root systems and are spaced comparatively far apart—tomatoes and grapes, for example.

Drip irrigation supplies are sold by agricultural supply stores, retail nurseries and garden supply centers, mail-order suppliers, and hardware stores.

Sprinkling. Using a good sprinkler that distributes water as evenly as possible is a time-saving way to water a garden, especially a large one. It's also a good way to leach excess salts from ridge and furrow plantings. For best coverage, overlap areas of wetting by about one-third.

Overhead sprinkling has a few disadvantages. Moisture on leaves may encourage diseases on some crops, especially in humid climates. Sprinkling also wastes water through evaporation, particularly in windy weather. Best times to use a sprinkler are in the morning (leaves will dry off during the day) and when the air is still.

Mulching your crops

A mulch is any material spread or laid over soil to help the growth of the desired plants and suppress growth of unwanted weeds. This definition covers the gamut from crushed rock, layered newspapers, and plastic sheeting to various organic materials such as grass clippings, straw, manure, leaves, and compost.

Mulching around your vegetables and berries will reduce evaporation, so the soil will stay moist longer for each application of water; keep soil temperature cooler and more stable during hot weather; and suppress the germination of weed seeds.

Many kinds of mulches provide a clean and fairly dry surface on which squash and melons, for example, may rest and ripen without risk of rot from contact with damp soil.

In addition, organic mulches, as they decompose, keep the top few inches of soil loose and crumbly. Such a soil surface allows easy penetration of water and dissolved nutrients and encourages free growth of surface feeder roots. It also provides a looser foothold for weeds that do sprout, so that weeding is easier.

Because most mulches will keep the soil beneath them cool, you should delay applying them until warm weather arrives. (Soil warmth is necessary to get most plants off to a good start.) Apply a mulch so it covers the soil completely but does not cover the bases of plants where they meet the soil. If kept too moist at their crowns, many plants will rot.

At least one kind of mulch can speed up the warming of the soil in spring: black plastic sheeting. After preparing the soil for planting, cover it with black plastic and cut small holes where you want to sow seeds or set out plants.

Black plastic sheeting is especially beneficial for growing warm-season crops where summers are cool or short. It also suppresses weed growth.

Black plastic sheet *used as mulch helps warm soil, conserve moisture. Good for heat-loving plants like melons.*

Fertilizing a garden

Dig a complete fertilizer into soil when you prepare it for planting. Nutrients will be available to give young plants an early growth push.

Plants, like other living things, must have nourishment if they are to thrive. Soil contains elements necessary for plant growth, but the supply gradually diminishes as plants use up the available nutrients. Fertilizing your garden replenishes the nutrients.

Organic or inorganic?

Depending on the source material of the nutrients, fertilizers can be grouped into two broad categories: organic and inorganic. To a plant's roots, the important point is whether or not a nutrient is present at the periods of critical need. The choice between organic or inorganic is a matter of personal preference, but the different ways they act will have a bearing on how and when you use either type.

Organic fertilizers, such as cottonseed meal, bone meal, and blood meal, are derived from the remains of living organisms. Rather slow to decompose and give up their nutrients, organic fertilizers work over a long period and some are not easily washed from the soil. You should work bone meal, for instance, into the soil well before planting time.

Keep in mind that many organic fertilizers are high in just one of the three major nutrients (see "Nutrients in the soil," page 99) and low or lacking in the other two. (Some are chemically fortified to increase their nutrient content.)

Gardeners sometimes confuse organic amendments with organic fertilizers. Sawdust and ground bark are primarily soil amendments, not fertilizers. Though they may contain small amounts of nutrients, they are best used to improve the texture of the soil.

Inorganic fertilizers—sometimes referred to as "chemical fertilizers"—are available in dry, liquid, and tablet form. With the exception of the slow or timed-release sorts, the inorganic fertilizers are effective for a shorter time than organic ones. But because their nutrients are usually released by dissolving rather than bacterial action, the nutrients are available to plants right away.

Inorganic fertilizers that contain all three major elements (see "Nutrients in the soil," page 99) are called "complete fertilizers." The ratios of the nutrients to one another may vary considerably, as explained further along in "Reading fertilizer labels." You can incorporate inorganic fertilizers into the soil as you prepare it, and you also can apply them after crops are growing. In general, inorganic fertilizers are less expensive—pound for pound of actual nutrient—than the organics.

Another way to apply fertilizer: Pour liquid fertilizer mixture from sprinkling can during growing season. Mixture is also effective for container plants.

Reading fertilizer labels. Nitrogen, phosphorus, and potassium occur in fertilizers in different amounts. The numbers on a fertilizer label refer to the percentage of these nutrients in the product: 5-10-10, for example, contains 5 percent nitrogen, 10 percent phosphorus, and 10 percent potassium. The order in which the elements are listed—nitrogen, phosphorus, and potassium—is always the same. Any fertilizer that contains all three primary elements is referred to as a complete fertilizer.

Your choice among fertilizers may seem bewildering at first, since formulas can vary so widely. Some are labeled "vegetable food" or are specifically recommended for food crops in general; these can be considered a fairly safe choice. But if you want to be really thorough about the matter, and possibly save money in the long run, you'll have your soil tested (see page 99) to learn what its nutrient deficiencies may be. Almost certainly any crop will need supplemental nitrogen. But a test may disclose that phosphorus or potassium or both are plentiful enough in your soil so that there is no need for a supplement.

How much to apply. Fertilizers packaged for home use generally specify the amount to be applied in terms of pounds per square feet of garden area. If, for example, directions specify 1 pound for each 100 square feet, you know that a 1-pound package will take

Apply a complete fertilizer during growing season in a band 4 inches away from plants. Scratch fertilizer into soil lightly, then water thoroughly.

care of a 10 by 10-foot plot, or one 5 feet wide and 20 feet long. Recommended amounts differ from one formulation to another; never assume that one recommended amount will hold for all fertilizers. Read the labels, then calculate your garden area.

Further advice. The description of each vegetable and berry mentions the crop's particular nutrient needs. Beyond that, the very best advice will come from your county farm advisor, who is familiar with local conditions.

Applying the fertilizer

Your first opportunity to apply fertilizer is when you prepare the soil for planting. Incorporate dry organic or inorganic fertilizer into the soil as you dig or till it: this puts nutrients into the anticipated root zone of the crops you intend to grow. This is especially important for applying phosphorous—it doesn't readily penetrate into the soil from surface application of a fertilizer.

You can scatter fertilizer over bare ground by hand (as though you were flinging out bird seed) or you can use a mechanical spreader, usually rentable from nurseries or garden equipment dealers. Scatter or spread the fertilizer as evenly as possible, then dig or till it into the soil. For general guidelines on amounts to use, see "How much to apply" on page 108.

Followup feeding. For many vegetables, the fertilizer dug into the soil will provide sustenance for the entire growing season. But some crops are heavy feeders, needing supplemental boosts during the growing season. (For more information, check the individual listings in the catalog section, pages 32–96.) These additional applications, often referred to as sidedressings, can be given in several ways.

If you use dry fertilizer, you can broadcast it over the soil surface (keep it off plant leaves), lightly scratch it into the soil, and water thoroughly. Or you might make a shallow trench about 4 inches from the plants alongside the row (or in a ring around widely spaced plants such as melons and squashes), scatter the fertilizer in the trench, cover with soil, and water it thoroughly.

If yours is a small garden, you may prefer to mix a solution of liquid fertilizer and use a watering can to sprinkle the nutrient solution on the soil.

Perennial vegetables and the various berries—because they remain in place for many years—receive surface applications of fertilizer year after year. At the start of each growing season, use the scattering or spreading method outlined under "Applying the fertilizer"; make any later applications if suggested in the individual description for each of these plants.

Staking berries

Most cane berries need staking and training so they won't become a tangled thicket of prickly canes.

Use the kind of trellis shown at upper left to train red and yellow raspberries and trailing blackberries. (Purple and black raspberries and erect blackberries usually aren't trained on a trellis.) The trellis shown at upper right is used to train red and yellow raspberries growing in a hedgerow.

For trellis supports, use posts that are 3 by 3 or 4 by 4 inches or, if round, 3 or 4 inches in diameter. Make sure that the posts are made of rot-resistant wood or are treated with a preservative such as copper naphthenate. Anchor posts well. Use number 10 or 11-gauge smooth galvanized wire between the posts or crossbars. (For trellises for grapes, see pages 57 and 120.)

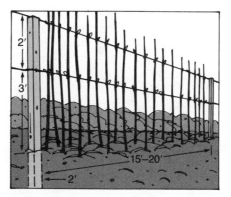

Tie canes of raspberries in a row to two horizontal wires for support.

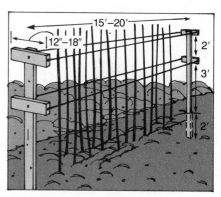

Keep hedgerow of raspberries in bounds with four wires on crossbars.

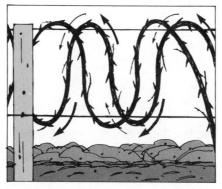

Weave long canes through wires to support long-caned blackberries.

Selectively tie canes upright or along wires for short-caned blackberries.

Staking vegetables

Some vegetables benefit from support: Climbing vegetables such as pole beans and peas, and sprawling vegetables such as tomatoes, cucumbers, and melons.

Not only will you save space by tying or propping up these crops, you'll also harvest more fruit—keeping fruit such as tomatoes and melons off the ground will keep them from rotting.

The best time for putting up stakes, poles, trellises, and other supports for vegetables is at planting time; because roots haven't yet formed, you needn't worry about disturbing them. Train or tie plants as they grow.

On this page are shown several ideas for training and supporting climbers and sprawlers. A word of caution: In hot climates, don't use metal frames, chickenwire, or galvanized clothesline wire for stringers. Plant leaves and tendrils can be burned when the metal becomes hot.

Wire cage, two stakes support tomato plant. Reach through mesh to harvest.

Strings stretched over A-frame made of 2 by 2s are for beans, peas to climb.

Bamboo poles in ground, tied together at crosspole, will hold tied-up tomatoes.

Tepee of bamboo poles tied together supports beans planted beside poles.

Sturdy frame leaning on wall makes trellis for cucumber or squash vines.

Tall wooden stakes hold up tomato plants. Use soft ties to fasten them.

Weeding techniques

Anyone who plants a garden sooner or later comes to grips with weeding. Removing weeds is a very important garden activity because weeds compete with productive plants for water, food, and light.

Weeding techniques

Hand-pulling, hoeing, and cultivating are time-honored ways of ridding gardens of weeds.

Pulling weeds by hand is the most time-consuming method. It is not too much of a chore if the weeds are few and are widely spaced, and is the safest way to remove weeds that are growing close to your plants. A scratcher or trowel may help you hand-pull by loosening soil a bit around weeds. Deep-rooted perennial weeds can be dug out with trowel, knife, or special weeding tools.

Hoeing works best on open patches of densely growing weeds. You get plenty of weeds with each hoe stroke, but you aren't working so close to crop plants that you risk harvesting them along with your weeds. Keep hoe blades sharp at all times. When hoeing, move forward, toward unhoed weeds. After hoeing, remove chopped-down weeds and compost them.

Cultivation—plowing weeds under— works best in large gardens with plenty of space between rows. Whether you use a hand cultivator or mechanical tiller, the goal of cultivation is to control weeds rather than to eliminate them totally. Weeds that are thoroughly plowed under will decay, but some always will regrow.

General points to keep in mind:

• Regardless of what technique you use, weeds pull out more easily when soil is moist.
• Pull weed seedlings as soon as you can. The smaller they are, the less they compete with crops and the more easily they come out.
• Gather and compost all pulled, hoed, and loose weeds to keep them from taking root again.
• Never let weeds become mature and go to seed.

Chemical weed controls

Herbicides—weed-killing chemical products—can be labor-saving aids to home gardeners if they are used with understanding and care. The critical point is to choose a herbicide that will remove the weeds without harming the crops you're growing. Select only herbicides that, according to the label, are safe to use on vegetables and berries, and *use them according to directions on the label.*

You can use pre-emergent herbicides (those that kill annual weeds as they sprout) among perennial crops such as asparagus, cane berries, and rhubarb. Don't use them in soil where you plan to grow from seeds.

If possible, avoid using herbicides that remain in the soil for a long time. A long-lived herbicide might be safe for a crop you plant in summer, but harmful to a different vegetable planted in the same soil in autumn.

Mulches

Weed seeds—like any seeds—need sunlight, warmth, and moisture to germinate and grow. Mulches help control weeds by depriving weed seeds of necessary sunlight (see page 107).

Black plastic sheeting is one of the most effective mulches.

Thick layers of organic material such as grass clippings and composted leaves discourage the sprouting of weed seeds. They also keep the soil surface loose and moist, making it easier to pull out any weeds that do sprout.

Another way to keep sunlight from soil is to blanket it with living plants. Closely planting some vegetables and berries (carrots, beans, and strawberries, for example) results in a dense cover of leaves, thereby denying sunlight to weed seeds and growing room to weed seedlings. Close planting is discussed more fully under French intensive gardening on page 125.

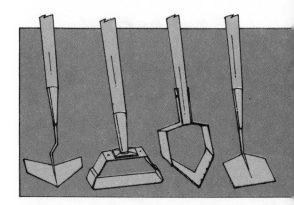
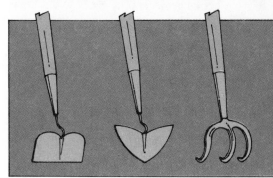

Some basic tools, both long and short-handled, for vegetable gardeners. Ones with prongs or comblike teeth are for cultivating soil; tools with blades hoe or cut out weeds; triangular blades will make furrows.

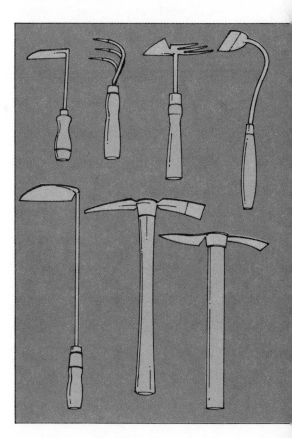

Harvesting & storage

Knowing when to pick the crop and how to store the excess for future use calls for as much know-how as the actual growing process.

When to pick?

The individual description for each vegetable and berry gives a general guideline for harvesting each at its peak of tenderness and sweetness. But for many vegetables and berries, the most certain test of readiness is to pick and taste a few.

Picked too soon, vegetables and berries may lose not just size but also sweetness. The resulting taste may be tart, bitter, or simply not flavorful.

If you wait too long, you may sacrifice flavor or texture, or both. The sugar of peas and corn turns to starch, beans become stringy, beets woody, and berries mushy, for example. Some vegetables even stop producing if their crop is not regularly harvested.

Storing the crops

Home-grown vegetables and berries have the kind of flavor you can't buy in a store—especially when you get them to the table immediately after picking. If you have more than you can eat, though, you may want to store the surplus.

The objective of storage is to keep the vegetable aging slowly. In storage the process of aging uses the vegetable's stored food; the faster this stored food is used, the faster the quality of the vegetable's flavor and texture declines. As aging continues, the vegetable eventually rots.

Vegetables and berries differ in the storage conditions needed to keep them in prime shape. The chart on the next page lists vegetables and berries according to the storage method appropriate for each. The shortest-lived crops must be refrigerated and used promptly; others, stored under the correct conditions, can last for many months.

To enjoy vegetables and berries the year around, preserve them. See the chart on the opposite page; for instructions, consult the *Sunset* book *Canning, Freezing & Drying.*

Cool and damp storage (32° to 40°F/ 0° to 4°C). Whether provided in a refrigerator or a root cellar, these conditions prolong the storage life of those vegetables and berries that have a high moisture content and fairly thin skins through which moisture transpires.

This storage slows the aging process in an atmosphere moist enough to prevent dehydration. Relative humidity of about 90 percent is satisfactory for most vegetables and berries in this category.

The major point of difference is length of successful storage time. The extremes range from several days for some berries and tender vegetables to a matter of months for root crops.

For the vegetables and berries with short storage life, the vegetable crisper in the refrigerator provides a good environment; for best flavor, use them as soon as possible. Bumper crops that overflow the crisper should be canned, frozen, or dried if they're not to go to waste.

Store the more long-lived vegetables in this category— root crops, for example—in a root cellar or coldframe.

In cold-winter areas, prepare crops for root cellaring before severe frosts hit. For root crops such as carrots, beets, turnips, rutabagas, and parsnips, dig the roots and remove the leaves. Dig—roots and all—cabbage, Brussels sprouts, and Chinese cabbage when their foliage is dry so they won't rot when piled up.

Knock the soil off the roots and remove the outer leaves, but don't wash the vegetables. Make a 6-inch layer of dry leaves or hay; lay the vegetables on it in a shallow layer. Mound a layer of hay 12 to 24 inches deep over the vegetables and cover them with a plastic sheet held down with soil to prevent the vegetables from freezing. Locate your root cellar under an overhang or in an area that's protected from extreme cold and heavy rains.

In a modern house, it's not easy to find a cool, damp room for storing vegetables. You can improvise a root cellar in a basement by insulating a special cool room from frost on the outside and from furnace heat on the inside. Use a window for ventilation. The crops can be stored on shelves or in wooden crates or bins.

It's important to prevent withering. To maintain adequate humidity, make use of natural evaporation from bare earth, gravel, or sand; or sprinkle the floor occasionally with water.

You can use a coldframe for fall storage of heading and rooting vegetables; fill the coldframe with dry leaves for insulation. Or store vegetables in a trash can sunk into the ground, a method that works particularly well with root crops. Dig a hole deep enough so you can recess the can to within 3 to 4 inches of the rim.

Use moist sand at the bottom of the can and between layers of vegetables to prevent drying out. A plastic-covered straw or leaf mulch over the can's cover provides additional insulation.

Cool and dry storage (35° to 50°F/ 2° to 10°C). This is the combination of conditions needed to store the two most widely grown bulb crops: onions and garlic. If kept moist, they would continue to grow or quickly decay—or both.

Both crops require an initial curing time at room temperature in a shady, dry spot—about a week and a half for garlic, up to 3 weeks for onions. Then store them where it's cool, dry, and well ventilated.

In colder parts of the country, a basement or garage may offer the ideal conditions. For good air circulation, spread bulbs out in shallow boxes or trays with slatted bottoms, tie them up by the stubs of their dried tops, or put them in mesh bags or in old nylon stockings.

Warm and dry storage (55° to 60°F/ 13° to 16°C). Pumpkins and hard-skinned winter squash store well under these conditions. Right after harvest, cure these crops at a fairly high temperature (80° to 85°F/27° to 29°C) for about 10 days. Then place them in an upstairs storage room or in a warm garage. Make sure the vegetables are not touching one another.

After they're picked

When you harvest more than you can possibly consume or even give away, prolong the pleasures of your garden for many months by storing or preserving your surplus. Careful storage of vegetables and berries allows you to enjoy them fresh for a period of time after they're picked. When they're preserved, vegetables and berries can grace your table throughout the year.

Check the lists below for the proper methods of storing and preserving your crops. You'll find a description of the various storage conditions on the facing page. Also see the *Sunset* book *Canning, Freezing & Drying*.

To store: Refrigerate unwashed; use as soon as possible

	To preserve
Artichokes	Freeze whole; can, freeze, or dry hearts
Asparagus	Can, freeze, or dry
Blackberries	Can or freeze
Blueberries	Can or freeze
Broccoli	Freeze or dry
Collards	Freeze
Corn	Can, freeze, or dry
Currants	Dry
Eggplant	Freeze or dry
Endive	Use fresh
Gooseberries	Can
Kale	Freeze or dry
Lettuce	Use fresh
Mustard greens	Dry
Okra	Can, freeze, or dry
Peas	Can, freeze, or dry
Radishes	Use fresh
Raspberries	Can or freeze
Spinach	Freeze or dry
Strawberries	Freeze
Swiss chard	Freeze or dry
Tomatoes	Can, freeze as purée, or dry

To store: Keep cool and damp for time indicated

	To preserve
Beets (3–10 weeks)	Can, freeze, or dry; freeze greens
Brussels sprouts (3–4 weeks)	Freeze or dry
Cabbage (12–16 weeks)	Freeze or dry
Carrots (16–20 weeks)	Can, freeze, or dry
Cauliflower (2–3 weeks)	Freeze or dry
Celery (8–16 weeks)	Can, freeze, or dry
Kohlrabi (2–4 weeks)	Freeze
Leeks (4–12 weeks)	Use fresh
Melons (2–4 weeks)	Freeze
Onions, green (4–12 weeks)	Use fresh
Parsnips (8–16 weeks)	Freeze
Peppers (4–6 weeks)	Can, freeze, or dry
Potatoes (12–20 weeks)	Can, freeze, or dry
Rhubarb (2–3 weeks)	Can or freeze
Rutabagas (8–16 weeks)	Freeze
Squash, summer (2–3 weeks)	Can, freeze, or dry
Turnips (8–12 weeks)	Can

To store: Keep cool and dry for time indicated

	To preserve
Garlic (24–32 weeks)	Use fresh
Onions, bulbing (12–32 weeks)	Can, freeze, or dry

To store: Keep warm and dry for time indicated

	To preserve
Pumpkins (8–24 weeks)	Can, freeze, or dry
Squash, winter (8–24 weeks)	Can, freeze, or dry

Pests & diseases

The joys of growing vegetables and berries can, from time to time, be temporarily interrupted by plant pests or diseases. You should know how to recognize the most common problems and know what remedies to use.

Pests or diseases that are likely to visit particular vegetables and berries are mentioned in the individual plant descriptions. Below and on the following pages, we present profiles of some troublemakers, along with appropriate controls. If you're uncertain about what is afflicting a particular crop, check with your county farm advisor.

Slight damage to crops is not a signal to begin chemical warfare. It is just a notice to be on alert and, if necessary, to take some first-step meas-

Crop-damaging pests

Here we present a rogue's gallery of common pests and suggested controls. The controls are grouped in order of preference: hand measures, homemade sprays, biological controls, botanical sprays, and manufactured chemicals.

Aphids. *Green, black, pink or yellow sucking insects feed on young leaves, stems. Controls: Hose off with jet of water; spray with soap solution, pyrethrum, rotenone, malathion, sevin.*

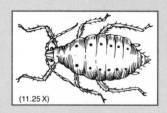
(11.25 X)

Armyworms. *Yellow green to gray green caterpillars are larvae of brownish gray moth. Feed in groups on young plants. Controls: Bacillus thuringiensis, malathion, sevin.*

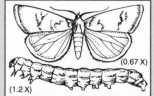
(0.67 X)
(1.2 X)

Asparagus beetle. *Adults are about ¼ inch long, shiny blue black with yellow markings on wing covers. Larvae are about ½ inch long, green or dark gray. Adults feed on shoots when they come up in spring, lay eggs on shoots. Larvae eat shoots, leaves. Controls: Hand-pick adults; spray adults and larvae with rotenone, malathion, or sevin.*

Borers. *Raspberry cane borers attack raspberries and blackberries. Currant borers attack currants and gooseberries. Adults lay eggs in tips of canes or stems. Eggs hatch into larvae that bore down into canes and stems, killing them. Look for wilting tips of canes and stems. Control: Cut off canes and stems 6 inches below dying tips and burn them.*

Cabbage looper. *Greenish caterpillars, also called inchworms, feed on cabbages, related crops. Controls: Bacillus thuringiensis, rotenone, diazinon, malathion, sevin.*

(1.17 X)

Cabbage root maggot. *White larvae of flies eat roots; plants wilt or are stunted. Controls: Put tarpaper collars on soil around stems to prevent egg-laying; dig diazinon into soil.*

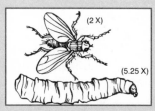
(2 X)
(5.25 X)

Cabbage worm. *Greenish caterpillars of white cabbage butterfly eat leaves of cole crops. Controls: Hand-pick large ones; Bacillus thuringiensis, rotenone, malathion.*

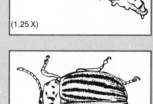
(1.25 X)

Colorado potato beetle. *Yellow and black-striped beetles and red larvae eat leaves of potatoes, tomatoes, eggplant. Controls: Hand-pick; rotenone, sevin.*

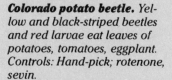
(2.5 X)

Corn borer. *Larvae of moth hatch from eggs laid on leaves of corn plants, tunnel into stalks both upward and downward. Larvae are 1 inch long, pink or brown, with rows of small dark brown spots. Look for signs of feeding first on leaves, tassels, and then in leaf whorl (funnel) of plant. Tunneling may cause corn stalks to collapse. Controls: Diazinon, sevin.*

Corn earworm. *Larvae of night-flying moth eat corn kernels under husks. Also green tomatoes. Controls: Apply mineral oil or sevin to corn silks; spray Bacillus thuringiensis on tomatoes.*

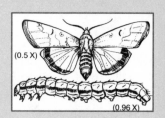
(0.5 X)
(0.96 X)

Cucumber beetles. *Oval-shaped beetles, greenish yellow with black spots or stripes, eat all parts of cucumbers, squashes, melons. Carry bacterial diseases. Controls: Rotenone, sevin.*

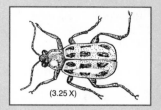
(3.25 X)

Cutworms. *Moth larvae live in soil, feed at ground level or on lower leaves of seedlings. Controls: Hand-pick; spread cutworm bait; drench soil with diazinon, sevin.*

(0.79 X)

ures. Packaged controls should be used only as last-resort procedures, when a specific pest or disease gets out of hand on a particular crop.

Here are some precautions you can take to offset or discourage crop damage.

• Plant disease-resistant varieties if available. Hybrids have been developed that are resistant to the most troublesome vegetable diseases. Many tomato hybrids, for example, are resistant to verticillium and fusarium wilts.

• Encourage healthy plant growth by providing the best possible growing conditions. A healthy plant is better able to resist pest or disease attacks.

• Mix up your planting. Large expanses of just one type of plant encourage large populations of any pest especially fond of that plant. A mixed planting of several kinds of vegetables and berries discourages large numbers of specific pests and also favors a larger and greater assortment of insects that prey on the damaging ones.

• Encourage natural controls. Toads, lizards, and many birds eat insects. You will find that there are helpful preda-

Flea beetles. *Tiny yellow, green, or black adults can jump like fleas. Adults chew holes in leaves; larvae feed on roots of potatoes and other crops. Controls: Rotenone, sevin.*

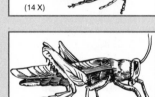
(14 X)

Grasshopper. *Large but often well-camouflaged pests with big appetites. Eat crops during the day. Controls: Hand-pick (during cool mornings when insects are sluggish); spray malathion, sevin.*

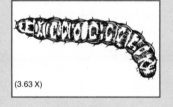
(0.55 X)

Grape berry moth larva. *Greenish larvae eat flowers and berries as they form; later generation eats mature berries. Controls: Rotenone or diazinon applied twice a season.*

(3.63 X)

Harlequin bug. *Adults are black with red orange markings. Nymphs (immature insects) suck juices from leaves, can kill plants. Controls: Hand-pick; spray adults, nymphs with sevin.*

(2.5 X)

Leafhoppers. *Green or brown adults hop about, feed on undersides of leaves, cause stippling of leaf surface. Spread leaf diseases. Beans are a favorite plant. Controls: Malathion, sevin.*

(10 X)

Leaf miners. *Adults—various flies, moths, or beetles—lay eggs on vegetables, cane fruits, strawberries. Eggs hatch into larvae, or leaf miners, that bore into leaves, making tunnels as they feed. Tunneling makes leaves of beets, cabbage, spinach unattractive for food. Controls: Remove infested leaves if few in number; spray rotenone, diazinon, malathion.*

Mexican bean beetle. *Adults, reddish yellow insects with black spots, and yellow larvae feed on undersides of bean leaves. Eat all but leaf veins. Controls: Hand-pick; spray malathion, sevin.*

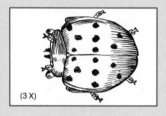
(3 X)

Mites. *Tiny spiderlike creatures (you need a magnifying lens to see them clearly) spin fine webs, suck juices on undersides of leaves. Controls: Blast leaves with water; spray diazinon, malathion.*

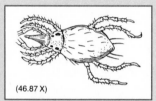
(46.87 X)

Nematodes. *Microscopic worms that live in the soil and feed chiefly on roots of plants. Some kinds cause plants to form root knots. All cause plants to be weaker, less productive. Controls: Before planting, fumigate soil with vapam or nemagon. Plant French marigolds as yearly rotation crop—they kill nematodes in soil.*

Rose chafer. *Tan beetles eat leaves, flowers, fruit of cane berries, grapes, strawberries. Occur mostly east of Rockies. Controls: Hand-pick; spray rotenone, diazinon.*

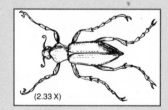
(2.33 X)

Snails, slugs. *Shelled and shell-less mollusks devour seedlings and leaves of many vegetables. Feed at night and on cloudy days. Controls: Hand-pick; metaldehyde bait.*

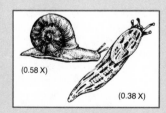
(0.58 X)
(0.38 X)

Squash bug. *Adults and nymphs feed on vines and fruit of squash, pumpkins, gourds, melons. Controls: Hand-pick adults, brown egg masses from leaves; spray sevin.*

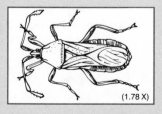
(1.78 X)

tory insects that will eat the plant damagers. Ideally the balance of nature will keep plant damagers in check by natural controls. Chemical sprays generally wipe out the helpful insects along with the troublemakers, leaving the garden wide open for a new attack by pests.

You can buy some beneficial insects (ladybugs, praying mantises, lacewings, trichogramma wasps) from mail-order sources. If you have a wide variety of pests for them to feed on, they may remain in and around your garden and cut down considerably on potential crop damage. The chance is just as great, though, that upon release in your garden they'll fly off to greener pastures without so much as sampling your aphids.

In any case, remember that predators won't appear—and imported ones won't stay—unless there is prey.

• Be vigilant on a daily basis. While you're watering, weeding, and harvesting your crops, keep a watchful eye out for the first signs of any damage. Hand-pick and dispatch the larger pests (snails, caterpillars, tomato hornworms). Try hosing off small pests, such as aphids, with a jet of water from the hose. Go on to stronger measures only if your first efforts fail.

Pests (continued)

Squash vine borer. *Larvae of moth bore into vines, cause sudden wilting. Look for entry holes in vines and yellowish castings. Control: Slit open vine with knife and kill borer.*

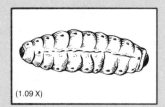
(1.09 X)

Strawberry root weevil. *Larvae feed on roots; adults chew holes in leaves of strawberries, cane berries. Difficult to control. Controls: Drench soil, spray leaves with diazinon, sevin.*

(3.75 X)

Thrips. *Thrips are common on onions; also damage other crops. Feed on leaves—whitish streaks are first sign of damage. Controls: Rotenone, diazinon, malathion.*

(17.5 X)

Tomato hornworm. *Fleshy green caterpillars with black and white stripes. Devour leaves of plants. Controls: Hand-pick; spray Bacillus thuringiensis, sevin.*

(0.63 X)

Whitefly. *Tiny, fluttery white insects cluster in great numbers on undersides of leaves of many plants, especially beans and tomatoes; fly about in clouds when plants are disturbed. Both larvae and adults suck juices from leaves. Difficult to eradicate from garden or greenhouse. Controls: Spray leaves with soap solution, rotenone, malathion.*

Wireworms. *Larvae of click beetles may damage root crops and roots of seedlings. Often found in soil where lawns were. Controls: Dig diazinon into soil.*

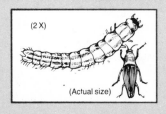
(2 X)
(Actual size)

Plant diseases

Club root. *Fungus disease causes roots to become swollen, twisted. Growth of plants is stunted. During hot days, plants wilt, eventually may wilt permanently. Controls: Avoid planting where cabbages and other cole crops were grown in last 3 years; apply terraclor solution to roots at planting time; at harvest, pull up and destroy swollen roots.*

Damping-off. *Various soil fungi cause damping-off diseases. Sometimes seeds rot in soil. Other times seeds sprout and start to grow, but then collapse. Controls: Plant seeds that have been treated with fungicide to prevent decay; apply captan or thiram to untreated seeds before planting; avoid planting seeds of warm-season crops when soil is still cold.*

Downy mildew. *Fungus disease causes odd-shaped brown spots on older leaves. Leaves turn dry, curl up, and die. It attacks melons, cucumbers, and watermelons. Look for outbreaks of disease when weather is cool, damp. Controls: Apply captan, maneb, zineb, or fungicide with fixed copper; plant disease-resistant varieties.*

Fusarium wilt. *Disease caused by a fungus that can live in soil for many years. Infection goes through roots, up into water-carrying system of plant. Lower leaves on stem turn yellow and die; gradually whole stem dies. Controls: No chemical controls available; plant disease-resistant varieties; avoid planting where disease has been a problem before.*

Powdery mildew. *Fungus thrives in humid weather, coating leaves and young stems with what appears to be a gray powder. Poor air circulation, crowding together of plants, shady locations all encourage growth of fungus. Controls: Spray plants with benlate, folpet, or sulfur. (Do not spray sulfur in hot weather; see label for temperature cautions.)*

Verticillium wilt. *Caused by a fungus that lives in soil for many years. Infection goes through roots up into water-carrying system of plant. Plants wilt in heat of day, may lose leaves, eventually die. Controls: No chemical controls available; plant disease-resistant varieties; avoid planting in soil where disease has been a problem before.*

Pest control choices

Control measures other than chemical sprays can be effective in many cases. Here we present courses of action available to you.

Hand measures. The larger pests (snails, grasshoppers, and some beetles, for example) are candidates for removal by hand. Pick them off the plant and destroy them. Some of the smaller pests, such as aphids and mites, can be dispatched by a blast of water from the garden hose. The job is easiest if you select a hose nozzle that will let you adjust the spray of water or a pistol type of nozzle that will give strong jets of water. To control the nearly microscopic mites, you need to aim the water at leaf undersides.

Homemade sprays. Some gardeners use a spray of soap solution to destroy aphids and whiteflies. Mix 3 tablespoons of soap flakes (not detergent) in 1 gallon of tepid water and spray onto insects that infest plants. Several hours later, rinse soap film off plants you have sprayed. Other homemade sprays include solutions of ground-up hot peppers and ground-up insects.

Biological controls. Some bacterial cultures can kill insects without harming warm-blooded creatures. Several manufacturers offer products containing *Bacillus thuringiensis,* a bacteria that controls various caterpillars by destroying their digestive systems. In areas where Japanese beetles are a problem, you may be able to buy products containing spores of milky spore disease, a disease that kills the beetle grubs.

Botanical sprays. Rotenone, pyrethrum, and ryania, derived from natural substances, are toxic to insects but relatively safe to humans. Because they have little residual effect on the plant, you must apply these sprays directly to the pests in order to kill them. Botanical sprays control some of the common sucking and chewing insects such as aphids and whiteflies.

Manufactured chemicals. Three manufactured insecticides that are available to home gardeners are suitable for use on vegetables and berries: malathion, diazinon, and sevin. All are fairly broad-spectrum insecticides, killing helpful insects as well as undesirable ones. These three are most effective against sucking insects such as aphids, thrips, leafhoppers, and whiteflies. Sevin also kills honeybees. Apply the chemicals strictly according to label directions.

Many sprays for vegetables contain a mixture of these chemicals. *Always* check the product label to be sure the pesticide is safe for edible crops. Never use any spray that isn't specifically labeled as safe for application to edibles. Be exact in following directions as to the length of time you must wait between spraying and harvesting.

Birds, deer, mammals

If your garden is likely to be bothered by birds, deer, rabbits, gophers or moles, your best approach to crop security lies in understanding their habits and using preventive defense.

In the air: birds. The presence of birds in the garden should be no cause for alarm; many are helpful in pest control, or are at least not harmful to your endeavors. But some birds are extraordinarily fond of berries and can tell about a day before you can that the fruit is ripe. Other birds may nibble on or devour tender seedlings.

In both cases the solution is netting of some sort, either wire or plastic. For berry protection, cover the plants with a broad-mesh plastic netting (½ to ¾ inch) several weeks before fruit is due to ripen. Protect rows of vegetable seedlings with a tent arrangement of wire or plastic mesh over the entire row—closed at both ends.

On the ground: rabbits and deer. Both can strip a garden overnight. The best preventive measure is fencing.

A rabbit fence need only be 2 feet high and, if wire, of a mesh small enough to keep rabbits from going through. But rabbits are burrowers, so you also have to keep them from going under a fence and into the garden. One solution is to extend a wire mesh fence at least 6 inches underground. A rabbit *can* burrow beneath this, in time.

Another way to foil rabbits is to fold out the bottom foot of a wire mesh fence and securely stake or weight it to the ground; rabbits won't be able to burrow at the edge of the fence.

In many cases, deer can be kept out of a garden by a 6-foot-high fence if the ground is level or slopes away from the garden on the outside of the fence. But a virtually foolproof deer fence should be 8 feet high.

If a fence that tall is out of the question, you may be able to take advantage of a deer's jumping limitations: it can leap high *or* wide but not both at once. Therefore, a 6-foot high fence with an almost-horizontal 3-foot extension at the top can keep deer out of a garden. The only other somewhat effective deer repellent is a large, barking dog.

Beneath the soil: gophers and moles. From tunnels beneath the soil, gophers feed on plant roots and bulbs. Signs of gopher sabotage include wilted plants that have no roots, and mounds of fresh, finely pulverized soil.

The greatest damage moles create is disturbing the soil—uprooting young seedling plants and introducing air pockets in the soil that dry out roots. Also, water can leave irrigation channels and follow moles' tunnels.

Moles travel in shallow tunnels, often so close to the surface that you can see the tunnels as raised ridges of soil. They also form soil mounds, but usually the soil is raised in a hump instead of the pulverized mound characteristic of gophers.

An effective preventive measure is to protect the roots of your crops with chickenwire or hardware cloth. To keep out gophers, a ½-inch mesh is necessary. If you plant in raised beds, wire mesh across the bottom will form a barrier. If you plant in the ground, you'll have to make individual mesh baskets for plant roots.

Various traps and poisoned baits are available commercially.

Pruning berries

Cane berries (raspberries, blackberries), shrubby berries (currants, gooseberries, blueberries), and grapes are all deciduous fruits that need annual pruning if they are to thrive. Pruning promotes the greatest yield of top quality fruit and, at the same time, encourages enough vigorous new growth to produce first-rate crops in the next year.

Most pruning should be done during the winter dormant period. In relatively mild-winter regions, the dormant pruning period is at any time when plants are out of leaf. Where winters are colder or severe, prune after coldest weather is gone but before plants begin to put on new growth.

Blueberry

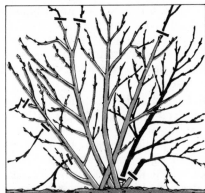

Blueberries produce fruit on short branches of stems for several years. During first 2 years, when plants are dormant, remove flower buds and prune lightly to remove drooping stems and crossing branches. Thereafter (see drawing) remove not only drooping stems and crossing branches, but also broken stems and branches and old twiggy stems—especially stems that are more than 5 or 6 years old. Cut back long stems to length where they can be easily harvested. Leave intact all vigorous stems that bear well, if they come up from ground or from base of plant.

Gooseberry

Gooseberries bear fruit on 1-year-old stems and on spurs (short side branches) on 2 and 3-year-old stems. First year, prune stems to short stubs with 3 to 4 buds per stem; top bud on each stem should face upward (if plant is spreading kind) or outward (if plant is upright kind). Second year, shorten 6 to 8 main stems to half their length (see drawing). Third year, remove weak stems, shorten main stems to half their length, shorten side shoots to 1 to 3 inches. Thereafter, each year remove weak and diseased stems and all stems more than 3 years old.

Currant

Currants bear fruit on 1-year-old stems and on spurs (short side branches) on 2 and 3-year-old stems. First year, cut back stems to short stubs with 3 to 4 buds per stem; top bud on each stem should face outward. Second year, shorten 5 to 8 main stems to 1/3 of their length (see drawing), cutting back to outward-facing buds. Third year, remove crowded stems leaving 8 to 9 sturdy stems; cut these stems to half their length and outward-facing buds. Thereafter, each year remove all stems more than 3 years old and any weak, diseased, or drooping stems.

Red/yellow raspberry—summer

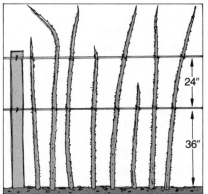

1) Summer-bearing red and yellow raspberries bear fruit once, on 2-year-old canes. During first year of growth (drawing above), tie new canes to trellis, or confine new canes in a hedgerow (not shown here; see page 109). Do not prune canes during first summer's growth.

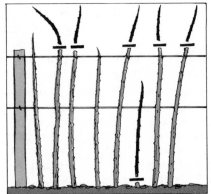

2) During second spring (see drawing), before new growth starts, cut to ground any weak, broken, and diseased canes. Also thin out canes, removing weaker ones until healthy canes stand 6 to 8 inches apart (both in row and hedgerow planting). Remove tops of remaining canes at 5 to 5½ feet height. (Canes of plants in hedgerow should be shortened to about 4 feet tall.) After crop is picked, cut to the ground all canes that bore fruit. During second summer, new canes will grow up to bear next year's crop; tie new canes to trellis as shown in drawing at left.

Purple/black raspberry

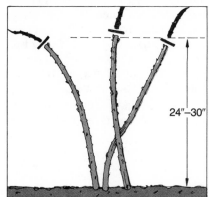

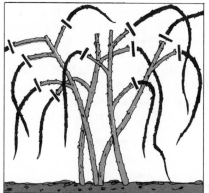

1) Black and purple raspberries bear fruit on 2-year-old canes. You can grow plants either freestanding or on a trellis. During first summer (drawing above) remove tips of new canes when black raspberries are 24 inches tall, purple raspberries are 30 inches tall. (For plants grown on trellis, remove tips of canes when black raspberries are 24 to 30 inches tall, purple raspberries are 30 to 36 inches tall.) Pruning off tips forces side branches to grow.

2) During second spring, before new growth starts, remove all weak canes (less than ½ inch thick) and dead and broken canes. If all canes are less than ½ inch thick, remove all canes but strongest two from each plant. Also (see drawing) shorten side branches of black raspberries to about 8 to 10 inches and side branches of purple raspberries to about 12 to 14 inches. Side branches will bear fruit. After crop is picked, cut to ground all canes that bore fruit. During second summer, remove tips of new canes as described at left.

Erect blackberry

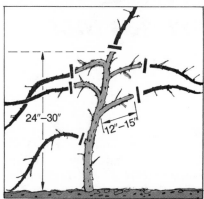

Upright blackberries bear fruit only on canes that are 2 years old. In summer of first year, cut off tops of new canes when they reach 24 to 30 inches tall to promote branching. In late spring of second year, as new growth starts, cut back side branches to 12 to 15 inches long (see drawing); also remove any dead or diseased canes. (New canes will be growing from ground and will need to be topped during summer at 24 to 30 inches.) After crop is picked, cut to ground level all 2-year-old canes that have fruited.

Red/yellow raspberry—fall

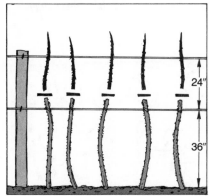

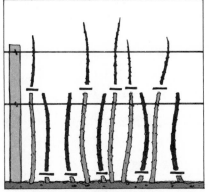

1) Fall-bearing red and yellow raspberries bear fruit on same canes twice, in autumn of first year, then in summer of second year. Grow either in rows or hedgerows. First year, let canes come up and tie to trellis. Canes will bear fruit on top third of each cane in autumn. After fruit is picked, cut off top part of each cane that bore fruit (see drawing).

2) During second year, after 1-year-old canes have borne summer crop of fruit on lower parts of canes, cut those canes to ground (see drawing). As new canes emerge during summer, tie them to trellis. After new canes have borne fruit in autumn, cut off top third of cane that bore fruit (see drawing).

Trailing blackberry

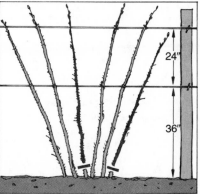

Trailing blackberries bear fruit only on canes that are 2 years old. First year, let canes grow unpruned. Where winters are cold, lay canes on ground and cover with protective mulch for winter. Where winters are mild, no mulch is needed. At start of growth in second year, tie canes to trellis, either cutting off tops of canes at 5 feet (shown above) or weaving long canes onto a trellis (see page 109). Remove weak, dead, or diseased canes. After harvest, cut to ground all canes that bore fruit. New canes that grew during summer will be tied to trellis next year.

Pruning grape vines

To have productive grapes, you must continually train (or direct) the vines to grow in the shape you want, and regularly prune the vines to achieve that shape.

There are two basic approaches to pruning table and dessert grapes: spur pruning and cane pruning. The choice of method depends on the variety.

The techniques of training on a two-wire trellis and of pruning (see first five drawings) are nearly the same for all grapes during the first 2 years of growth.

Training on a trellis. Set stout posts in the ground 15 to 20 feet apart (farther apart for the more vigorous grapes) so that they project 5 feet above the soil. String sturdy wire—10 or 11 gauge—across the post tops and also at the 2½-foot level. Four "arms"—canes—of each grape plant will be trained on these wires.

Spur pruning works for most European grapes ('Thompson Seedless' and 'Lady Finger' are among the exceptions) and for muscadine grapes. The object is to create short spurs, each of which develops two bearing canes (armlike branches). After bearing, these canes are cut back and new spurs grow out. This method is illustrated in the drawings below.

Cane pruning is used for 'Thompson Seedless', 'Lady Finger', and a few other European grapes and for most American grapes, such as 'Concord', 'Delaware', 'Niagara', and 'Pierce'. These kinds produce sparsely when cut back to short spurs, since most of their fruit is borne from buds farther out on the canes—the part that's cut off when branches are spur pruned.

You can distinguish new from 1-year-old canes by looking at the bark: new

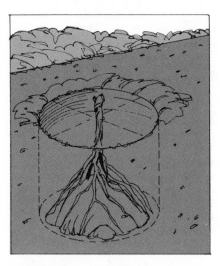

1) Plant bare-root grape during dormant season (December to May, depending on severity of winter). Set plant deep, leaving one bud above soil level. This promotes deep rooting and one strong cane for future trunk.

2) During first year, let vine grow as it chooses. The more leaves it develops, the more food is manufactured to help root development. Here is typical plant at end of first year, after leaves have fallen.

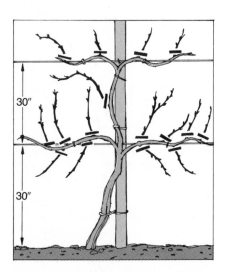

6) Second winter. Dormant vine looks something like this. Lower two arms have made most growth, upper two are shorter, less branched. Cut off all lateral canes, then tie arms to wires. Remove any other branches from trunk.

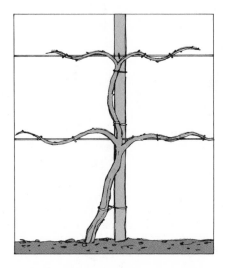

7) End of second winter. Pruned vine has one trunk, two arms on each wire. Basic structure is now established so pruning in subsequent years can be aimed at fruit production. New canes will grow on arms during summer.

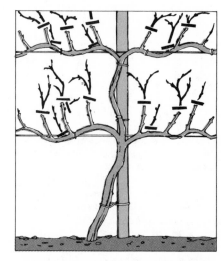

8) Third winter. Trunk and arms are thicker, arms are longer and have many lateral canes. Canes grew from buds where old canes were cut off. Cut each cane back to two buds. Bars show where to make pruning cuts.

canes have smooth, tight bark; 1-year-old branches have rough, loose bark.

In the vine's second winter, remove all but two to four side shoots; cut these shoots back severely to form two-bud renewal spurs. Each renewal spur will grow two long branches by the end of the third growing season.

During the third winter, shorten one of the two canes that grew from each renewal spur, cutting back until 8 to 15 buds remain. They will become the fruiting canes for the fourth summer. Then shorten the second canes that grew from each renewal spur, cutting them back to stubs with just two buds; these stubs are renewal spurs that will produce canes that will bear fruit in the fifth summer. Cut off all other canes growing from the main trunk.

In the fourth winter and each following year, cut off the old fruiting canes. Each renewal spur will have sent out two shoots; prune the lower shoot as a fruiting cane (eight to fifteen buds long), the upper shoot as a renewal spur with two buds. Keep four spurs as renewal spurs, and keep the same number of fruiting canes.

3) First winter, *during dormant season, select future trunk by cutting off all but strongest cane. Loosely tie it upright to the stake, then cut it back to bud close to lower wire at 30 inches above ground.*

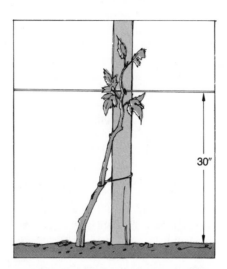

4) During second spring, *new growth will come from uppermost buds. Select strongest shoot (preferably the uppermost) to grow up to top wire. Leave two lower shoots to form arms to grow along wire. Pinch out any others.*

5) Growth during second year. *When strong shoot reaches top wire, pinch out the tip. Let two shoots grow just below pinched-off tip to train along top wire. Arms growing on lower wire may form laterals. Pinch back laterals to 10 inches.*

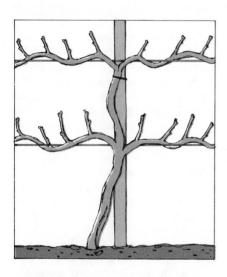

9) Third winter, pruned vine. *All weak lateral canes were cut from arms. Remaining canes are 6 to 10 inches apart along arms. Each lateral cane was cut back to two buds, forming a spur. No side sprouts remain on trunk.*

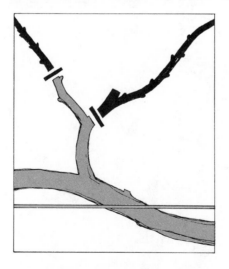

10) Fourth winter. *Closeup of pruned lateral (above) after 1 year of growth (branches bore fruit during summer). Remove upper branch totally; cut back lower branch to two buds. Repeat pruning technique yearly on new growth.*

11) Fourth winter. *Well-pruned arm has laterals spaced 6 to 10 inches apart. Those that are 1 year old are cut back to two buds. Laterals that were cut to two buds during third winter are pruned as in previous drawing.*

Specialty gardening

Containers

Lack of space for a garden plot or the lack of suitable soil need not deprive you of the pleasure of growing your own "farm-fresh" vegetables and berries. Many vegetables, strawberries, and some shrubby berries can be productive in containers. You can have your own mini-farm on a patio, deck, or balcony. You can also use containers to overcome problems of poor garden soil, heavy root competition, or shade.

In order to successfully grow crops in a container, you will need to consider the location and size of the container, the soil mixture within the container, and the watering and fertilizing needs of the container-grown plants.

Location. Nearly all vegetables and most berries require a place with full sunlight. Crops will grow faster and produce more in full sunlight than in a partly shaded spot. Plants grown for their fruits, such as tomatoes, squashes, and strawberries, need as much sunlight as possible. If all you have is a partly shaded site, you can still get a harvest of root and leaf crops. The point is to match the crop to the location of the container.

Container choice. Nearly anything that will hold soil and let water drain from it can be used as a container. The most important consideration is that the container should offer enough room for the roots of the crop you plan to grow. You could raise a fine stand of chives in an 8-inch clay pot but fail resoundingly with squash in the same container. Most crops will need soil that is at least 8 inches deep.

Large wooden boxes, wooden barrels or metal drums cut in half, pressed pulp tubs, and large (1 foot in diameter or greater) clay and plastic pots will hold enough soil for all but the largest vegetables. Remember that the smaller a container is, the faster it will dry out and the more subject it will be to changes in temperature.

Hanging containers—in which you might plant tomatoes, for example—can dry out rapidly because they are so thoroughly exposed to sunlight and wind. Since they become quite heavy when filled with mature plants, be sure to use sturdy hooks and wire or chain for suspending them.

Soil mixture. A good container soil must provide free penetration of water and air, but ideally it should be moisture-retentive as well. A liberal quantity of organic matter in the soil mixture will help.

Gardeners who make their own compost may find that compost alone will work well as a container soil. Nurseries and garden centers carry artificial soil mixes—usually containing some combination of peat moss or other organic material and sand, perlite, or vermiculite; these can be used right from the sack. If you prefer, you can mix your own container soil. A satisfactory mixture consists of two parts good garden soil (but not clay soil), one part sand, and one part peat moss, ground bark, or similar organic material.

Watering and fertilizing. Soil in a container dries out more rapidly than a comparable volume of soil in the ground. A container is exposed on the top and sides to drying effects of sun and wind, and often to reflected heat from a paved surface. Therefore, you need to be watchful of your container vegetables and berries.

At first, when plants are small and weather is just warm, you may need to water only every 2 to 3 days. But in the heat of summer and when plants are mature, daily watering may be needed. Apply enough water each time so that water runs out the container's drain holes.

To maintain steady growth, container vegetables need a steady nutrient supply. One method is to use a controlled-release fertilizer that releases small nutrient amounts every time you water. Or you can use a granular vegetable fertilizer in the amounts and frequency recommended on the label of the product. Some gardeners prefer to use liquid fertilizers, applying them every week to two weeks.

For a list of vegetables and berries that do particularly well in containers, turn to page 30.

Containers—pots, half-barrels, planter boxes—make successful garden plots for such vegetables as tomatoes, beans, lettuce, corn, beets, spinach.

Coldframes

A coldframe is a low-profile structure that has a slanting, transparent roof. Its purpose is to provide a protected area for starting seedlings, for rooting cuttings, and for hardening off young plants in early spring and late autumn, when the temperature is uncertain. It works by capturing solar heat during the day and holding some of it through the night.

Construction can be as simple or elaborate as you choose. Sides are usually made of decay-resistant wood or concrete blocks; the roof can be made from glass, fiberglass, acrylic plastic, or clear plastic sheeting. (Old window sashes are the traditional coldframe roof.) There is no standard size.

Since the coldframe is heated by the sun, put it in a sunny location and slant the roof toward the south. If cold north winds prevail during the months you will use your coldframe, locate it where it will be protected on the north side by a wall or hedge.

Cover the floor of the coldframe with a thick layer of sand, which will let water drain away quickly from the plants. If you want to start seeds directly in the coldframe soil rather than in individual containers, spread a 3-inch layer of potting mix on top of the sand. Sow seeds in the mix.

A coldframe will give some protection against freezing, but you'd be wise to play it safe and cover the frame with a tarpaulin, a piece of old carpeting, or a sheet of styrene foam when the temperature is expected to drop below 32°F/0°C. On warm days, prop open the roof.

A hotbed is merely a coldframe with special electric heating cables buried in the floor. It's useful for germinating seeds early and quickly. You can sow seeds directly in the soil above the heating cables and actually raise crops of cold-season vegetables when outdoor temperatures would prohibit this.

To set up a hotbed, first spread a 2-inch-deep layer of sand on the floor of your coldframe. Then loop the special

Simple coldframe gets vegetable plants off to early start by holding warmth.

heating cable back and forth over the sand, and cover the cable with a ½-inch wire mesh. If you're going to put containers in the hotbed, add a 2-inch layer of sand on top of the mesh. If you intend to plant directly in the hotbed, spread about a 4-inch layer of potting soil, instead of the sand, over the mesh.

Greenhouses

Greenhouse is aid to raising vegetables that need warmth or longer season.

The word "greenhouse" suggests a profusion of tropical plants, exotic orchids, and a steamy atmosphere. But remember that the purpose of a greenhouse is simply to provide a more favorable environment for plants that won't live out-of-doors during a particular season.

Tomatoes are a favorite greenhouse crop. They do best in a warm greenhouse, where it is possible to maintain the temperatures they need for good growth and fruit set. Generally this is in the 55° to 70°F/13° to 21°C range at night and up to 85°F/29°C during the day. Cucumbers and peppers also are good bets for a warm greenhouse.

If you have a cool greenhouse (night temperature from 40° to 55°F/4° to 13°C and daytime highs of 70° to 75°F/21° to 24°C), you might try cool-season crops such as lettuce, broccoli, and carrots. During winter these will need full sunlight. For summer production in hot-weather regions, they will need some shading and good ventilation.

Most greenhouse growing will be in containers or raised beds. (See page 122 for details on container growing.) Using containers in the greenhouse allows you to place crops where they will receive the right amount of sunlight or shading.

For vining crops—cucumbers and tomatoes, for example—you can make the most of available space by training the plants on stakes or on the greenhouse roof supports. Because greenhouse space is usually at a premium, smaller vegetables or dwarf varieties will often give greater rewards for the space they occupy.

Vegetables that need pollination of their flowers to produce a crop may need some assistance because greenhouses lack the natural outdoor pollinators: wind and insects. You can ensure pollination in three ways: use a camel's hair brush to transfer pollen from one flower to another; gently shake or tap the plant to release pollen into the air; or run a fan to simulate a natural breeze.

Hillsides

Sloping land isn't a complete obstacle to the growing of vegetables and berries, but it does present several challenges that must be met so plants will have the conditions they need for best production. Applying water is the number one hillside challenge. You want to have well-watered plants without water runoff and soil erosion.

Terracing

For a gentle slope, you can run planting rows across the slope, following the land's contour lines. Each row becomes, in effect, a natural miniature terrace.

On moderate to steep slopes, however, you'll need to construct terraces—a steplike series of level planting areas. The soil for each is kept level and in place by a retaining wall, ideally of wood, concrete block, brick, or stone. The illustration on this page shows the use of decay-resistant lumber in a permanent garden.

Any solid retaining wall needs drainage holes at its base about every 2 feet to allow excess water to escape from the terrace. Otherwise, water may build up in the soil and buckle or break down the retaining wall.

When you remove soil to make the terraces, set it aside so you can return it to make the level planting beds behind the retaining walls.

Bottomless boxes

A somewhat less ambitious solution to the challenge of hillside gardening is to make some bottomless boxes and set them into the hillside so the soil within them can be made level and watered easily. Each box can be made large enough to accommodate several vegetable plants. Make small bottomless boxes (about 1½ feet square), or buy large-diameter, shallow flue tiles. Set them into the slope to provide individual "containers."

Convert hillside land for vegetable growing by building level terraces.

Landscapes

Just because you grow some vegetables and berries for food doesn't mean that you have to separate them from the rest of your plants. If there's no room in your yard for a plot of edibles, or if an orderly plot of vegetables and berries just wouldn't fit into your landscape plans, then consider growing the crop plants among your ornamental garden favorites.

Vegetable versatility

The secret to incorporating crop plants into the landscape is to look at them with a fresh eye. Foliage, shapes, or fruits of many vegetables are very attractive. Try to picture vegetables as a part of your overall garden scheme, rather than always in farm-style rows.

Some, such as lettuce and greens, can be grouped into clumps of several-to-many plants rather than strung out in rows. These clumps can be incorporated into plantings of annuals or perennials. Some plants with low and appealing foliage, such as leaf lettuce and green onions, can edge a bed of ornamentals or line a pathway. Bold-foliaged vegetables, such as rhubarb, Swiss chard, and artichokes, can be used as accent plants; vining vegetables and berries can be used as backdrops or as featured vertical emphasis points.

Consider the quantity

When you're planting vegetable or berry crops as landscape components, it's important to correctly estimate the quantity that your planting will produce. Zucchini plants, for example, have handsome, bold-textured foliage. But if you use them as a low hedge along a driveway or property boundary, you'll have enough squash to supply the neighborhood beyond the saturation point. On the other hand, one large clump of corn, featured as a tall and grassy accent, may not be enough to satisfy your needs.

Use care with "one-shot crops"

Remember, too, that some vegetables are a one-shot proposition—you harvest the entire plant. If you use carrot plants to furnish a fernlike border or edging, you'll totally remove the effect when you harvest. But parsley, used in the same situation for the same effect, would last all season.

Many vegetables, berries are attractive enough to be tucked into landscapes.

French intensive gardening

Growing vegetables by the French intensive method requires more hand labor than other modes do, but the production per square foot of soil is greater. Some gardeners feel that the vegetable quality is superior also.

There are three points that, in combination, distinguish this system from all others: 1) very thorough soil preparation, incorporating all nutrients before planting; 2) preparation of beds rather than rows, each bed mounded up above normal grade to form a body of soil that warms quickly, drains well, and takes in air easily; and 3) close planting.

At almost all stages of growth, leaves completely shade the soil, reducing moisture loss and preventing extreme fluctuations in soil temperature. In other words, the vegetable plants act as a living mulch. The fast, steady growth produces tender, full-flavored vegetables.

Preparing the soil

First, divide the area to be planted into beds running north to south. Beds for plants that need vertical support—beans, peas, cucumbers, tomatoes—should be only 1½ feet wide. Though the beds for other vegetables are made wider, keep them narrow enough for easy reaching (3 to 5 feet across).

Double dig the soil as shown in the illustration below, incorporating organic matter and sand to make a planting mix that's approximately ⅓ organic matter, ⅓ sand, and ⅓ original garden soil. Leave the surface rough for 2 to 5 days to air out, and then break up the clods and work the surface to a fine texture, maintaining the mounded profile. Set aside enough soil to cover seeds.

Next, sprinkle a thin dusting of bone meal on the soil, followed by a dusting of wood ash (if possible) or potash and a 1 to 2-inch layer of well-rotted manure. Dig these materials into the top 6 inches of the bed; then rake the soil into a smooth mound.

Sowing seeds

You will have to sow some kinds of vegetables directly into a bed because they don't transplant well. Sow seeds of bush beans, dwarf peas, and various root crops, for example, at about the same distance apart as recommended for row sowing, but scatter them over the entire bed (be sure to cover the corners and edges). Just barely cover the seeds with the soil you set aside.

Sowing crops like beets, bush beans, dwarf peas, and spinach is simple because their seeds are large enough that you can see how thickly they are sown. Fine-seeded crops like carrots and turnips are trickier. (Some gardeners mix seeds into sand or fine soil, and then sow the mixture.)

You can plant root crops such as carrots closer than is usual for other types of crops because you begin harvesting them when they are fingerling size. Thin the crop so that the remaining plants can mature to normal size.

When planting chard, do not broadcast its seeds; instead plant them in furrows on top of the bed, leaving a 1-foot space between furrows. When seedlings are about 2 inches tall, thin them to about 3 inches apart.

Some plants grow so tall or large that solid coverage of a wide mound isn't practical. You can still grow such plants in mounds, but you plant them in the usual way—clusters (hills) of seeds for melons and squash, and rows for climbing peas and beans, corn, cucumbers, potatoes, and tomatoes.

Setting out transplants

In the French intensive method, spacing between plants is important. Setting out young plants gives you much more control over spacing than sowing does. The goal is to set the plants at intervals so their outer leaves will touch as they approach mature size.

Double digging *involves digging series of adjoining trenches two spades deep across width of bed (see page 100). Amend soil throughout. Soil that came from first trench goes to fill in last one.*

Once double digging *is complete and soil amended, contour soil into a mound that is highest in center of bed, tapers down at all four edges. Water soil, let settle, then plant.*

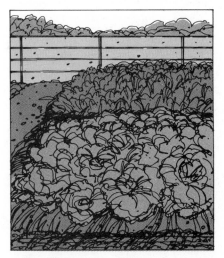

Close planting *gives greater crop productivity, stifles weeds, and acts as a living mulch—conserving moisture and regulating soil temperature. Repeatedly thin plants as they grow.*

Mail-order nurseries

*T*he racks of seed packets and bins of young plants at your local nursery or garden center may give you a sufficient selection to provide the crop garden you need, but you're missing a lot of fun if you don't send out for a few mail-order catalogs.

The big seed companies publish catalogs that contain many more offerings than the average nursery will stock. Inevitably, they will feature the latest hybrids. On the other hand, some companies sell plants of old-fashioned or hard-to-find varieties—hard to find not because they are inferior (quite the contrary) but because they don't ship well to produce markets, or are not as widely adapted or disease resistant as modern commercial varieties.

Some of these catalogs feature color photographs; others are mere lists. A few companies, though they send out quality seeds, print their offerings on not-very-glamorous newsprint. In addition, many companies request a small fee for their catalog, which often is applied as credit toward purchase.

Catalogs are ready for mailing well in advance of planting season, and you should order your seeds or plants early for best availability. Plants of perennial vegetables and the various berries are sent through the mails at their appropriate planting time. They will arrive with their roots encased in moisture-retentive material.

Archias Seed Store Corp.
P.O. Box 109
Sedalia, MO 65301

Bountiful Ridge Nurseries, Inc.
P.O. Box 250
Princess Anne, MD 21853

Brittingham Plant Farms
Salisbury, MD 21801

Buckley Nursery Co.
646 N. River Avenue
Buckley, WA 98321

Bunting's Berries
Selbyville, DE 19975

Burgess Seed & Plant Co.
905 Four Seasons Road
Bloomington, IL 61701

Burpee (W. Atlee) Seed Co.
300 Park avenue
Warminster, PA 18974

Burrell Seed Growers Co.
P.O. Box 150
Rocky Ford, CO 81067

California Nursery Co.
Niles District
P.O. Box 2278
Fremont, CA 94536

Columbia Basin Nursery
Box 458
Quincy, WA 98848

Comstock, Ferre & Co.
263 Main Street
Wethersfield, CT 06109

The Cook's Garden
Box 65054
Londonderry, VT 05148

Dave Wilson Nursery
4306 Santa Fe Avenue
Hughson, CA 95326

Dean Foster Nurseries
511 S. Center Street
P.O. Box 127
Hartford, MI 49057

De Giorgi Co., Inc.
P.O. Box 413
Council Bluffs, IA 51502

Earl May Seed & Nursery Co.
2130 Elm Street
Shenandoah, IA 51603

Ed Hume Seeds, Inc.
Box 1450
Kent, WA 98032

Exotica Seed Company
P.O. Box 160
Vista, CA 92083

Farmer Seed and Nursery
Faribault, MN 55021

Fowler Nurseries, Inc.
525 Fowler Road
Newcastle, CA 95658

Garden City Seeds
Box 297
Victor, MT 59875

Glecklers Seedsmen
Metamora, OH 43540

Grace's Gardens
10 Bay Street
Westport, CT 06880

Gurney Seed & Nursery Co.
Yankton, SD 57079

Harris Co., Inc.
Moreton Farm
3670 Buffalo Road
Rochester, NY 14624

Hastings
434 Marietta St. N.W.
P.O. Box 4274
Atlanta, GA 30302-4274

Henry Field Seed & Nursery Co.
Shenandoah, IA 51602

Henry Leuthardt Nurseries, Inc.
Montauk Hwy.
P.O. Box 666
East Moriches, NY 11940

Herb Gathering
5742 Kenwood
Kansas City, MO 64110

High Altitude Gardens
Box 4238
Ketchum, ID 83340

Horticultural Enterprises
P.O. Box 810082
Dallas, TX 75381-0082

Inter-State Nurseries
Hamburg, IA 51644

Ison's Nursery & Vineyard
Brooks, GA 30205

J. E. Miller Nurseries, Inc.
Canandaigua, NY 14424

J. L. Hudson, Seedsman
P.O. Box 1058
Redwood City, CA 94064

Jackson & Perkins Co.
1 Rose Lane
Medford, OR 97501

John Brudy's Exotics
3411 Westfield Drive
Brandon, FL 33511

Johnny's Selected Seeds
299 Foss Hill Road
Albion, ME 04910

Jung Seed Co.
Randolph, WI 53956

Kalmia Farm
Box 3881
Charlottesville, VA 22903

Kelly Bros. Nurseries, Inc.
Danville, NY 14437

Kilgore Seed Co.
P.O. Box 2158
Sanford, FL 32772

Kitazawa Seed Company
356 West Taylor Street
San Jose, CA 95110

Landreth's Seeds
180 West Ostend Street
Baltimore, MD 21230

Le Jardin du Gourmet
P.O. Box 5
West Danville, VT 05873

Le Marché Seeds International
Box 566
Dixon, CA 95620

Lockhart Seeds, Inc.
Box 1361
Stockton, CA 95205

Mellingers
2130 W. South Range Road
North Lima, OH 44452

Mountain Seed & Nursery
Box 9107
Moscow, ID 83843

**New York State Fruit Testing
Cooperative Association**
Geneva, NY 14456

Nichols Garden Nursery
1190 North Pacific Hwy.
Albany, OR 97321

Otis Twilley Seed Co., Inc.
P.O. Box 65
Trevose, PA 19047

Owen's Vineyard & Nursery
Georgia Highway 85
Gay, GA 30218

Park Seed Co., Inc.
Hwy 254 N.
Greenwood, SC 29647-0001

Piedmont Plant Co., Inc.
P.O. Box 424
Albany, GA 31702

Plants of the Southwest
1812 Second Street
Santa Fe, NM 87501

Porter & Son, Seedsmen
P.O. Box 104
Stephenville, TX 76401

R. H. Shumway Seedsman, Inc.
628 Cedar Street
P.O. Box 777
Rockford, IL 61105

Redwood City Seed Co.
P.O. Box 361
Redwood City, CA 94064

Seedway, Inc.
Hall, NY 14463-0250

Shepherd's Garden Seeds
7389 W. Zayante Road
Felton, CA 95018

Southmeadow Fruit Gardens
Lakeside, MI 49116

Spring Hill Nurseries
110 West Elm Street
Tipp City, OH 45371

Stanek's Garden Center
East 2929 27th Avenue
Spokane, WA 99203-4494

Stark Brothers Nurseries
Louisiana, MO 63353

Steele Plant Company
Gleason, TN 38229

Stokes Seeds, Inc.
Box 548
Buffalo, NY 14240

Sunrise Enterprises
P.O. Box 10058
Elmwood, CT 06110

Thompson & Morgan Inc.
P.O. Box 1308
Jackson, NJ 08527

Tsang and Ma International
P.O. Box 295
Belmont, CA 94002

The Urban Farmer
Box 444
Convent Station, NJ 07961

Van Well Nursery
P.O. Box 1339
Wenatchee, WA 98801

Vermont Bean Seed Co.
Garden Lane
Bomoseen, VT 05743

Vita Green Farms
217 Escondido Avenue
Vista, CA 92803

Waynesboro Nurseries
P.O. Box 987
Waynesboro, VA 22980

Willhite Seed Company
P.O. Box 23
Poolville, TX 76076

Wyatt-Quarles Seed Co.
P.O. Box 739
Garner, NC 27602

Index

**Boldface numbers refer to the
individual vegetable
and berry descriptions.**